Military Badge Collecting

DEDICATION

For my children – for the late Iain, for Fiona and for Andrew:
They don't come any better

John Gaylor

Military Badge Collecting

Fifth Edition

First published in Great Britain by
Seeley Service & Company
1971
Reprinted 1973
Second Edition 1977
Third Edition 1983
Fourth Edition 1991
Reprinted in this Fifth Edition 1995 by
Leo Cooper
190 Shaftesbury Avenue, London WC2H 8JL
an imprint of Pen & Sword Books Ltd.,
47 Church Street, Barnsley, S. Yorks S70 2AS

A CIP catalogue record for this book is
available from the British Library

Copyright © John Gaylor, 1971, 1977, 1983, 1991, 1995

ISBN 0 85052 438 5

Printed in Great Britain by
Redwood Books, Trowbridge, Wilts.

Contents

APPENDICES

Illustrations

(Appearing after page 160)

Acknowledgements

Whilst it is normal to acknowledge one's indebtedness to all sources of help and advice these are so numerous that it will be fairer if I collectively thank all those members of the Military Historical Society who have helped me in many ways on questions of dates, identifications, etc.

If it is not invidious to single out one name I must mention the late Hugh Harper of Edinburgh, a man of infinite patience, with a splendid collection far in advance of my own and an admirable tolerance of my more naïve questions.

This is not a catalogue of badges but rather a guide-book. As a young collector finding unidentifiable badges or inexplicable variations of known patterns I searched in vain for some book which would shed some light on these mysteries but found none. I hope that this book may serve to answer some of the questions of the budding collector.

JOHN GAYLOR

Introduction

The collecting of regimental badges is by no means a new hobby and for many years old soldiers have been seen in barracks wearing belts carrying metal titles, buttons and badges picked up from other units beside whom they served in the past. Generally speaking, once the belt was full the interest lapsed.

The hobby may be said to have begun just before the turn of the century when the complete range of distinctive cap badges came into being. Some firms made cheap copies and replicas of earlier patterns. These 'restrikes' still appear from time to time and it is a matter of choice whether one decides to include them in a collection, even assuming that you can spot them.

When I first wrote this book in 1971, badges were not highly regarded by the antiques trade, but one might hazard the opinion that the market has now made an about turn and is convinced that the commonest infantry or Corps cap-badge can now command a sum in double figures. However, happily, the plentiful militaria fairs which have sprung up in the past decade provide ample opportunities for the budding collector to buy the more common varieties at prices which I understand to be within the range of today's pocket-money.

Once started, the collector can extend his interests to embrace all the insignia of the soldier, including metal shoulder titles, collar and cap badges, waist-belt clasps, cross-belt badges, helmet and shako plates, buttons and arm badges. The field is limitless but most collectors restrict themselves to one category such as helmet plates or to a certain regiment or group of regiments. My own collection consists of head-dress badges only and most collectors seem to start with these.

The Hobby I

The Evolution of the Cap Badge

In order to define and recognize the British Army cap badge it is necessary to see how it evolved.

Full dress for the bulk of the army ceased in 1914; its head-dress was the spiked infantry helmet of German pattern, introduced in 1878. This was worn by most of the infantry and the Corps as well as the Royal Artillery and the Royal Engineers, by some with a ball rather than the spike. The infantry head-dress badge was an eight-pointed star with the regiment's number, consisting of detachable brass numerals, in the centre of the Garter placed on the middle of the star.

In 1881 the British infantry consisted of 109 separate regiments of foot, numbered consecutively from 1 to 109, and some bore regional or territorial designations. What are usually described as the Cardwell Reforms took effect in that year and gave a regional title to every regiment. They instituted the two-battalion regimental system whereby one battalion of the newly-constituted regiment served abroad and the other remained in the United Kingdom as a draft-producing and training unit as well as fulfilling its largely nominal internal security role. A list of the titles allocated is given in *Appendix B*. The system was that at infrequent intervals the two battalions would change places and the roles would be reversed. Like most such reforms these produced some unfortunate and unhappy marriages but in the main they were accepted; the old numbers were dropped but not forgotten and the new titles adopted. These titles were the common currency of the South African and the two World Wars and can be the basis of a collector's plan.

The 1881 reforms made it necessary to discard the old numbers in the helmet plate and a new, universal star plate was produced with a one and seven-eighths inches diameter space in the centre, designed to take a standard pattern badge. This consisted of a circle bearing the new title with the regimental device, often a collar badge, in the centre.

Concurrently with the helmet, the glengarry was worn as the undress cap. This is usually thought of as exclusively a Scottish head-dress but it was adopted in about 1870 for walking out by all troops and was worn by English, Irish and Welsh as well as Scots. It was not popular and was supplanted in the mid-1890s by the field-service cap of Austrian pattern which seems, like an old soldier, never to die. It was in use again in 1939 by the new Militia and later by the rest of the army. Replaced by the general service cap and the beret during the Second World War it has again come to light in its many coloured variety for wear with No. 2 Dress (the barathea, officer-type, service dress uniform in current use).

Until 1881 the badge in the glengarry had embodied the numeral and usually some regimental device, like a sphinx, a bugle-horn, a castle, etc., but after that date the badge was replaced by the helmet-plate centre (called HPC by collectors, the helmet plates themselves being HPs) and when so worn, a detachable crown was set above the HPC. The War Office of the day, as paternal and considerate as now, issued a back-fitting or template to ensure that these two should be positioned correctly. The HPC also appeared in India, worn on the foreign-service helmet, and the odd HPC is often found with a long prong fastener, suggesting that it may have been used for this purpose, tucked in the folds of the pagri or folded muslin wound around the helmet.

When the field-service cap became general wear the HPC was found to be too large and at first a collar badge was worn. Cavalry, having no collar badges, wore brass numerals and letters such as '4 DG' and 'VIII H'. The new infantry cap badges dropped the constraining circular band of the HPC and displayed the regimental motif more clearly. There is no certain date for the changeover since the battalion abroad was always far slower to adopt new fashions, and slower still if such fashions were disliked by the CO. India was a long way from the War Office in the nineteenth century! But by about 1898 sealed patterns had been evolved for most regiments, cavalry and infantry.

How does one recognize a cap badge? The infallible indicator used to be the vertical prong or slide-fastener, a narrow tongue of metal whereby the badge was slid into the glengarry, field-service cap, service-dress cap or beret. But some regiments favour two loops secured by a split-pin so that the badge does not fall from the cap when the head-dress is removed. If in doubt, one can usually judge from the size since collar badges, or collar dogs as the soldier inexplicably calls them, are obviously much smaller having been designed originally to fit on the narrow stand-up collar of the jacket.

Apart from the size and the prong-fastener there is no common feature but one soon develops an eye for the cap badge.

The nearest thing to a standard work on the subject for the British Army was Major T. J. Edwards' *Regimental Badges*, now out of print, but the first edition published in 1951 is best for the beginner. This, for instance, gives a clearer idea of the Infantry of the Line as it was during the two World

Wars, whereas the latest edition deals with the more recent changes which are as far-reaching in their effects as were the 1881 reforms: the Brigade System born in the 1957 White Paper and the subsequent Infantry Divisions.

How to start a collection

I began collecting in 1939 when at school and at a time when the school-boy hobby enjoyed a topical popularity. I cast about among my father and uncles who mustered their own badges from the First World War. One day an older boy arrived at school whose father had a collection of ninety-six badges that he was prepared to sell for a pound. This was a considerable sum for a schoolboy in 1939 and six of us decided to pool our resources. I invested two-and-six which entitled me to twelve of the badges. For one new penny each I added, among others, the Guards Machine Gun Regiment and the Huntingdonshire Cyclist Bn. badges.

I do not suggest that you will get a similar offer but in these days it is an unusual family which has not had some member who either served in the Second World War or who subsequently did National Service. With some prompting they can probably be persuaded to look out their old badge or badges and so you have a start. The most reluctant soldier usually kept his cap badge. A search of local markets and old furniture shops will very likely unearth others at fairly modest prices. These general dealers will put any old military brassware aside for you if you show signs of becoming a reg-ular visitor. When they do this you should take it whether you need it or not. This will encourage them and you will have items for exchange or sale to other collectors. I have carried such pieces around in my spares box for months and then had them snapped up eagerly by someone who had long been in search of just such specimens.

As badge-collecting is still an unsophisticated hobby you will probably find yourself the only local enthusiast. 'Cash and contacts' are my two hints for assembling a collection. Most badges can be bought once you have found them. If you have the resources, watch the auction sales at Bosley's, 42, West Street, Marlow, Bucks, SL7 1NB or Messrs Wallis and Wallis, West Street Auction Galleries, Lewes, Sussex BN7 2NJ. Since the average collector cannot afford the time or the money to do this he must resort to contacts. These probably can best be found in the Military Historical Society, National Army Museum, Royal Hospital Road, London, SW3 4HT. The Society was founded by a collector in 1948 and now embraces all aspects of military history and interests. Membership is worldwide, a meeting is held monthly and the quarterly journal usually has an article of interest to badge collectors. The Society has branches based in the East and West Midlands and Dorchester.

Having amassed a quantity of badges there is the problem of how and where to mount them. I suggest that you put them on a sheet of white or black cardboard until you have enough to start to classify them. This would be a good time to buy Major Edwards' book or to beg or buy an old Army List which gives a great deal of very useful information. Major Edwards' book has drawings of most of the badges in use during and immediately after the Second World War so that you will be able to identify some of the problem items which do not carry their designation on the scroll or title-band.

For badges of earlier vintage *Twenty Years After* had a series of plates and the *Boys' Own Paper* once produced a folding plate of illustrations of those in use during the First World War. These, of course, included the Irish regiments which ceased to exist in 1922 on the formation of the Irish Free State. Some of the illustrations from the former may be suspect as the drawings were made twenty years after and some post-1920 patterns purport to be those worn during the war.

As there are many badges that cannot be illustrated in this book I will try to explain some of the varieties which you will encounter to help you to identify them.

Regimental histories are inconsistent in their treatment of badges, some giving a full description while others gloss over or ignore the subject entirely.

Like many other collectors I restrict my own collection to 'other ranks' badges. Exceptions are the Royal Army Chaplains' Department and the Army Legal Corps which consist of officers only.

The 'other ranks' limit is mainly because of cost but was originally for interest's sake. Officers' badges on service dress were given a bronzed finish that was not very interesting. When service dress was supplanted by battle dress and became the undress uniform, badges were made more attractive and burst into coloured enamels and precious metals. These must necessarily be more expensive than the plain die-struck badges of the rank and file and are, in any case, far harder to find. Nevertheless, if a collector proposes to specialize in one particular regiment or corps he will have to have officers' badges as well.

Crowns

These are a first rough guide to the date of usage of a badge. Around 1898, when most cap badge designs emerged, Queen Victoria was on the throne. There were several variations of her crown but all are easily recognized. There is the angular one (shown in the 18th Hussars badge in Plate 4), the curved one (shown in the 4th Hussars badge in Plate 3) and the flat-topped variety (shown in both 21st Lancers badges in Plate 4) said to have been awarded to those units with most service in India at the time of the 1897 Jubilee because it was similar to that depicted in the Order of the Star of India. In the text I have followed the custom of collectors and dealers in referring to crowns of this period as 'QVC', qualifying it as 'flat-topped' when necessary.

When Edward VII came to the throne in 1901 the crown changed to the Tudor Crown, a 'domed' pattern (seen in the '1914' plates). It was retained by George V, Edward VIII and George VI (normally referred to as 'K/C').

With the accession of Elizabeth II in 1952 the crown changed to St, Edward's Crown, a 'dropped centre' type (referred to as 'Q/C'). Wherever a badge included the Royal Cypher, this naturally changed for a new monarch.

There are others, mural crowns, naval crowns and various types of coronet, as well as Saxon crowns, which will be encountered from time to time. Possession of these always has some significance whereas the possession of the sovereign's crown does not. There are Regiments such as the Suffolks and Corps such as the Intelligence which each have a crown but are not Royal. Conversely, others such as the Royal Scots Greys and the Royal Wiltshire Yeomanry do not bear the crown on their badge although they have 'Royal' in their title.

In this connection there is a story, current in the Intelligence Corps, that George VI when examining the possibilities of various corps becoming 'Royal' in 1946 enquired about the services performed by this one. He said that while obviously deserving of the honour, there were several aspects of the Corps' work which it was better should not be acknowledged by the Crown. So it seems unlikely that the Intelligence Corps will ever become 'Royal'.

Metals

To simplify things I refer to the metals of which other-rank badges are normally made as white metal (which looks like silver) and brass. Major Edwards in his book refers to gilding metal but practically all collectors overlook this purism and speak of brass badges, w/m badges and bi-metal badges – those made of both metals.

In 1952 there appeared the 'Staybrite' badge, of anodized aluminium (a/a) which did not need cleaning. If they are rubbed the brass or white-metal-seeming dye comes off baring the grey metal underneath. Most badges in use then and since have been made in this finish. Contrary to official belief they are not popular with soldiers. One of their claimed advantages is that, in the case of collar badges, they would not need to be removed from the tunic for cleaning and so obviate wear and tear on clothing. Most serving soldiers and most collectors dislike them for their bright tinsel look but one cannot logically refuse to collect them if one intends to have an unbroken collection.

For the most part I have not mentioned in the text that all badges in current use are made in a/a but it may safely be assumed that they are.

In the past decade there is evidence that some regiments and corps are turning against the a/a badges to the extent that they are commissioning metal badges and purchasing them privately.

Dates

Difficult though it is to be accurate with the dates of usage of badges I have quoted dates in most cases. These can be easily refuted or contradicted but it is a very difficult matter on which to be precise. Sealed patterns were often not brought into use for many years and sometimes not at all; some badges were worn but never sealed or approved. Old soldiers will generally be hard pushed to remember when badges changed pattern or size and photographs are far from a good indication. I cannot recall that anyone took a photograph of me in uniform in 1966 but if so his grandchildren will have irrefutable photographic evidence that this depicted a pre-1953 soldier since I was still wearing a K/C badge! Soldiers are conservative and sentimental, preferring their old badges: ERE soldiers (extra regimentally employed, i.e. serving away from their own units at a headquarters or a transit camp or with another arm) would often be found wearing old badges and formation signs long out of use in their own regiments but retained for sentiment's sake.

Forgeries

In the past few years the number of restrikes appearing has grown and the collector has had to be careful when offered a scarce or unusual item. Some dealers have even gone to the extent of 'weathering' their products by exposing them to the English climate in an attempt to secure instant tarnish. One's attitude to restrikes again must be a purely personal one. If you are content to have a copy of a badge, made from the original die, in your collection then this is your own decision. I do not doubt that many present-day collectors, loud in their denunciations of recent restrikes, proudly cherish specimens of Fox restrikes of the pre-territorial glengarry badges made over ninety years ago (and sold for 7½p each) and now made respectable by the passing years!

But cast metal badges must be mentioned. In 1914–15 many Territorial Force units were sent to India to relieve regular battalions who were sent to serve in France. In India the Territorials needed badges and some were made locally in the bazaars under semi-official arrangements. Later, enterprising merchants in Pakistan produced a range of cast badges none of which can be regarded as authentic.

I do not claim to have mentioned all patterns, all badges, nor all units in the pages which follow but I hope that what there is will help to solve a few problems and give an idea of the scope of the hobby. It is easy to amass a collection of badges in a jackdaw fashion but the real interest comes from learning the stories behind them, the regimental past, the regimental politics and the regimental mistakes. It is a hobby capable of great expansion if it is extended to Commonwealth countries but once embarked upon you may well find that the British Army provides challenge enough.

I have purposely avoided discussing cash values because intrinsically it is a matter of coppers only. But values have become inflated in recent years and simple cap badges once priced at twopence halfpenny in Ordnance Vocabularies are now pursued by people with folding money in their hands. It would be nice to think that collectors were building their collections out of interest and not as investments. However there is little satisfaction in knowing that one has an appreciating asset if it is never to be realized.

2 The Cavalry and Royal Armoured Corps

The Cavalry did not have the traumatic experiences of the infantry in the 1881 Reforms: their shocks were to come later. Plates 1 and 2 show the badges worn by the Household Cavalry and the Cavalry of the Line at the outbreak of war in 1914. The titles in heavy type in each paragraph are those in use in 1914.

At that time, the **Household Cavalry** consisted of the **First Life Guards, Second Life Guards** and **Royal Horse Guards**. The badges shown are those worn in the khaki service-dress cap. In the forage cap, the blue, flat-topped, red-banded cap with the brass-bound peak, all three regiments wore the Household Cavalry badge, the Royal Cypher within the Garter (Plate 3). There were no Life Guards, Royal Horse Guards or Household Cavalry badges bearing either VR or ERVII Royal Cyphers as until the 1913 manoeuvres, the regiments had worn pillbox caps above blue undress uniforms with lofty disdain for considerations of camouflage. King George V noticed that they had no badge when in khaki and the resulting patterns are shown.

After the First World War it was found that the Army had far too many cavalry regiments and the total was reduced by nine. This was done in 1922 by merging pairs of regiments and the senior two to be so linked were the First and Second Life Guards. The initial badge bore the title 'The Life Guards (1st and 2nd)' (Plate 3) but this soon gave way to 'The Life Guards', as worn today, only the cypher changing, to GRVI and then to ERII. The Royal Horse Guards badge remained unchanged until 1969 when they merged with the 1st Royal Dragoons to form **The Blues and Royals (Royal Horse Guards and 1st Dragoons)**. It ranged through the Royal Cyphers of all the monarchs including ERVIII (Plate3). The new bronzed badge follows the same pattern with title 'The Blues and Royals' (Plate 3).

It must be stressed again that badges are not an exact science: approved badges are often unworn while others are worn without approval. The badges of both Life Guards regiments were in brass and those of the Royal Horse Guards bronzed, although I have found the latter in polished brass. Some badges, although struck, do not necessarily reach the intended wearers. Edward VIII's was a short reign and old Household Cavalrymen have assured me that they never saw badges bearing his Cypher yet I have specimens for both regiments. Stocks may have come to hand after the Abdication in 1936 and not been issued but a few escaped the melting-pot. (See also chapter 20).

The Cavalry of the Line in 1914 consisted of twenty-eight regiments, seven heavy and twenty-one light cavalry. **The 1st (King's) Dragoon Guards**, the senior heavy regiment, wore until 1915 the brass eagle from the Arms of the Emperor Francis Joseph I of Austria who was their Colonel-in-Chief from 1896 to 1914, with title scroll below. During the First World War the Emperor was on the other side and the Austrian insignia was dropped in 1915. It gave place to an inoffensive bi-metal star until 1937 (Plate 4) when a brass eagle was resumed but this time without the title scroll. Later, possibly in the Second World War, the brass eagle became white metal and remained so even after amalgamation with the Bays in 1959 to form **The Queen's Dragoon Guards.**

The Queen's Bays (2nd Dragoon Guards) kept the same pattern brass badge for just over sixty years, differing only in the successive three crowns. They lost their badge on the merger with the King's Dragoon Guards (Plate 1).

The 3rd (Prince of Wales's) Dragoon Guards badge was simply white-metal plumes and motto, brass coronet and scroll, although two different strikes used varying patterns of the numeral '3', one rounded and the other flat-topped. There was nothing significant in this, possibly only a change of maker. In 1922 they merged with the Carabiniers (6th Dragoon Guards).

The senior Irish cavalry regiment, **The 4th Royal Irish Dragoon Guards**, wore the Star of the Most Illustrious Order of St. Patrick in white metal with a brass title scroll superimposed. After amalgamation in 1922 with the 7th Dragoon Guards (Princess Royal's) it lost all reference to its Irish services.

At one time in its history **The 5th Dragoon Guards** also had an Irish title, the 2nd (or Green) Irish Horse, but all trace of this has long since disappeared. The badge shown, a white-metal centrepiece with brass crown and outer band carrying the motto, originally appeared with Queen Victoria's crown. In 1922 they merged with the Inniskillings (6th Dragoons).

The Carabiniers (6th Dragoon Guards) badge had an abbreviated title in white metal within a brass Garter, brass crown above, all superimposed upon crossed carbines carrying a white-metal scroll across their butts. A previous badge had borne a Queen Victoria's crown. The merger with 3rd (Prince of Wales's) Dragoon Guards brought a pleasing combination: white-metal plumes, carbines and motto scrolls, brass coronet and title scroll (Plate 3). The new title was **3rd Carabiniers (Prince of Wales's Dragoon Guards).**

In 1971 the Regiment was amalgamated with The Royal Scots Greys to form **The Royal Scots Dragoon Guards (Carabiniers & Greys)**, the badge embodying the Greys' Eagle, the Carabiniers' crossed carbines and a title-scroll below (Plate 48). Following the return of a Conservative government to power in 1970 it was felt that both regiments might have been preserved but they decided finally to effect the merger.

Earl Ligonier was Colonel of **The 7th (Princess Royal's) Dragoon Guards** for twenty-nine years and in 1898 his crest was authorized in white metal above a title scroll '7th Dragoon Guards'. In 1906 the badge was changed to a brass one (Plate 3) with Ligonier's crest above his motto *Quo Fata Vocant**. After the merger with the 4th Royal Irish Dragoon Guards the St. Patrick's star was kept but the central cross was moved through 45 degrees into a St. George's Cross and the Princess Royal's coronet placed on it to illustrate her association with the Regiment. The new title was simply **4th/7th Dragoon Guards** but they became **4/7th Royal Dragoon Guards** in 1936 with no change in the badge (Plate 3). (See also chapter 20).

The 1st (Royal) Dragoons, the senior light cavalry regiment, took the French 105th Regiment's eagle at Waterloo in 1815 and its use as a badge was authorized in 1838. But when cap badges were agreed upon in 1898 the Regiment took into use the Royal Crest with Queen Victoria's Crown. The same design but with the King's Crown was in use until about 1915. The Kaiser had been the Regiment's Colonel-in-Chief until the outbreak of war when King George V became the new royal patron. The Regiment had long wanted to adopt the eagle and early in the war they had brass badges made privately by a firm in Hythe. This was a small brass eagle (Plate 3). It was worn until 1919 when they returned to Hounslow from the Rhineland and the Royal Crest was again resumed under pressure. Finally, in 1948 the eagle was officially sanctioned and a more dignified brass bird was adopted with w/m wreath and tablet (Plate 3) until the merger with the Royal Horse Guards in 1969.

Also among the eagle-snatchers at Waterloo were **The 2nd Dragoons (Royal Scots Greys)** who took that of the French 45th Regiment. The w/m eagle above a brass scroll remained unchanged until 1971 except that in the recent anodized aluminium issues there is a differing number of leaves in the wreath on the eagle's breast, hardly a significant change. Bandsmen in the Regiment wore in the cap a small brass flaming grenade with a plain body to the bomb (Plate 3) and this is still worn by bandsmen of The Royal Scots Dragoon Guards (Carabiniers & Greys).

The 3rd (King's Own) Hussars wore a rather splendid, spirited White

---

*A list of mottoes and their translations will be found in Appendix G.

Horse of Hanover above a brass title scroll '3rd King's Own Hussars'. In 1920 the title was slightly changed as were those of so many other cavalry regiments and a new badge followed, the horse kept but reduced in size. The new scroll read '3rd The King's Own Hussars'. In 1958 the Regiment merged with the 7th Queen's Own Hussars.

The 4th (Queen's Own) Hussars first badge in 1898 (Plate 3) was similar to the pattern worn in 1914 except, of course, for the QVC and for the w/m motto scroll (Plate 1). After the accession of King Edward VII the K/C issue appeared. In 1906 the motto *Mente et Manu* was authorized and the motto scroll was added to the badge. A Q/C version of this badge exists but I do not believe that it was ever worn. In 1958 the Regiment was merged with the 8th King's Royal Irish Hussars.

Raised in 1689 **The 5th (Royal Irish) Lancers**, as they became, suffered almost sixty years of disbandment in the nineteenth century. Their badge, brass except for w/m lower half of the pennons and the numeral in the centre, bore only the motto *Quis Separabit* to indicate its Irish connections. The red and white traditional colours of British lance-pennons derived from the national colours of Poland, homeland of the lancers. Another issue exists in which only the numeral in the centre is in w/m, the remainder brass. In 1922 they merged with the 16th The Queen's Lancers.

In 1914 **The 6th (Iniskilling) Dragoons** were wearing the splendid castle of Inniskilling in w/m above a brass scroll. On amalgamation with the 5th Dragoon Guards in 1922 the title became 5/6th Dragoons but no badge appeared. In 1927 the title changed to the **5th Inniskilling Dragoon Guards** and in 1935 became Royal. The badge evolved was simply 'VDG', below K/C, all w/m, a functional abbreviation of the title, abandoning both the White Horse and the Castle of the component regiments (Plate 3). A Q/C issue appeared in about 1955. (See also chapter 20).

The 7th Queen's Own Hussars badge – w/m monogram 'QO' on brass, as worn in 1914 had only one predecessor which bore what is popularly described as the Albert Crown (Plate 3) instead of the more usual QVC. A Q/C version of the badge appeared in about 1957 shortly before the merger with the 3rd The King's Own Hussars to form **The Queen's Own Hussars.** After this merger the old 7th badge was for–saken in the adoption of the 3rd's White Horse above a scroll 'The Queen's Own Hussars' (Plate 48) (See also Chapter 20).

The 8th (King's Royal Irish) Hussars 1914 badge also had only one predecessor, bearing the QVC. The w/m harp with brass crown and title scroll clearly expressed the Irish connection. The merger in 1958 with the 4th Queen's Own Hussars to form **The Queen's Royal Irish Hussars** produced an agreeable design incorporating the harp of the 8th with the brass circle and w/m title scroll of the 4th, in a/a (Plate 48). The first badge was flat, struck in one process, but a couple of years later another badge appeared with harp and royal crest superimposed on the title band. This succeeded in making the old 4th Hussars' part of the badge more obvious. A Q/C badge exists for the 8th but it is doubtful if this was worn. (See also chapter 20). (See also notes on Pipers.)

A pleasingly uncomplicated w/m badge was that of **The 9th (Queen's Royal) Lancers.** The Victorian period badge had embodied the flat-topped crown favoured by certain regiments. In about 1956 a Q/C issue appeared but in 1960 the 9th Queen's Royal Lancers disappeared from the Army List on amalgamation with the 12th Royal Lancers (Prince of Wales's).

The 10th Royal Hussars (Prince of Wales's Own) wore simply the w/m Prince of Wales's plumes and motto with brass coronet above a brass title scroll until they merged in 1969 with **The 11th Hussars (Prince Albert's Own),** The latter unit was styled the 11th (Prince Albert's Own) Hussars in 1840, having furnished an escort to Prince Albert when he came to London to marry Queen Victoria. Their badge became the crest of the House of Saxe-Coburg-Gotha above a motto scroll *Treu und Fest* all in brass. The Regiment when wearing their brown beret with a crimson band did not wear a badge. On the merger with the 10th in 1969 to form **The Royal Hussars (Prince of Wales's Own),** the new Regiment took the old 10th badge with 'The Royal Hussars' on the scroll (Plate 48). (See also chapter 20).

Unusual among Lancer regiments which normally bore fairly obvious evidence of their calling, **The 12th (Prince of Wales's Royal) Lancers** badge was the Prince of Wales's Plumes and motto in w/m with brass coronet and a brass title scroll below, inscribed 'XII Royal Lancers'. In 1903 this was changed to the pattern shown, brass K/C, crossed lances, coronet and numerals 'XII' with plumes and lower half of the pennons in w/m. It had doubtless occurred to them that the Prince of Wales's plumes, for all that they were a royal distinction, were hardly distinctive when shared with other cavalry, Yeomanry, infantry, both Welsh and Irish, plus sundry colonial units. The Q/C version appeared in about 1958. After the merger with the 9th the new regiment, the **9/12th Royal Lancers (Prince of Wales's),** kept the basic 12th badge but a scroll across the lance-butts reads simply 'IX-XII', in a/a (Plate 48).

Uncluttered by titular garnishings **The 13th Hussars** wore from 1898 to 1901 a similar badge to the one shown, w/m numerals in a brass QVC badge with motto *Viret in Aeternum.* The small brass badge with 'Z' scroll in Plate 3 was described in the 1900 Dress Regulations as a field-service cap badge but photographs indicate that the larger badge was more often used. In 1922 the 13th merged with the 18th Royal Hussars (Queen Mary's Own).

Another regiment whose badge fell victim to anti-German feeling in

1915 was **The 14th (King's) Hussars.** The w/m eagle on an oval brass disc gave way that year to the Royal Crest within the Garter, a title scroll below, all in brass. Three versions of this badge were struck, small with voided centre and large, with both voided and solid centres (Plate 3). The large type, known as 'The Cartwheel' within the Regiment, was extremely unpopular and was soon discarded. In 1922 the 14th merged with the 20th Hussars.

The 15th (King's) Hussars also carried the Royal Crest, but in w/m, within the Garter: below, 'XV.KH', standing on a scroll *Merebimur* all in brass. The earlier pattern of course carried QVC. In 1922 the 15th merged with the 19th Royal Hussars (Queen Alexandra's Own).

Another lancer regiment's badge based on a simple graphic design was that of **The 16th (The Queen's) Lancers.** Two patterns preceded the one shown in the 1914 photograph: one was the same design, with QVC, but with 'Queen's Lancers' on the scroll. This was in use from 1898 to 1903 when a K/C version followed. In 1905 'The' was added, as shown. The merger in 1922 with the 5th Royal Irish Lancers subordinated the 5th. The title became **16/5th Lancers** but the badge remained that of the 16th. The sixty years break in the last century made the 5th a junior partner. A Q/C version appeared in about 1958. In 1954 the title was amended to the **16/5th The Queen's Royal Lancers** but the badge was unchanged. (See also chapter 20).

Probably the best-known British badge is that of **The 17th (Duke of Cambridge's Own) Lancers.** The skull resting on a pair of crossed bones above a scroll *Or Glory* all in w/m, is stark, simple and distinctive. In 1922 the 17th merged with the 21st Lancers (Empress of India's).

The 18th (Queen Mary's Own) Hussars took the w/m badge shown in 1911 – 'XVIII' superimposed upon an 'H' within a circle reading 'Queen Mary's Own', flanked by laurels, and surmounted by a K/C. From 1898 to 1911 there were four other badges and these are probably accounted for by the plethora of title changes:

1861–1904	18th Hussars
1904–05	18th Princess of Wales's Hussars
1905–10	18th (Victoria Mary, Princess of Wales's Own) Hussars
1910–19	18th (Queen Mary's Own) Hussars

Plate 4 shows the QVC badge, w/m '18H' in a brass badge with motto *Pro Patria Conamur*, worn from 1898 to 1902. It was succeeded for a year or two by a K/C version until the next pattern came into use in 1904, an all-brass badge embodying the numerals in the centre, now in roman figures, an enlarged motto *Pro Rege, pro Lege, pro patria Conamur* and the Princess of Wales's scroll. In 1906 the same badge crammed an extra word on the last scroll and became 'Princess of Wales's Own' until 1911 when the Princess became Queen Mary and the badge changed to the fifth pattern in use by one regiment in thirteen years. The merger of 13th and 18th in 1922 to form the **13th/18th Royal Hussars** produced a functional design embodying the letters 'QMO' and the letter 'H' (Plate 4) but it proved somewhat fragile and yielded to the present brass pattern, with K/C in the first place, of course (Plate 4), in 1938. The Q/C badge appeared in about 1957. (See also chapter 20).

It was an unusual pattern which **The 19th (Princess of Wales's Own) Hussars** wore, a w/m elephant brought from India – they were an old Honourable East India Company regiment – and wore from 1898 to 1902 when the design changed a little to become a more friendly-looking beast above a double scroll inscribed '19th Alexandra P.W.O. Hussars' (Plate 4). Then in 1909 in consequence of a change in title the previous year to 19th (Queen Alexandra's Own Royal) Hussars they cast aside the distinctive elephant to assume the Dannebrog.(Danish national device) in w/m. In 1922 on merging with the 15th, elephants and Dannebrog vanished: the **15/19th Hussars** took the badge of the 15th, dropping the 'KH' and substituting 'XIX' (Plate 4). In 1933 the title changed to 15/19th King's Royal Hussars but no badge-change resulted. The a/a Q/C version follows the K/C pattern but later bi-metal issues have appeared with the motto scroll in both brass and in w/m. (See also Chapter 20).

The 20th Hussars badge at the outbreak of war in 1914 was simply the 'XHX' and K/C in brass. The same badge in 1898 had carried the flat-topped Victorian crown. On merging with the 14th in 1922 the 20th's badge was discarded and the new **14/20th Hussars** simply added '20' to the scroll (Plate 4). In 1931 they reassumed the brass eagle, or 'The Hawk' as it is known within the Regiment (Plate 4). In 1936 the title changed to **14/20th King's Hussars** but no badge alteration was made until 1968 when it became a black eagle with gilt coronet, orb and sceptre. (See also chapter 20).

In 1898 **The 21st Lancers** took the crossed lances, flat-topped QVC and the numerals 'XXI', all brass except for the w/m lower half of the lance-pennons (Plate 4), and this was worn until the following year. In recognition of its brilliant services at Omdurman the Regiment had become **The 21st (Empress of India's) Lancers** in 1898 and the badge changed in 1899 to the upright lances enclosing the 'VRI' Royal Cypher and 'XXI', again all in brass except for the lower half of the pennons. In 1901 another change took place and they crossed the lances, mounted the cypher on the intersection and placed the 'XXI' below. Hardly had this appeared than the monarch changed and the badge was amended to the appropriate K/C, in use until the merger with the 17th in 1922 (Plate 2). The merged regiment, the **17/21st Lancers** – took the badge of the old 17th. A slightly smaller badge of identical design appeared after 1945 for beret wear. (See also Chapter 20).

Not all the regiments merged in 1922 took up new badges immediately. The junior partner of the merger, in most instances far below strength following the First World War, kept a squadron – which was known, for example, as the 21st Lancer Squadron. All ranks of this squadron wore the 21st's insignia for several years; other squadrons wore that of the 17th. Finally, in 1929 it became mandatory for all personnel of the merged regiments to wear the new badges.

Early in the Second World War it became necessary to create more armoured regiments and even in darkest 1940, someone was prepared to search for six numbers and seek to breathe life into war babies by reviving old cavalry traditions for some of them. Badges are shown in Plates 4 and 5.

The 22nd Dragoons, 23rd Hussars and **24th Lancers** were all created on 10 December, 1940.

There had been several other bearers of the number 22nd but none since 1819. However, there was nothing traditional about the badge, a 'D' enclosing 'XXII', K/C above and scroll 'Dragoons' below, all in w/m.

The 23rd Hussars whose most recent predecessor disappeared in 1817 were little better off, having an 'H' in w/m with brass K/C above and brass scroll '23rd Hussars' below.

Before inspiration ran riot and an 'L' was coupled with the figures '24' someone realized that Lancers can usually display some trade motif, hence **The 24th Lancers** badge with crossed lances on a circle enclosing the numerals 'XXIV', K/C above, all in w/m. Their most recent antecedents were the 24th Light Dragoons, disbanded in 1819. It was in the 24th Light Dragoons that John Shipp, that remarkable soldier of the early nineteenth century, reached the rank of RSM between his two spells of commissioned service.

The 25th Dragoons and **26th Hussars** were both raised in India in 1941, the former from personnel of the 3rd Carabiniers. Its badge con–sisted of w/m crossed swords, the remainder brass. An earlier 25th Light Dragoons was disbanded in 1818.

The Prussian eagle in brass adopted by the 26th Hussars doubtless arose out of their being formed from a cadre of the 14/20th King's Hussars. Plate 5 shows four badges, one of the 25th Dragoons and three of the 26th Hussars. These were trial patterns made but not adopted and the chosen designs were far better. The third pattern projected for the 26th was cast in India, an eagle standing on a rectangular tablet inscribed 'XXVI'.

The 27th Lancers were authorized in December 1940 and took the elephant's head won by the 27th Light Dragoons in the Mahratta War of 1803. The old 27th was renumbered 24th in 1804 and disbanded in 1819. The elephant's head was in w/m, the rest of the badge brass. A version also exists with the lower half of the lance-pennons in w/m.

All six wartime cavalry regiments were disbanded in June 1948.

One is not alone in wondering why anybody in 1940–41 was willing to spend time updating regiments dead over a century before. In *The Grand Alliance*, the third volume of Churchill's *The Second World War* he comments to the CIGS: 'Surely it was a very odd thing to create these outlandish regiments of Dragoons, Hussars and Lancers, none of which has carbines, swords or lances, when there exist already telescoped up the 18th, 20th and 19th Hussars, 5th Lancers and 21st Lancers. Surely all these should have been revived before creating these unreal and artificial titles. I wish you would explain to me what was moving in the minds of the War Office when they did this.'

Junior to all the cavalry regiments was **The Royal Tank Corps**, formed in July 1917 from the Heavy Branch of the Machine Gun Corps. Its first badge as the Tank Corps was of brass (Plate 5). In 1922 the motto *Fear Naught* and the title *Royal* were awarded and in 1924 a new badge appeared, in w/m. Unfortunately the tank, when the badge was worn in the beret, was obviously going to the rear. As this was clearly not good for morale a new badge was struck later in the year, with the tank going to the wearer's right (Plate 5). A brass version of this was worn by the Corps Band. Early in the 1950s a Q/C version was issued.

The Royal Tank Corps became **The Royal Tank Regiment** in April 1939 when it was decided to form a **Royal Armoured Corps to** embrace the mechanized cavalry regiments and the RTC. In due course all Cavalry and Yeomanry except The Household Cavalry became part of The Royal Armoured Corps. The first RAC badge was simply 'RAC', within a laurel wreath, K/C above, all brass (Plate 5). In 1941 a new design was chosen (Plate 5), a mailed, right-hand gauntlet, fist clenched, palm to the front with a tablet 'RAC' on the wrist. From the wrist ran two concentric circles with arrowheads on either side of the K/C, all in w/m. Armour purists pointed out that the palms of gauntlets were not normally mailed but subsequent Q/C issues do not appear to have been affected by the revelation.

The badge was worn at recruit training depots and in the wartime numbered regiments of the Corps.

The Brigade of Guards 3

The Grenadier Guards, Coldstream Guards and Scots Guards were the only three of the five Regiments of Foot Guards in existence at the turn of the century. The Irish Guards were formed in 1900 and the Welsh Guards not until 1915. As badges were not worn on bearskins the pill-box cap required only a small badge and the same one remained in use on the service-dress cap and the beret. As might be expected, Her Majesty's Foot Guards are extremely conservative in their badges (Plate 20).

The plain brass grenade is worn by all ranks of the **Grenadier Guards** up to, but not including, full Serjeant. Musicians and serjeants wear the grenade embossed with the Royal Cypher and topped with the appropriate crown, all in brass. Warrant Officers, Orderly Room Serjeants and Band Serjeants wear the same badge but with w/m Cypher and crown on a brass grenade. The final Grenadier badge shown is that which was worn on the foreign-service helmet, the Royal Cypher (GR) reversed and entwined within the Garter, with K/C above, all in brass.

The badge of the **Coldstream Guards** is the Star of the Order of the Garter, granted to them in 1696 by King William III. It is worn in plain brass by all other ranks except Warrant Officers, Drum Majors, Orderly Room Serjeants and Band Serjeants. They wear the attractive badge shown: an eight-pointed, diamond-cut star in silver, the cross in red enamel and the motto on a blue ground. The large, brass, elongated star shown was worn in the foreign-service helmet as recently as 1939–40 in Egypt and a more elaborate rendering of it in the same finish as the Warrant Officers' cap-star was authorized for the helmets of serjeants and above.

Not surprisingly, the **Scots Guards** wear the Star of the Order of the Thistle and this is in brass for all ranks up to but not including full Serjeant. For musicians, full Serjeants and Colour-Serjeants, the Star is in w/m and the centrepiece in brass, while Warrant Officers, Drum Majors, Orderly Room Serjeants and Band Serjeants wear a more attractive badge, similar in finish to that worn by the Coldstream, a diamond-cut star in silver with a gilt centre and a green enamelled backing to the Thistle. The slightly larger brass star was authorized for wear in the foreign-service helmet (see notes on pipers).

Rudyard Kipling wrote in 1918 of the **Irish Guards** that

> 'We're not so old in the Army,
> But we're not so young at our trade,
> For we had the honour at Fontenoy
> Of meeting the Guards Brigade.'

However, at Fontenoy the Irish Brigade who sold their swords in Europe were in the pay of the French. It was not until 1900, by Army Order 77, that Queen Victoria gave authority for the raising of the Irish Guards 'to commemorate the bravery shown by the Irish Regiments in the operations in South Africa in the years 1899 and 1900'. The badge granted was the Star of the Order of St. Patrick and this is worn in brass by all other ranks below Warrant Officer. The latter wear the silver and gilt badge shown with a red enamelled St. Patrick's Cross in the centre, a green shamrock and a blue circular band. The circle carries the motto *Quis separabit* and the date 'MDCCLXXXIII' (1783, when the Order was founded). In the foreign-service helmet the Irish Guards wore a large brass Star of the Order, similar in size to that worn by the Coldstream in the helmet (see notes on pipers).

Raised in wartime, in the same way as the Irish Guards, the **Welsh Guards** were formed in 1915 by order of King George V. The badge chosen was the leek and this is worn in brass by all other ranks. The leek is an ancient Welsh device and is mentioned by Shakespeare in *Henry V*. Welshmen under the Black Prince wore leeks in their caps and on St. David's Day the Welsh Guards wear imitation leeks. The other Welsh badge shown was worn on the foreign-service helmet, a leek within a circular scroll inscribed *Cymru am Byth* backed by red felt.

In 1916 the **Guards Machine Gun Battalion** (or Machine Gun Guards) was formed and their badge was a w/m star, the five points being bullets whilst the grenade, rose, thistle, shamrock and leek between were representative of the five Regiments of Foot Guards. In the centre was a monogram 'GMG' and the year '1916'. Subsequent epansion in May, 1918, to form the **Guards Machine Gun Regiment** embracing dismounted Household Cavalrymen meant a change of badge. This, in brass, embodied the Garter upon crossed Vickers machine guns with the title scroll below. Both badges are illustrated in Plate 20.

The final badge shown is that of the **Guards Officer Training Unit** of 1914–18. In the centre was the GRV Royal Cypher within a chain circle. An outer white enamelled band carried the gilt letters 'lLG2LGRHGGGCGSGIGWG'. Household Cavalry and Foot Guards were together in this venture and the cryptogram, unravelled, stood for: 1st Life Guards, 2nd Life Guards, Royal Horse Guards, Grenadier Guards, Coldstream Guards, Scots Guards, Irish Guards and Welsh Guards.

Regular Infantry of the Line before 1958 4

The great infantry reorganization, finalized in 1881 and generally referred to as the Cardwell Reforms converted 109 numbered regiments of Foot into territorially-titled regiments, each of two battalions. (A list of these is given in *Appendix B*.) The different titles are given in the section on cap badges later in this chapter. Some of the titles were quickly changed.

The regiments up to and including the 25th Foot already had two battalions; the 26th to 109th were linked in pairs, except for the 79th which became the 1st Bn. Queen's Own Cameron Highlanders and remained a one-battalion regiment until a second battalion was formed in 1897. Another exception was the 60th which had four battalions. This process was known as the Territorial System, not to be confused with the Territorial Force in 1908 which created a military body for home defence.

Under the system the 28th Foot, for instance, became the 1st Bn. The Gloucestershire Regiment and the 61st Foot became the 2nd Bn. The Royal South Gloucestershire Militia became the 3rd Bn. and The Royal North Gloucestershire Militia became the 4th Bn. Local Rifle Volunteers were brought under the regimental umbrella and formed Volunteer Battalions, numbered 1st, 2nd, 3rd Vol. Bns. etc., of the county regiment. The two regular battalions normally wore the same badge and one of them was to remain in England whilst the other soldiered abroad. After a fairly lengthy tour overseas the foreign-service battalion returned and the other, made up to strength, went abroad.

At this point it might be expedient to point out that an infantry regiment is not a tactical unit and does not go to war. It consists of a number of battalions which are the held force units: an infantry regiment is a sort of family. In wartime an infantry regiment can be expanded almost infinitely but all the battalions formed are part of the regiment and all regard the regimental depot as home. But regiments of cavalry, artillery, engineers, signals and transport *are* tactical units and the 999th Field Regiment, Royal Artillery goes to war as such.

The Helmet Plate

When the Territorial System was unveiled in 1881 the spiked infantry helmet, adopted in 1878, continued to be worn by most of the Infantry.

Highlanders wore the bonnet and fusiliers wore the fur cap, as did Riflemen. On the front of the helmet was an eight-pointed universal brass plate with QVC, perforated to take the helmet-plate centre (HPC). The plate and a selection of centres are shown in Plate 6. After 1901 a plate was struck bearing a K/C (Plate 7) and correspondingly the centres which bore a crown such as the Royal Irish Regiment (same plate), changed to K/C. So even in the comparatively short life of the HPC, 1881 to 1914, there were several regiments which had two or more patterns following a change of crown, title or, simply from regimental preference.

A list of the centres in use from 1881 to 1914 follows. Badges are in brass unless specified otherwise. The titles quoted are those commonly used and are not necessarily always the full one.

THE ROYAL SCOTS

1. On circle: 'Lothian'. Centre: Star of the Order of the Thistle with St. Andrew bearing his cross thereon. Above, QVC; below, a Sphinx. This pattern was only worn for about a year, giving way to pattern 2 on change of title.
2. As 1 but, on circle 'The Royal Scots', worn 1882–89.
3. A complete break from the format. The badge taken is that now worn and as shown in plate 10, a w/m Star of the Order of the Thistle with brass centrepiece. In 1902 the helmet was replaced by the Kilmarnock bonnet and the HPC retained alone. The badge has been worn ever since, apart from 1959–69 when the Lowland Brigade badge was in use.

THE QUEEN'S (ROYAL WEST SURREY REGIMENT)

1. On circle: 'West Surrey'. Centre: Paschal Lamb in w/m with banner on right shoulder.
2. On circle: 'The Queen's'. Centre: Paschal Lamb in w/m but banner on left shoulder. The sealed pattern for this was dated 1904 but the centre appears to be little known and may not have been in use from 1904 to 1914 – or, indeed, at all (Plate 6).

BUFFS (EAST KENT REGIMENT)

1. On circle: 'East Kent'. Centre: A Dragon.
2. As 1, but, on circle, 'The Buffs East Kent Regiment'. Worn 1911–14.

THE KING'S OWN (ROYAL LANCASTER REGIMENT)

On circle: 'Royal Lancaster'. Centre: The Lion of England.

THE ROYAL WARWICKSHIRE REGIMENT

1. On circle: 'Warwickshire'. Centre: w/m moving Antelope, forefoot raised.
2. As 1 but, on circle, 'Royal Warwickshire'. This antelope is standing. Again, this was dated 1904 on the sealed pattern but is so little known that there is some doubt whether it was ever worn (Plate 6). The old 6th Foot became 'Royal' in 1832 so it is odd that the title was not on the HPC when first worn in 1881.

THE KING'S (LIVERPOOL REGIMENT)

On circle: 'Liverpool'. Centre: White Horse in w/m.

THE NORFOLK REGIMENT

1. On circle: 'Norfolk'. Centre: in w/m, Britannia seated, right hand resting on the knee, and holding a laurel branch. This was known Regimentally as the 'Honolulu pattern', based upon the supposed location of the lady's hand.
2. As 1, but Britannia has the right hand raised (Plate 7).

THE LINCOLNSHIRE REGIMENT

On circle: 'Lincolnshire'. Centre: Sphinx on tablet 'Egypt' w/m.

THE DEVONSHIRE REGIMENT

On circle: 'Devonshire'. Centre: Exeter Castle above scroll *Semper Fidelis*. Two variants of this exist: in one, the walls linking the three towers are bricked; in the other, the walls are smooth but the difference is not significant.

THE SUFFOLK REGIMENT

1. On circle: 'Suffolk'. Centre: Castle (with two turrets) and Key of Gibraltar below scroll 'Gibraltar'.
2. As 1, but the castle is of the 'standard' pattern. In 1900 the War Office noted that the four regiments bearing Gibraltar Castle on their badges, Suffolks, Dorsetshires, Essex and Northamptonshires – seemed unable to agree on their concept of the Castle. With a proper sense of order, the authorities laid down that the pattern depicted on the coinage of Gibraltar was to be used: a castle with three turrets and key suspended below the central gate. All four regiments took new HPCs shortly after the new design was agreed upon.

PRINCE ALBERT'S (SOMERSET LIGHT INFANTRY)

1. On circle: 'Somersetshire'. Centre: Stringed bugle below a mural crown and a scroll 'Jellalabad'; sphinx within the bugle-strings.

2. As 1, but on circle 'Somerset'. Again, although the sealed pattern is dated 1912 it is doubtful if this was worn to any great extent (Plate 6).

THE PRINCE OF WALES'S OWN (WEST YORKSHIRE REGIMENT)

On circle: 'West Yorkshire'. Centre: White Horse in w/m (Plate 6).

THE EAST YORKSHIRE REGIMENT

On circle: 'East Yorkshire'. Centre: Rose of York in w/m inside a laurel wreath upon an eight-pointed brass star.

THE BEDFORDSHIRE REGIMENT

On circle: 'Bedfordshire'. Centre: Garter Star with, in centre, a w/m hart crossing a ford.

THE LEICESTERSHIRE REGIMENT

On circle: 'Leicestershire'. Centre: Tiger below a scroll 'Hindoostan'.

THE ROYAL IRISH REGIMENT

1. On circle: 'Royal Irish'. Centre: Harp, surmounted by QVC.
2. As 1, but K/C after 1901 (Plate 7).

ALEXANDRA, PRINCESS OF WALES'S OWN (YORKSHIRE REGIMENT)

1. On circle: 'Yorkshire'. Centre: The letter 'A' (for Alexandra, Princess of Wales) linked with the Dannebrog bearing the date '1875'. Above, a crown (Plate 7).
2. As 1, but central device in w/m (worn by bandsmen).

THE CHESHIRE REGIMENT

On circle: 'Cheshire'. Centre: Eight-pointed star with a w/m Prince of Wales's Plumes and brass coronet superimposed (Plate 6).

THE SOUTH WALES BORDERERS

On circle: 'South Wales Borderers'. Centre: Laurel wreath encircling a Welsh Dragon.

THE KING'S OWN SCOTTISH BORDERERS

1. On circle: 'King's Own Borderers'. Centre: Edinburgh Castle above scroll *Nisi Dominus Frustra*. Worn 1881–84.
2. W/m badge similar to the pattern shown in Plate 11 but slightly larger and with QVC. Central circle, however, reads 'King's Own Borderers'. Worn 1884–87.

3. W/m badge similar to the pattern shown in Plate 11 but slightly larger and with QVC. Worn 1887–1901.

4. As 2, but with K/C after 1901 and slightly smaller.

Until 1887 the Regiment had been the King's Own Borderers, but in that year the Scottish Borderers Militia had been brought into the Regimental family as the 3rd Bn. making a change of title necessary.

THE GLOUCESTERSHIRE REGIMENT

On circle: 'Gloucestershire'. Centre: Sphinx on tablet 'Egypt' w/m.

THE WORCESTERSHIRE REGIMENT

1. On circle: 'Worcestershire' at top and *Firm* in box at bottom. Centre: Eight-pointed star, resting on two points, with tower superimposed on star. Worn 1881–83.

2. As 1, but star resting on one point. Worn 1883–90.

3. As 1, but within circle, an elongated eight-pointed star with Lion in centre, surrounded by Garter and above a scroll *Firm*.

THE EAST LANCASHIRE REGIMENT

On circle: 'East Lancashire'. Centre: Sphinx on tablet 'Egypt' w/m.

THE EAST SURREY REGIMENT

On circle: 'East Surrey'. Centre: Eight-pointed star bearing the arms of the City of Guildford.

THE DUKE OF CORNWALL'S LIGHT INFANTRY

On circle: 'Duke of Cornwall's Light Infantry'. Centre: Stringed bugle-horn; superimposed, a castle upon two crossed feathers (Plate 6).

THE DUKE OF WELLINGTON'S (WEST RIDING REGIMENT)

On circle: 'West Riding'. Centre: Demi-lion issuing from a coronet (the Duke of Wellington's crest).

THE BORDER REGIMENT

1. On circle: 'Border'. Centre: Tablet 'China' above Chinese Dragon within laurel wreath.

2. Large w/m badge (as in middle of bottom row in Plate 7); cross carrying eleven battle honours. In the centre, a Chinese Dragon below the word 'China': around the Dragon, a band 'Arroyo dos Molinos' and '1811'. Below, the Regiment's name on scroll.

THE ROYAL SUSSEX REGIMENT

On circle: 'Royal Sussex'. Centre: Laurel wreath surrounding cross carrying the Garter superimposed upon the Rousillon plume (Plate 7).

THE HAMPSHIRE REGIMENT

On circle: 'Hampshire'. Centre: Tiger.

THE SOUTH STAFFORDSHIRE REGIMENT

On circle: 'South Staffordshire'. Centre: Sphinx on tablet 'Egypt' in w/m (Plate 7).

THE DORSETSHIRE REGIMENT

1. On circle: 'Dorsetshire'. Centre: Gibraltar Castle with two turrets. Above, scroll 'Gibraltar': below, scroll *Primus in Indis* (Plate 6).
2. As 1, but after 1900, redesigned castle (Plate 7).

THE PRINCE OF WALES'S VOLUNTEERS (SOUTH LANCASHIRE REGIMENT)

On circle: 'South Lancashire'. Centre: Sphinx on tablet 'Egypt', w/m.

THE WELSH REGIMENT

1. On circle: 'The Welsh'. Centre: w/m Prince of Wales's plumes and brass coronet; below, a long brass scroll *Gwell angau neu Chywilydd*, overlapping the circle.
2. As 1, but scroll reads *Gwell angau na Chywilydd* (Sealed pattern 1890.)
3. As 1, but scroll reads *Gwell augau neu Chwilydd*.
4. As 1, but scroll reads *Gwell angau neu Chwilydd*.

THE OXFORDSHIRE AND BUCKINGHAMSHIRE LIGHT INFANTRY

1. On circle: 'Oxfordshire'. Centre: Stringed bugle-horn.
2. As 1, but on circle: 'Oxfordshire and Buckinghamshire'. (Sealed pattern 1909.) This change of title took place in 1908. In that year the Buckinghamshire Militia disappeared, as did the rest of the Militia but was reborn as 3rd Bn. and the county included in the new title (Plate 7).

THE ESSEX REGIMENT

1. On circle: 'Essex'. Centre: Gibraltar Castle with two turrets above motto *Montis Insignia Calpe* above Castle, Sphinx on tablet 'Egypt'.
2. As 1, but after 1900, redesigned Castle.

THE SHERWOOD FORESTERS (NOTTINGHAMSHIRE & DERBYSHIRE REGIMENT)

1. On circle: 'Derbyshire'. Centre: Cross surmounted by QVC; in centre of cross, a stag within an oak wreath. On the lower arm of the cross, a scroll 'Derbyshire'; on the horizontal arms, two scrolls 'Sherwood – Foresters'.
2. As 1, but with K/C.
3. On circle: 'Notts & Derby'. Centre: as 1, but K/C and title on lower scroll amended to 'Notts & Derby'.
   The two counties were linked in the title in October 1902.

THE LOYAL NORTH LANCASHIRE REGIMENT

1. On circle: 'Loyal North Lancashire'. Centre: Royal Crest, QVC, above the rose of Lancaster.
2. As 1, but K/C in Royal Crest.

THE NORTHAMPTONSHIRE REGIMENT

1. On circle: 'Northamptonshire'. Centre: Gibraltar Castle. Above, scroll 'Gibraltar': below, scroll 'Talavera'.
2. As 1, but after 1900, redesigned Castle.

PRINCESS CHARLOTTE OF WALES'S (ROYAL BERKSHIRE REGIMENT)

1. On circle: 'Berkshire'. Centre: Stag beneath an oak tree, the badge of the old Royal Berkshire Militia. Worn 1881–88.
2. As 1, but 'Royal Berkshire'. Worn 1888–1914. The Regiment became the 'Royal' in 1885 following the 1st Bn.'s conduct at the battle of Tofrek in the Sudan earlier in the year (Plate 6).

THE QUEEN'S OWN (ROYAL WEST KENT REGIMENT)

On circle: 'West Kent'. Centre: White Horse of Kent in w/m above a brass scroll *Invicta*. Above, a brass scroll *Quo Fas et Gloria Ducunt,* the county motto.

THE KING'S OWN (YORKSHIRE LIGHT INFANTRY)

1. On circle: 'South Yorkshire'. Centre: Stringed bugle-horn with Rose of York between the strings and below, a scroll *Cede Nullis*. Worn 1881–87.
2. On circle: 'Yorkshire Light Infantry'. Centre: French horn enclosing a w/m rose.

THE KING'S (SHROPSHIRE LIGHT INFANTRY)

On circle: 'Shropshire'. Centre: Stringed bugle-horn.

THE DUKE OF CAMBRIDGE'S OWN (MIDDLESEX REGIMENT)

On circle: 'Middlesex'. Centre: Coronet and Cypher of the Duke of Cambridge below w/m Prince of Wales's plumes, Coronet and Cypher, all above a scroll *Albuhera* and within a laurel wreath.

THE DUKE OF EDINBURGH'S (WILTSHIRE REGIMENT)

On circle: 'Wiltshire'. Centre: Coronet and Cypher of the Duke of Edinburgh in centre of a cross pattée.

THE MANCHESTER REGIMENT

On circle: 'Manchester'. Centre: Arms of the City of Manchester (Plate 7).

THE PRINCE OF WALES'S (NORTH STAFFORDSHIRE REGIMENT)

On circle: 'North Staffordshire'. Centre: Prince of Wales's plumes and motto in w/m, coronet in brass.

THE YORK AND LANCASTER REGIMENT

On circle: 'York & Lancaster'. Centre: Combined Red and White roses in brass and w/m.

THE DURHAM LIGHT INFANTRY

On circle: 'Durham'. Centre: Stringed bugle-horn.

THE CONNAUGHT RANGERS

1. On circle: 'Connaught Rangers'. Centre: Harp of Erin above a scroll *Quis Separabit*. Worn 1881–90.
2. As 1, but harp noticeably wider.

THE PRINCE OF WALES'S LEINSTER REGIMENT (ROYAL CANADIANS)

On circle: 'Leinster'. Centre: Prince of Wales' plumes in w/m, coronet in brass above two maple leaves and a scroll 'Central India'. (Plate 6.)

Jersey and Guernsey

Although these are not Regular Infantry they are included here as they are in the same format as the standard HPC and are found fairly often.

ROYAL MILITIA OF THE ISLAND OF JERSEY

On circle: 'Royal Jersey Light Infantry'. Centre: Stringed bugle-horn but no tassels to the cord.

ROYAL GUERNSEY MILITIA

On circle: 'Royal Guernsey Light Infantry'. Centre: Arms of Guernsey surmounted by laurel spray; draped across the spray is a scroll *Diex aie*.

The centres can also be found with the long prong-fastener indicating its use on the topi or foreign-service helmet. It will be seen that many of these had common features, the Sphinx, the ubiquitous Prince of Wales's plumes and the stringed bugle-horn, so that recognition was not always easy unless you were well versed in facing-colours. (Facings were the coloured collars and cuffs on the scarlet tunics, differing between regiments, now largely a matter of record so far as other ranks' clothing is concerned.) When cap badges were finalized in 1898 many of the designs were radically changed, as will be seen.

Fusilier regiments wore a sealskin cap instead of a blue helmet. In the front of this was worn a brass grenade of a shape common to all fusiliers, with a rounded body and long, pointed flames as shown in Plate 9. These are usually referred to as fur-cap grenades in contrast to the brass glengarry grenades which had a flat body and round flames, again common to all fusilier regiments, also shown in Plate 8.

The grenades, encountered in w/m, are those worn by Volunteer Battalions of the regiments.

Although the shapes were similar, the motif on the body of the grenade varied between regiments:

NORTHUMBERLAND FUSILIERS

St. George and Dragon within circle bearing title.

ROYAL FUSILIERS

Rose within the Garter, surmounted by the appropriate crown. There was no K/C Glengarry grenade as this head-dress was not worn at that time.

LANCASHIRE FUSILIERS

Sphinx on tablet 'Egypt' within laurel wreath, all inside circle bearing 'Lancashire'.

ROYAL SCOTS FUSILIERS

Royal Coat of Arms with appropriate crown. The QVC variety shows crown only whereas the post-1901 badge carries the Royal Crest above the Arms.

ROYAL WELSH FUSILIERS

Prince of Wales's Plumes.

ROYAL INNISKILLING FUSILIERS

Enniskillen Castle inside circle bearing 'Inniskilling'.

ROYAL IRISH FUSILIERS

There were two patterns for this regiment:
1. French Eagle on tablet inscribed '8' within circle bearing title.
2. Eagle on tablet only, no circle or title. (Sealed pattern 1903.)

ROYAL MUNSTER FUSILIERS

Three crowns on shield within a laurel wreath.

ROYAL DUBLIN FUSILIERS

Three castles, the badge of the old Royal Dublin City Militia on a shield.

The Cap Badge

It will be seen that the cap badge, evolving in the nineties, was worn con-currently with the helmet plate, albeit sometimes of very different design, until 1914 when full dress disappeared for the bulk of the army, never to return. I believe that the helmet has never officially ceased to be the full-dress head-wear for the majority of the infantry; in fact, many infantry bands have now returned to the helmet for appropriate occasions.

The following notes attempt to describe the badges worn by the British Regular Infantry of the Line. Territorial and Volunteer badges are dealt with in a later chapter.

Plates 10, 11, 12, 14 and 15a show the badges worn by the Infantry of the Line when war broke out in August 1914. In general, designs proved more stable than the cavalry's once they were chosen. But in 1915 the nickel shortage made itself felt and badges worn in bi-metal finish and some w/m issues were frequently struck in all-brass, also for economy as badges could then be struck in one process only. They were most unpopular and as soon as opportunity offered in 1919 they were replaced by bi-metal issues again.

As with the cavalry, I have felt it unnecessary to mention in each case the existence of an all-brass badge of a regiment. Some years ago a group of the more active collectors held a survey to try to ascertain which all-brass issues had existed. As no official list could be traced I have included this listing as *Appendix D*. Where the standard badge of a regiment was issued in all-w/m (for those normally in brass or bi-metal), these are less simple to account for and there is no common denominator. Mostly, these were worn by Militia battalions. Frequently, the first Volunteer Battalion of a regiment wore a w/m version of the badge while the second and sub-sequent battalions had to make some change or addition to it to show their identity. I have a w/m version of the King's Own Royal Regiment (Lancaster), worn when their 5th Battalion was a Royal Armoured Corps regiment during the Second World War. After that war the 1st Bn. The Middlesex Regiment had their Serjeants and Warrant-Officers wearing w/m badges. Regiments sometimes had them made specially for their Bandsmen and so there is no official record. (Plate 16 shows the fourteen regiments which had changed their badges by September 1939.)

The title at the head of each regimental paragraph is the one which was in use in 1914. Previous and subsequent changes of title are recorded in the text.

The Royal Scots (Lothian Regiment) continued to use their HPC, the w/m Star with voided brass centre piece. A piece of red cloth was normally worn behind the badge by the 1st Bn. to show through the voided centre. The 2nd Bn. wore a piece of mid-green cloth. There was no change in 1920 when they became The Royal Scots (The Royal Regiment). In 1958 the Brigade System meant that the Regiment wore the Lowland Brigade badge but authority was granted in 1969 for the Regimental badge to be resumed. (See also notes on pipers). (See also Chapter 20).

The Queen's (Royal West Surrey Regiment) wore a brass Paschal Lamb above a w/m scroll 'The Queen's' until 1920 when the title changed to The Queen's Royal Regiment (West Surrey). The badge was altered and the swallow-tailed banner became a flag, the Lamb changed the flag to his other paw, squared his shoulders, discarded the scroll as being quite unnecessary for such a distinguished and well-known animal and, all in brass, mounted what is inexplicably called a wreath in heraldic terms (Plate 16). This pattern appeared at the end of the Second World War in about two-thirds size for beret wear. The origin of the Paschal Lamb is obscure as a regimental device but the Queen's were once The Tangier Regiment and it may have been felt that this was a suitable badge for a regiment crusading against heathens in North Africa. In 1958 the Regiment assumed the Home Counties Brigade badge, and in October of that year merged with the East Surrey Regiment to form **The Queen's Royal Surrey Regiment.**

The Buffs (East Kent Regiment) have a Dragon described in the Army List simply as 'The Dragon' but Clothing Regulations of 1747 record it as a green one. He appears on the ground above a scroll 'The Buffs' all in brass and was worn thus until 1958 when the Home Counties Brigade badge was assumed. Early in this century the Dragon was worn as a pagri badge in the foreign-service helmet but not in precisely the same form. The forepaw dropped to the horizontal and the wings became more ruffled, perhaps not surprising since he is balancing on a wreath (Plate 17). There was no change in the badge when the Regiment became the Buffs (Royal East Kent Regiment) in 1935. The Regiment merged with the Queen's Own Royal West Kent Regiment in 1961 to form **The Queen's**

Own Buffs, Royal Kent Regiment, wearing the Home Counties Brigade badge.

The King's Own (Royal Lancaster Regiment) wore as a badge the Lion of England above the voided inscription 'The King's Own', all in brass. In 1920 the title was reshuffled to The King's Own Royal Regiment (Lancaster) but there was no change in the badge. When an anodized version of the badge was struck, the letters would have been too fragile to stand alone and they were produced on a solid block. After 1958 the Regiment adopted the Lancastrian Brigade badge and in October 1959 amalgamated with the Border Regiment to form **The King's Own Royal Border Regiment.**

The Northumberland Fusiliers were the possessors of another ancient badge; St. George and the Dragon, was worn on the base of a flaming grenade inside a circle bearing the title, all in brass. In 1935 they became **The Royal Northumberland Fusiliers** and the badge changed to bi-metal, St. George and the Dragon in w/m within a band, also w/m, bearing the motto *Quo fata vocant* all on a restyled brass flaming grenade (Plate 16). The Regiment was authorized to wear a red and white feather hackle, red uppermost, in 1829 and this was worn until 1968 when the **Royal Regiment of Fusiliers** embraced all the English fusiliers, and then assumed the same hackle for itself. The hackle was worn on the fur cap as a longer plume but it was not suitable for wear on either the khaki service-dress cap or the field-service cap. Taken into use once more after the Second World War in the beret it was worn even after the Regiment was compelled to accept the Fusilier Brigade badge in 1959.

The Royal Warwickshire Regiment wore an elegant w/m antelope, with a coronet around its neck and chain attached, standing on an heraldic wreath over a brass title scroll. This badge continued to be worn, unchanged in design until the Regiment was nominated to the Midland Brigade in 1958. Before a badge could be struck for the Brigade it was restyled the Forester Brigade but, even so, lasted a very short time. In 1962 the Royal Warwickshire Regiment became the **Royal Warwickshire Fusiliers** as an administrative convenience, the Forester Brigade ceased to exist and the new fusiliers joined the Fusilier Brigade to wear a blue and orange feather hackle above the Brigade badge.

The Royal Fusiliers (City of London Regiment) wore on their grenade the Garter with a rose in the centre and above, a K/C, all in brass (Plate 10). Its predecessor bore a QVC, but this was placed below the neck of the grenade and was not very clearly defined, looking more like a ducal coronet. After 1952, the new Q/C was placed on the neck as was the K/C before it. Another difference is in the rose. In the most recent issue the rose is so placed that a full petal is immediately below the Crown: previous issues showed the Crown above a division between two petals (Plate 17). Specimens of other Regimental devices in the Regimental Museum show no uniformity in the positioning of the rose. However, it is said that the rose derives from a mark cast on old cannon up to the time of Queen Anne which has the petal uppermost, directly below the Crown. In 1958 the creation of the Fusilier Brigade meant that The Royal Fusiliers assumed the Brigade badge although they continued to wear their own white feather hackle above it.

The King's (Liverpool Regiment) were awarded the White Horse of Hanover in 1716 by King George I. The first-pattern badge (Plate 10) was a w/m horse on ground above a brass scroll inscribed, rather oddly, 'The "Kings"', in roman letters. In 1926 the design changed slightly and a rather larger w/m horse mounted that popular heraldic perch, the wreath, surmounting a brass scroll carrying, in Old English lettering, 'Kings' (Plate 16). This badge was issued in about two-thirds size for beret wear in 1952 but in 1958 The King's Regiment (Liverpool), as it had become in 1920, amalgamated with The Manchester Regiment to form **The King's Regiment (Manchester & Liverpool)** and to wear the Lancastrian Brigade badge.

The Norfolk Regiment has the figure of Britannia, traditionally regarded as an award by Queen Anne following the battle of Almanza in 1707, during the War of the Spanish Succession. The first cap badge showed the figure seated within a laurel wreath, all in w/m, above a brass scroll (Plate 10). In 1935, their 250th anniversary, the Regiment became Royal and in 1937 the plain, brass Britannia shown in Plate 16 came into use. This pattern was worn in larger size by Warrant Officers and Serjeants of the Regiment as a pagri badge between 1881 and 1900. In common with some other regiments, a smaller beret badge appeared in about 1950. The East Anglian Brigade engulfed the Royal Norfolk Regiment in 1958 and in 1959 it merged with the Suffolk Regiment to form **1st East Anglian Regiment (Royal Norfolk & Suffolk)** and wore the Brigade badge.

The Lincolnshire Regiment won The Sphinx as the 10th Foot in Egypt in 1802. The badge shown in Plate 10 was the w/m Sphinx upon a tablet inscribed 'Egypt' in Old English lettering above a brass scroll 'Lincolnshire'. In November 1946 the Regiment was granted the Royal title for past services and a new badge was issued. This differed in that the name 'Egypt' below the Sphinx was in roman lettering and they contrived to cram 'Royal Lincolnshire Regiment' on to the brass scroll (Plate 17). In 1958 the Regiment went to the East Anglian Brigade to merge, in 1960, with the Northamptonshire Regiment, forming **2nd East Anglian Regiment (Duchess of Gloucester's Own Royal Lincolnshire and Northamptonshire).**

Exeter Castle, adopted by **The Devonshire Regiment** in 1883 had been the badge of the Devon Militia for many years. The badge was the w/m castle above a scroll *Semper Fidelis* inside a brass circle bearing the title and surmounted by QVC, upon an eight-pointed w/m star. After 1901 the badge changed to accommodate the new crown and again about 1956 when an anodized version bore the Q/C. In 1958 they merged with The Dorset Regiment, forming the **Devonshire & Dorset Regiment**, wearing the Wessex Brigade badge.

The Suffolk Regiment was the senior Gibraltar regiment and the first pattern badge was as shown in Plate 17. It carried the pre-1900 version of Gibraltar Castle inside a circle inscribed *Montis Insignia Calpe* within an oak wreath, surmounted by QVC, all in w/m above a brass title scroll 'The Suffolk Regt'. Dress regulations for 1900 show the badge, with QVC and, in the centre, the 'new' castle to be used by all four regiments carrying the honour. I have not seen one of these but I do have a K/C badge, thus obviously issued after 1901, still with the old, Regimental-pattern castle (also in Plate 17). But this soon gave way to the issue bearing the correct castle as in Plate 10 and this was worn until the Regiment adopted the East Anglian Brigade badge in 1958 and merged with the Royal Norfolk Regiment in 1959. No Q/C badge was issued between 1952 and 1958, but it was approved and made.

The Prince Albert's (Somerset Light Infantry) bore the distinctive horn of the light infantry, a distinction conferred upon the 13th Foot in 1822. Between the strings the letters 'P.A.' signified Prince Albert whilst the mural crown above with scroll 'Jellalabad' commemorated the defence of that fort during the First Afghan War in 1842. The w/m badge was worn unchanged (except for a slight reduction in size after 1950) until the merger with the Duke of Cornwall's Light Infantry in 1959 when the Light Infantry Brigade badge was taken into use. Changes of title, from Prince Albert's (Somersetshire Light Infantry) in 1912 and to The Somerset Light Infantry (Prince Albert's) in 1920 did not affect the design.

The Prince of Wales's Own (West Yorkshire Regiment) wore the w/m Horse of Hanover above a brass scroll 'West Yorkshire'. The badge continued in use until 1958 when they amalgamated with the East Yorkshire Regiment and adopted the Yorkshire Brigade badge. The change of title to The West Yorkshire Regiment (The Prince of Wales's Own) in 1920 necessitated no change of badge.

The East Yorkshire Regiment displayed a w/m Rose of York superimposed upon a brass star within a laurel wreath above a title scroll 'East Yorkshire'. In 1935 the Regiment became The East Yorkshire Regiment (The Duke of York's Own) without change in the badge. The combined East & West Yorkshire Regiments became **The Prince of Wales's Own Regiment of Yorkshire**, wearing the Yorkshire Brigade badge.

The Bedfordshire Regiment's badge was based upon a Maltese Cross, superimposed upon the Star of the Order of the Garter. In the centre were the (Garter and motto, and within, a hart crossing a ford, all in w/m. Across the lower arm of the cross was a brass scroll 'Bedfordshire'.

In 1919, to recognize the number of Hertfordshire men who had served in The Bedfordshire Regiment the title became **The Bedfordshire and Hertfordshire Regiment.** The badge altered a little, approximating the cross to that used in the insignia of the Order of the Bath whilst the scroll, reading 'Bedfordshire & Hertfordshire' dropped below the star. The badge was all in w/m (Plate 16). It was worn until 1958 when the Regiment was merged with The Essex Regiment to wear the East Anglian Brigade badge, forming the **3rd East Anglian Regiment (16/44th Foot)**, a notable reversion to the use of the old numbers.

The Leicestershire Regiment's Royal Tiger was granted to them as the 17th Foot for distinguished service in India 1804–23. The tiger on the ground is in brass whilst the 'Leicestershire' scroll below and the scroll 'Hindoostan' above are in w/m. In November 1946 the Regiment was granted the Royal title and the badge was re-struck with a 'Royal Leicestershire' scroll in standard size and later in small pattern for beret. The 1958 changes put the Regiment into the Midland Brigade, subsequently redesignated the Forester Brigade. In 1962 the Brigade was dispersed and the **Royal Leicesters** went to become the fourth battalion in the East Anglian Brigade.

The Harp and Crown worn by **The Royal Irish Regiment** were said to have been conferred by King William III. It is odd that the Harp of Erin was chosen for the cap badge when previous Regimental appointments had borne the Angel Harp. They were worn above a three-part scroll 'The Royal Irish Regiment', in brass. The crown initially was QVC but changed after 1901 to K/C. In 1922 the Regiment was disbanded, together with four other Irish regiments, on the formation of the Irish Free State.

Alexandra, Princess of Wales's Own (Yorkshire Regiment) wore at first the attractive badge shown in Plate 17. The Dannebrog and the Princess's coronet are in brass and the remainder of the badge in w/m. The date 1875 on the badge refers to the granting of the Royal title to the old 19th Foot. In 1908 another badge with the Dannebrog and coronet was produced in w/m but this time incorporating the name 'Alexandra' in consequence of a change of title in 1902 from The Princess of Wales's Own (Yorkshire Regiment). This badge is shown in Plate 10. Within the Regiment it was referred to as the 'Eiffel Tower' badge because of its slender and distinctive appearance. The change of title in 1920 to The Green Howards (Alexandra, Princess of Wales's Own, Yorkshire Regiment) brought no change in the badge but during the Second World War, probably when badges were being produced in haste and in quantity, a variant appeared with a crown in place of the coronet (Plate 17). This was described by an officer of the Regiment as an example of regimental incompetence but was, after all, only a repetition of a mistake made in the HPC which bore a crown in place of the princess's coronet intended (Plate 17). In 1952 a small, more squat badge appeared, in w/m, but with

'The Green Howards' on the scroll for the first time (Plate 17). The intended coronet was again supplanted by a crown of the flat-topped variety. In the regiment this was not a popular badge. The Yorkshire Brigade embraced **The Green Howards** in 1958 but in early 1969 it was announced that they would be permitted to resume their Regimental badge. However, in 1970 yet another badge was issued (Plate 49) and this embodied the coronet and the numerals 'XIX', the first reappearance since 1881 of the old numbers. (See also chapter 20).

The Lancashire Fusiliers wore on their brass grenade the Sphinx on a tablet inscribed 'Egypt', awarded for the service of the old 20th Foot in the 1801 campaign, above a w/m three-part scroll 'The Lancashire Fusiliers'. The Sphinx is within a laurel wreath, said to have been awarded for service at Minden in 1759. The badge continued unchanged from its introduction until the Regiment joined the Fusilier Brigade following the 1958 changes. However, after the Second World War a cloth badge was worn in the beret (the same as worn in the foreign-service helmet – these were originally cut from the shoulder-straps of the scarlet tunic): the letters 'L' and 'F' below a grenade, embroidered in white on red cloth (Plate 17). The Regiment wore a primrose feather hackle.

The Royal Scots Fusiliers continued to wear their old brass glengarry badge for as a Scottish regiment, they were still wearing the glengarry. The only changes were from QVC to K/C to Q/C. A white feather hackle was worn. In 1959 the Regiment, a Lowland one, merged reluctantly with the Highland Light Infantry to form **The Royal Highland Fusiliers**. This, incredibly, became a unit of the Lowland Brigade and wore the Lowland Brigade badge. (See also notes on pipers.)

The acorn carried by **The Cheshire Regiment** is popularly said to derive from services at the battle of Dettingen but no reliable evidence exists that they were there. Whatever the origin, the brass acorn and oak leaves appeared on an eight-pointed w/m rayed star above a scroll 'Cheshire' (Plate 11). Plate 17 shows the change of badge in 1922. The acorn and oak leaves remained in the centre of a title band, all in brass, superimposed upon an eight-pointed diamond-cut w/m star. Following the 1958 changes the Regiment went to the Mercian Brigade and wore their badge until 1969 when a return to the old Regimental badge was authorized. (See also chapter 20).

The Royal Welsh Fusiliers inevitably wore the grenade, a small brass one and superimposed upon the body a w/m circular band carrying the title, surrounding the Prince of Wales's plumes with a brass coronet. The older form of spelling was taken into use again in 1920 and badges were changed to read 'Royal Welch Fusiliers'. As part of the Welsh Brigade after 1958 they adopted the Brigade badge until 1969 when authority was granted to revert to their old badge. A white feather hackle is worn.

The South Wales Borderers' badge consisted principally of a brass wreath of immortelles, described somewhat illogically as silver immortelles. This wreath was directed by Queen Victoria to be borne upon the staff of the Queen's Colour of the 24th Foot to commemorate the gallantry of Lieutenants Coghill and Melville who saved that Colour after the battle of Isandlwana and for the battle of Rorke's Drift in 1879. In the centre was a w/m Sphinx on a tablet inscribed 'Egypt', for services in 1801, and on the lower part of the wreath the letters 'SWB', also in w/m. The Regiment was taken into the Welsh Brigade in 1958 and wore the Brigade badge.

The King's Own Scottish Borderers wore in the glengarry the w/m badge that was adopted as the HPC in 1887, changed slightly after 1901, becoming smaller and bearing the K/C. This continued unchanged until after 1958 when the Borderers adopted the badge of the Lowland Brigade. In 1969 reversion to the Regimental badge was sanctioned and a Q/C version appeared shortly afterwards. (See also Chapter 20).

The Cameronians (Scottish Rifles) was a merger of the old 26th (Cameronians) Regiment and the 90th (Perthshire Volunteers) (Light Infantry). The badge (Plate 11), was a simple w/m one, the star – a mullet or spur-rowel coming from the arms of the Douglas family (the Earl of Angus who formed the Regiment in 1689 was a Douglas). This represented the 26th who became the 1st Battalion, while the stringed bugle-horn denoted the 2nd Battalion, the old 90th. The first title of the combined regiment in May 1881 was The Scotch Rifles, changed in July to The Cameronians (Scotch Rifles), and again in December to The Cameronians (Scottish Rifles). But until after the First World War the two battalions styled themselves 1 st Cameronians and 2nd Scottish Rifles. Serjeants wore a cast w/m badge in the same design but slightly larger – three inches wide against the standard two-and-a-half inches. Paradoxically, when most regiments adopted a pagri badge it was normally a larger version of the cap badge. In the Cameronians' case theirs was smaller, being only two inches wide. All three are shown in Plate 17 and there are one or two very minor points of difference. However, the bonnet badge continued in use until 1958 when the Lowland Brigade badge was reluctantly adopted. In 1968 the Regiment was disbanded. (See also notes on pipers.)

The Royal Inniskilling Fusiliers bore on their brass grenade badge a w/m Castle of Enniskillen from the central tower of which flew St. George's flag, blowing to the viewer's left, above a scroll 'Inniskilling'. The castle badge was awarded to commemorate the original defence of Enniskillen in 1689. About 1926 the grenade motif was discarded and the w/m castle with 'Inniskilling' scroll above and flag flying to the viewer's right (Plate 18) took its place until 1934 when the old badge returned but with flag flying to the viewer's right (Plate 16). In the late 1940's a similar badge appeared with the mis-spelling 'Inneskilling'. The Regiment wore a grey feather hackle which it took with it to the North Irish Brigade after 1958. (See also notes on pipers.)

The Gloucestershire Regiment wore the Sphinx on a tablet 'Egypt' for their service in 1801, above a laurel spray with a scroll 'Gloucestershire' below, all in w/m. It was worn unchanged until induction into the Wessex Brigade after 1958 when the Brigade badge was taken. The Regiment is unique in that it was also permitted to wear a badge on the back of the head-dress to commemorate the gallantry of the old 28th at the Battle of Alexandria when they were attacked by the French from both front and rear. The rear rank turned about and drove them off. The brass back-badge (Plate 11) was the first pattern worn in the cap, both field-service and service-dress (approx. half-inch diameter). In 1918 to commemorate the 1st Battalion's back-to-back stand at Festubert a larger badge was authorized, approximately one inch in diameter, with a w/m Sphinx on a tablet 'Egypt' within a brass laurel wreath. But this distinction proved unpopular and in 1935 permission was given to revert to the old, smaller brass badge. When the Wessex Brigade was formed in 1958 the Brigade badge was adopted but the back-badge was retained. (See also Chapter 20).

The Worcestershire Regiment initially wore the all-brass badge shown in Plate 11 but in 1925 changed to the elongated star which had been the third pattern HPC. The central lion on a tablet *Firm* was in w/m surrounded by a brass Garter, superimposed on the w/m elongated star (Plate 16). The 1st Battalion, the old 29th, was raised in 1694 by an ex-Coldstream Guards officer who brought with him the Star of the Order of the Garter for his new Regiment. In 1958 the Worcestershire Regiment accepted the Mercian Brigade badge but in 1969 was again wearing its own badge.

The East Lancashire Regiment wore as their badge the pattern shown in Plate 11 but with QVC. The Sphinx on a tablet 'Egypt' commemorates service in 1801 while the rose was the red one of Lancaster. The rose was in brass, the remainder of the badge w/m. The badge was also made in brass with a w/m rose and this pattern was worn by the 3rd (Militia) Bn. in both QVC and K/C strikes. This battalion, of course, ceased to exist as Militia in 1908 but the badge continued to be worn. After the First World War it was issued again but the Regular battalions refused to wear it and stocks were passed to the TA. The introduction of the Brigade System in 1958 compelled The East Lancashire Regiment to amalgamate with The South Lancashire Regiment (Prince of Wales's Volunteers) to form **The Lancashire Regiment (Prince of Wales's Volunteers)** and to wear the Lancastrian Brigade badge.

As might be expected, **The East Surrey Regiment** bore in the centre of their badge the Arms of Guildford (the county town) in w/m on a brass shield superimposed on a w/m eight-pointed star; the scroll 'East Surrey' below, was in brass. The first issue bore the flat-topped QVC, yet a pagri badge worn by the 1st Battalion 1891–93 (Plate 18) and struck in brass bore the more normal Victorian crown. The bi-metal badge continued with a K/C after 1901 and was reduced to about two-thirds size after the Second World War for beret wear. Q/C issues in both sizes followed. In October 1959 the Regiment amalgamated with The Queen's Royal Regiment (West Surrey) to form the **Queen's Royal Surrey Regiment**, wearing the Home Counties Brigade badge.

The Duke of Cornwall's Light Infantry wore the normal light infantry stringed bugle-horn with a ducal coronet above, set on a scroll 'Cornwall', all in w/m. In my early days as a collector I was told that the tassels on the ends of the strings were in fact thistles commemorating the connection of the old 32nd Foot, the defenders of Lucknow during the Indian Mutiny, with the 93rd Highlanders who fought through to their relief. This is a splendid story and other collectors will know plenty more, equally insubstantial. If you try holding almost any other Light Infantry badge upside down you can see the same 'thistles'. The design came into use in 1901 and continued in use until the merger with The Somerset Light Infantry in 1959 to form **The Somerset and Cornwall Light Infantry.** Prior to 1901 the pattern shown in Plate 18, made in brass, was worn. Behind the w/m badge a piece of red felt was worn to commemorate the action of Brandywine in 1777 during the American War of Independence.

The Duke of Wellington's (West Riding Regiment) was the linking of the 33rd and 76th Regiments of Foot. The Duke had served as a sub-altern in the 76th and as a major, later colonel, in the 33rd. The first title in 1881 was The Halifax Regiment (Duke of Wellington's), but changed after a few weeks to The Duke of Wellington's (West Riding Regiment) and again in 1920 to The Duke of Wellington's Regiment (West Riding). The badge shows the crest and motto of the Duke in w/m: a demi-lion issuing from a ducal coronet above the motto *Virtutis Fortuna Comes* all over a brass scroll 'The West Riding'. It continued in use until the creation of the Yorkshire Brigade in 1958 when the Brigade badge was adopted. In early 1969 permission was given for the Regimental badge to be assumed once more.

The Border Regiment wore a distinctive w/m badge (Plate 12), a cross similar to that of the Order of the Bath, superimposed upon a laurel wreath upon a star similar to that of the Order of the Garter, topped by a K/C with, below, a scroll reading 'The Border Regt.' The four arms of the cross carried battle honours: in the centre, was a circle inscribed 'Arroyo dos Molinos 1811' and, within the circle, a Dragon with 'China' above, on a ground, part white (the upper part) and part red (the lower). The lower part, in fact, is voided and backed by a piece of red felt. This represents the two-thirds red and one-third white shako pom-pom of the French 34th Regiment defeated at Arroyo dos Molinos. The honour 'Arroyo dos

Molinos' was only borne by The Border Regiment. The badge passed through the sequence of crowns until October 1959 when The King's Own Royal Regiment (Lancaster) and The Border Regiment were linked to form **The King's Own Royal Border Regiment**, wearing the Lancastrian Brigade badge.

The Royal Sussex Regiment carried as the dominant feature of their badge the Star of the Order of the Garter deriving from the Royal Sussex Militia in 1881. This was in w/m, as was the plume worn behind it. The plume was said to commemorate the action of the 1st Battalion, the old 35th Foot, when they defeated the French Regiment of Royal Roussillon who wore the long white plume. Below the star was a brass scroll 'The Royal Sussex Regt.' When the Brigade System was introduced in 1958 the Regiment assumed the Home Counties Brigade badge.

The badge of **The Hampshire Regiment** was known to its wearers as the 'Cat and Cabbage'. Dominant features were a w/m Royal Tiger (to record the old 37th's service in India 1805–26) above a brass Hampshire rose and it was to these that the affectionate description referred. Tiger and rose were surrounded by a w/m laurel wreath while a brass scroll below read 'Hampshire'. In 1946 the Regiment became **The Royal Hampshire Regiment** and in 1949 the new badge was announced. The old Cat and Cabbage remained intact, a K/C was added to the top of the badge and the new scroll read 'Royal Hampshire' (Plate 18). In due course, a Q/C issue appeared and then, in the 1958 changes, the Regiment adopted the Wessex Brigade badge. Early in 1969, the Regimental badge was assumed again. (See also chapter 20).

The South Staffordshire Regiment had the ideal badge, simple in concept and execution and instantly recognizable. The knot was the badge of the de Stafford family and has been incorporated into county and local authority heraldry. Crown and knot were in w/m and the scroll 'South Staffordshire' in brass. The bi-metal design ran from QVC to K/C to Q/C until, in January 1959, they merged with The North Staffordshire Regiment to form **The Staffordshire Regiment (The Prince of Wales's)**, wearing the badge of the Mercian Brigade. It was customary to wear behind the Regimental badge a piece of brown holland material. In the early part of the eighteenth century the 1st Battalion, the old 38th Foot, spent almost sixty years in the West Indies during which time they were so forgotten that they had to mend their clothing with holland instead of the appropriate cloth.

The Dorsetshire Regiment was another of the Gibraltar regiments and their first badge (Plate 18) bore the old Regimental-pattern, two-towered castle with key in w/m above scroll 'Primus in Indis' (as the old 39th Foot was the first line infantry regiment to serve on operations in India – with Clive at Plassey in 1757) and Sphinx above, on tablet 'Marabout', commemorating the services of the 2nd Battalion, the old

54th Foot, in Egypt in 1801. Surrounding, was a brass laurel wreath with, on the top half, a scroll 'Dorsetshire'. Dress Regulations for 1900 show the new pattern (Plate 12): the Castle became standard pattern but the Sphinx was lirted up and rested between the ends of the wreath while the title scroll moved to the bottom. In 1951 when the title changed to The Dorset Regiment the name on the scroll became 'Dorset'. In May 1958 the Regiment amalgamated with The Devonshire Regiment to become **The Devonshire and Dorset Regiment**, wearing the badge of the Wessex Brigade.

The Prince of Wales's Volunteers (South Lancashire Regiment) were formed from the 40th Foot and the 82nd Foot in 1881 and the first title was **The South Lancashire Regiment (Prince of Wales's Volunteers)**, but only a few weeks elapsed before it was changed to the sequence at the head of this paragraph. In 1920, the title changed a little when the word 'Regiment' was dropped from inside the bracket and eighteen years later the original title was restored. However, the badge shown in Plate 12 incorporated both parts of the title on two scrolls, top and bottom, linked by laurel branches: in the centre, the w/m Sphinx on a tablet 'Egypt' (commemorating the service of the old 40th Foot in 1801) is below the Prince of Wales's plumes and motto in w/m with a brass coronet. The 1958 changes saw the amalgamation with The East Lancashire Regiment to form **The Lancashire Regiment (Prince of Wales's Volunteers)**, wearing the Lancastrian Brigade badge.

The Welsh Regiment, as might be expected, wore the Prince of Wales's plumes with scrolls *Ich Dien* in w/m, a brass coronet and a scroll below, 'The Welsh'. In 1920, the spelling of the title was changed to an older style and the badge was issued with 'The Welch' on the scroll. The Welsh Brigade, formed in 1958, embraced **The Welch Regiment** who assumed the Brigade badge.

The Black Watch (Royal Highlanders), the senior Highland regiment, wore the Star of the Order of the Thistle, with St. Andrew and his cross in the central oval, surrounded by the band with motto *Nemo me impune lacessit* and a thistle wreath. Above, flanking the QVC, were two scrolls 'The Royal' and 'Highlanders' while, below was the Sphinx on a blank tablet (commemorating the Egyptian service of the 1st Battalion, the old 42nd Foot, in 1801) flanked by two scrolls 'Black'-'Watch' all in w/m. After Queen Victoria died the badge was reissued with K/C (Plate 12). In 1934 the title changed to The Black Watch (Royal Highland Regiment) and it was decided to reverse the titles to read 'The Black Watch' at the top and 'Royal Highland Regiment' at the bottom. When it was found that the lower scrolls were too small to carry the subsidiary title it was decided to drop the scrolls completely. The resultant badge is shown in Plate 16. It was reissued subsequently with Q/C. Before 1881 Serjeants of the 42nd wore a bi-metal badge (Plate 18), w/m star, gilt centrepiece with '42' in w/m. This continued to be worn by Serjeants of the 1st Battalion The Black Watch (Royal Highlanders) and later, in a K/C version until 1926. A curious feature of all Black Watch badges appears to be an inability to decide upon the spelling of *Lacessit* on the motto band: it is sometimes struck *Lacesset*. Despite the discarding of title scrolls shortly after the change of title in 1934 I believe that badges continued to be struck from the old die for many years after. Lately, the badge has only been worn in the glengarry. Other head-dresses have carried the red feather hackle in its place. The Highland Brigade badge was prescribed for wear after 1958 but in 1969 permission was granted to revert to the Regimental badge.

The Oxfordshire and Buckinghamshire Light Infantry, when first created in 1881 from the old 43rd and 52nd Foot were styled The Oxfordshire Light Infantry, the reference to Buckinghamshire being added in 1908. The 52nd were the first regiment to be converted to the Light Infantry role and the 43rd followed shortly after. The Badge, the stringed bugle-horn with the strings tied in three loops, was in w/m. It continued unchanged through the 1908 amplification of the title and was issued slightly smaller as a beret-badge after 1945. When the Brigade System took effect in 1958 it was found necessary to put the Regiment into The Green Jackets Brigade with The King's Royal Rifle Corps and The Rifle Brigade to ensure adequate numbers for the Brigade: the Light Infantry Brigade, the logical spot for the oldest Light Infantry regiment, already had four regiments.

The Essex Regiment was another of the Gibraltar regiments and Plate 18 shows the badges before and after 1900 to illustrate the differences in the castles. In this case, the two patterns are more similar than in the other regiments affected. The castle was in brass as was the oak wreath while the Sphinx on tablet 'Egypt' and the title scrolls 'The Essex Regt.' were in w/m. The Sphinx was won by the 1st Battalion, the old 44th, for their services in 1801 and the Castle and Key of Gibraltar came from the old 56th Foot, the 2nd Battalion, for service at the siege in 1779–82. A version of this badge with reversed metals was worn by the 3rd (Militia) Bn. of the Regiment until 1908. The badge shown in Plate 12 continued in use until June 1958 when The Essex Regiment merged with The Bedfordshire and Hertfordshire Regiment to form **3rd East Anglian Regiment (16/44th Foot)**, wearing the badge of the East Anglian Brigade.

The Sherwood Foresters (Nottinghamshire and Derbyshire) Regiment began life as a combination of the 45th (Nottinghamshire Sherwood Foresters) Regiment and the 95th (The Derbyshire) Regiment so that it is something of a surprise to learn that the first title, The Sherwood Foresters (Derbyshire) Regiment – omitted reference to Nottinghamshire. This was rectified in 1902. The badge shown in Plate 18 was the first pattern, a w/m Maltese Cross with, in the centre, a white hart within an oak wreath; above, QVC; across the left- and right-hand arms of the cross, two scrolls 'Sherwood'-'Foresters'. The lower scroll, in brass, was inscribed 'Derbyshire'. Briefly, a K/C badge existed in this format but these were in use for a very short time only and are seldom seen. The next badge (Plate 12) had K/C and 'Notts & Derby' on the brass scroll. A Q/C badge was issued shortly before the 1958 changes which put the Regiment into the Midland Brigade. This was soon renamed the Forester Brigade but in 1962 the Brigade was warned for dispersal and The Sherwood Foresters found themselves wearing the Mercian Brigade badge.

The Loyal North Lancashire Regiment bore the red rose of Lancaster, with the petal uppermost, above a scroll, in brass, inscribed 'Loyal North Lancashire', all surmounted by the Royal Crest with QVC in w/m. After 1901, a K/C issue came into use and in 1920 the title was reshuffled to The Loyal Regiment (North Lancashire). The rose shifted through 36 degrees to a position where a gap between petals was uppermost and the scroll was amended to read 'The Loyal Regiment' (Plate 16). A Q/C issue was made just before the Lancastrian Brigade badge came into use in 1958.

The Northamptonshire Regiment was the fourth of the Gibraltar regiments and Plate 18 shows the badges before and after 1900 illustrating the differing Castles. It will be seen that in the earlier pattern the Castle has a flag and that the Key is larger, superimposed upon the 'Talavera' scroll and turned in the opposite direction to its successor. The Castle, 'Talavera' and 'Gibraltar' scrolls, the Key and the laurel wreath are in w/m while the 'Northamptonshire' scroll is in brass. The constituent elements of the Regiment were the 48th who contributed the Talavera honour and the 58th who were at Gibraltar. In 1958 the Regiment went into the East Anglian Brigade and, in June 1960, amalgamated with The Royal Lincolnshire Regiment to form **2nd East Anglian Regiment (Duchess of Gloucester's Own Royal Lincolnshire and Northamptonshire).**

Princess Charlotte of Wales's (Royal Berkshire Regiment) was formed in 1881 from the 49th (Princess Charlotte of Wales's) and the 66th (Berkshire) Regts. The Dragon of China was brought to the union by the 49th for service in China 1840–42. In 1885, following the battle of Tofrek in the Sudan, the Regiment became Royal. The badge, in brass, had the Dragon above a scroll 'Royal Berkshire'. It continued in use until the Wessex Brigade saw the Regiment merge with The Wiltshire Regiment (Duke of Edinburgh's) in June 1959 to form **The Duke of Edinburgh's Royal Regiment (Berkshire and Wiltshire).**

The Royal Marine Light Infantry and **The Royal Marine Artillery** in 1914 had separate existences and separate badges. The Light Infantry wore the traditional bugle-horn above the Globe, showing the Eastern Hemisphere, within a laurel wreath, in brass (Plate 13). The Globe was awarded by King George IV in 1827 to symbolize the worldwide service of the Corps and the laurels for the capture of the island of Belleisle in the Bay of Biscay in 1761. The Artillery used the plain brass grenade shown until 1922 when the design changed to bring them more into line with the Light Infantry, placing the grenade above the Globe and Laurel. In 1923, the two elements were merged into one Corps of Royal Marines wearing one badge, the Royal Crest, with K/C, above the Globe and Laurel, in brass. Serjeants wear the same badge in gilt while Colour-Serjeants have the same badge, also in gilt, but in two parts, the Royal Crest separate and worn above the Globe and Laurel. These three appeared with K/C and Q/C. In 1962 the Corps adopted a new uniform of lovat green and bronzed badges were issued with Q/C in two styles: in one piece for all ranks up to and including Serjeants and in two pieces for Colour-Serjeants.

Royal Marine Bandsmen at the Royal Naval School of Music wore the Globe and Laurel with a lyre above in brass and senior NCOs wore the same pattern with slightly larger lyre, in gilt. The various bands, despite changes of title, wore badges as follows:

Chatham Division: 1902–23. Badge of the RMLI in brass, with silver York Rose separately above.
1923-50. Three-part badge consisting of brass Globe and Laurel: above, silver York Rose: above, brass Royal Crest K/C.
In 1950 this was disbanded, personnel being transferred to other Bands.

Plymouth Division: 1920–23. Badge of RMLI in brass, with silver Prince of Wales's plumes, coronet and motto separately above.
1923–52. Three-part badge consisting of brass Globe and Laurel; above, silver Prince of Wales's plumes, coronet and motto; above, brass Royal Crest, K/C.
1952 to date: as above, but Q/C.
Portsmouth Division: 1890–1923. Badge of the RMLI in brass, with silver Prince of Wales's plumes, coronet and motto separately above.
1923–55. A gilt grenade surrounded by laurel wreath: on the body of the grenade, in silver plate, the Royal Cypher GRV and K/C. This was the cap-badge of the old Royal Marine Artillery Band, transferred to the Portsmouth Band on the creation of the Corps of Royal Marines in 1923. 1955 to date. As above but following the Royal Tour of the Commonwealth in 1953–54 the Band, which is also known as The Royal Yacht Band was awarded an additional distinction: the combined Cyphers of the Queen and Prince Philip in silver plate worn separately above. I have this badge also with the GRV cypher on the grenade but topped by a Q/C. I understand that this was a mistake and it was withdrawn.

The Royal Marines have been included here as when they serve under the Army Act, they rank in seniority after The Royal Berkshire Regiment (all badges are shown in Plate 13).

The Queen's Own (Royal West Kent Regiment) wore as a badge a White Horse, not the more familiar horse of Hanover but, appropriately, a hopping horse of Kent upon a scroll *Invicta*, in Old English lettering above a three-part scroll 'Royal West Kent', all in w/m. A change of title in 1920 to The Royal West Kent Regiment (Queen's Own) and another in 1921 to The Queen's Own Royal West Kent Regiment brought no changes in the badge and it continued in use until the adoption of the Home Counties Brigade badge in 1958. Amalgamation of the Regiment with The Buffs (Royal East Kent Regiment) followed three years later when **The Queen's Own Buffs, Royal Kent Regiment** was created.

The King's Own (Yorkshire Light Infantry) wore the smallest badge in the army, a brass French horn with a w/m Rose of York in the twist. A very much larger pattern of it, twice the width and twice the height, was worn in the pagri (Plate 18). Removal of the brackets in the title in 1920 brought no change in the badge. Shortly after the Second World War the badge was reissued, wholly in w/m. On absorption into the Light Infantry Brigade in 1958 the Regiment assumed the Brigade badge.

The King's (Shropshire Light Infantry) was the title adopted in 1882. The badge was simply the brass letters 'KSLI' within the cords of a w/m stringed bugle-horn. The brackets were removed from the Regimental title in 1920 but, as the King's Shropshire Light Infantry, the Regiment continued to wear the same pattern, reduced after 1950 to a smaller, beret badge until embodied in the Light Infantry Brigade in 1958.

The Duke of Cambridge's Own (Middlesex Regiment) stuck to the design in the HPC: Prince of Wales's plumes and motto in w/m, brass coronet; below, brass coronet and cypher of the Duke of Cambridge above the honour scroll 'Albuhera'; surrounding all, a brass laurel wreath and, below, a w/m scroll 'Middlesex Regt'. It was at Albuhera in 1811 that the wounded Colonel Inglis of the 57th Foot positioned himself near the colours, shouting 'Die hard, my men, die hard'. This gave rise to their nickname 'The Diehards'. The title was changed in 1920 to The Middlesex Regiment (Duke of Cambridge's Own) but the badge was unchanged. This badge was worn, entirely in w/m, by Serjeants and Warrant-Officers of the 1st Battalion after the Second World War. In the 1958 changes The Middlesexx Regiment was swept into the Home Counties Brigade and wore the Brigade badge.

The King's Royal Rifle Corps wore a most distinctive badge, a black Maltese Cross with QVC above, all on a red cloth backing. The arms of the cross carried battle honours with, in the centre, a circle bearing the full title and inside it a stringed bugle-horn. The crown actually rested, not on the upper arm of the cross, but on a tablet inscribed *Celer et Audax,* reputedly given as reward for the Regiment's services before Quebec in

1759. The badge was struck again after 1901 to incorporate the K/C but honours for South Africa were awarded in 1905 and yet another K/C badge was issued with Defence and Relief of Ladysmith on the lower arm of the cross. In the 1950s when a Q/C version was produced, no attempt was made to add any more; in any case, there was no room. The surprising feature about this last badge was that it was made in black plastic, the only one so produced since the days of the Second World War. The 1958 changes allocated The King's Royal Rifle Corps to the Green Jackets Brigade.

The Duke of Edinburgh's (Wiltshire Regiment) wore a brass cross pattée, surmounted by the late Duke of Edinburgh's coronet; in the centre, on a disc, the Duke's coronet and monogram 'AEA' (Alfred Ernest Albert, second son of Queen Victoria); below, a title scroll, 'The Wiltshire Regiment'. When the present Duke of Edinburgh became Colonel-in-Chief in 1954 a new coronet, that of a Prince Consort, was to appear above the cross and also in the centre, over the letter 'P', reversed and entwined, in brass (Plate 19). In 1920 the title was changed to the Wiltshire Regiment (Duke of Edinburgh's). The Wessex Brigade badge was worn following the 1958 changes when the Regiment amalgamated with The Royal Berkshire Regiment (Princess Charlotte of Wales's) to form **The Duke of Edinburgh's Royal Regiment (Berkshire and Wiltshire).**

The Arms of the City were worn by **The Manchester Regiment** in w/m above a brass title scroll 'Manchester'. This was known as the 'Tramconductor's badge' for obvious reasons and few people seem to have been sorry in 1923 when the change was made to the simple brass fleur-de-lys which commemorated service in the French island of Martinique by the old 63rd Foot over a hundred years before (Plate 16). After the Second World War the brass badge changed to w/m. In the 1958 changes, The Manchester Regiment merged with The King's Regiment (Liverpool) to become **The King's Regiment (Manchester and Liverpool)**, wearing the badge of the Lancastrian Brigade. During the period 1881–1895, warrant-officers of the Regiment wore a distinctive badge (Plate 19), embodying the w/m Sphinx gained by the old 96th in Egypt in 1801 above a brass title-scroll.

The Prince of Wales's (North Staffordshire Regiment) also wore the Stafford knot, in brass, above a w/m scroll 'North Stafford'. This perpetuated the 1st Battalion, the old 64th Foot, secondarily titled '2nd Staffordshire'. The 98th Foot was The Prince of Wales's and so the w/m Prince of Wales's plumes and motto, with brass coronet, appeared above the knot. In 1920 the title was reshuffled to The North Staffordshire Regiment (The Prince of Wales's) but no change of badge was necessary. The two Staffordshire regiments amalgamated in January 1959 to form **The Staffordshire Regiment (The 'Prince of Wales's)** and to wear the Mercian Brigade badge.

44

The York and Lancaster Regiment, like the Royal Hampshire Regiment, included a tiger and a rose in their badge and this was also called the 'Cat and Cabbage'. The brass Royal Tiger was brought to the 1881 union of the 65th and 84th Foot by the former Regiment: it stood below a brass and w/m Union Rose, representing the Yorkist and Lancastrian roses; above, a brass ducal coronet, stemming from the Duchy of Lancaster, all surrounded by a laurel wreath and a title scroll 'York and Lancaster' in brass. The 1958 changes saw the Regiment in the Yorkshire Brigade where they remained until disbandment in 1969.

The Durham Light Infantry wore the stringed bugle-horn with the flat-topped QVC above and the letters 'DLI' within the strings. In due course, the crown changed to K/C and in the 1950s to Q/C. The badge continued in use in reduced size for the beret until the Regiment was incorporated into the Light Infantry Brigade in 1958.

The Highland Light Infantry, created in 1881 from the 71st (Highland) (Light Infantry) and the 74th (Highlanders) Regiment of Foot, wore the Star of the Order of the Thistle and on it, the French bugle-horn of the 71st above the Elephant granted to the 74th for services in India, especially at the Battle of Assaye in 1803. The Elephant had a scroll 'Assaye' above and in the centre of the bugle-horn the monogram 'HLI'. Above the bugle-horn at first was a flat-topped QVC, changing after 1901 to K/C. The badge, all in w/m, did not change in 1923 when (City of Glasgow Regiment) was added to the title. The Regiment is another which bore the honour 'Gibraltar', but this was not granted until 1908 by which time the badge was already full and without room for the Castle and Key. A Q/C badge was later made. When the Brigade System came into being in 1958 the Regiment was ordered to amalgamate with The Royal Scots Fusiliers. Despite considerable opposition the merger took place in January 1959 when logic was ignored and the new regiment, **The Royal Highland Fusiliers**, donned the Lowland Brigade badge.

The Seaforth Highlanders (Ross-shire Buffs, The Duke of Albany's) was the second title of this Regiment, the merger of the 72nd (Duke of Albany's Own Highlanders) and the 78th Highland Regiment of Foot (or Ross-shire Buffs). The first, Seaforth Highlanders (Ross-shire Buffs), was held only from July to November 1881. The badge, the stag's head, and the motto *Citdich'n Righ* are those of the Mackenzies and were said to have been given to the chieftain of the clan for having saved King Alexander II of Scotland from a wounded stag. The clansman severed the stag's head immediately behind the antlers and was awarded this trophy as a personal device. A descendant became the first Earl of Seaforth in 1623. The badge was worn in w/m and Warrant-Officers wore the stag's head alone in silver plate, in relief. The Regiment was the only one in the army with a Gaelic motto. In 1958 the Seaforths adopted the Highland Brigade badge and in February 1961 were amalgamated with The Queen's

Own Cameron Highlanders to form **Queen's Own Highlanders (Seaforth and Camerons).**

The Gordon Highlanders also bore a stag's head in a w/m badge. The Regiment was a union of the 75th Stirlingshire Regiment and the 92nd (Gordon Highlanders) Regiment of Foot. The latter was raised in 1794 by the Marquess of Huntly, later Duke of Gordon, and the stag's head issuing from a ducal coronet is the family crest. The ivy was the badge of the Gordon family. The 75th did not appear to feature in the head-dress badge. The motto *Bydand* below the coronet is not Gaelic but Lowland Scots dialect, loosely translatable as 'Watchful'. There is a version of the badge in which the motto appears as two words, *By dand*, but this is simply a manufacturer's error. Serjeants and Warrant-Officers wore what is normally described as the 'Staff badge' (Plate 19) which shows the stag's head in relief, of silver plate. In 1958, when the Highland Brigade came into being, the Brigade badge was adopted but 1969 saw the Regimental badge authorized for use once more. (See also chapter 20).

The Queen's Own Cameron Highlanders were the old 79th and they kept what was their old badge. It showed St. Andrew and his Cross within a wreath of thistles, all in w/m. The pattern shown in Plate 15 embodies also a scroll 'Cameron'. The sealed pattern for this latter badge was dated 1897 but an account from the Regiment contends that it was first issued in 1912. However, the 1st Battalion who received these while at Aldershot, did not protest and so, the official Regimental badge in use in 1914 bore the scroll, although we may be sure that most of the Jocks continued to wear the old nameless pattern. In fact, it was the ambition of every Cameron Highlander to wear one of these and at least one officer was still doing so in February 1961 when The Queen's Own Cameron Highlanders merged with the Seaforth Highlanders (Ross-shire Buffs, The Duke of Albany's) and adopted the Highland Brigade badge. The brass Cameron badge, which is in the Scottish United Services Museum in Edinburgh and which was issued as a first World War economy measure, came apparently from the old die and had no scroll. The Camerons badge shown in the set of drawings in *Twenty Years After* has no title scroll which may suggest that this pattern was still in general use at that time.

The Royal Irish Rifles was created in 1881 when the 83rd (County of Dublin) Regiment of Foot and the 86th (Royal County Down) Regiment were linked. The badge was the Angel Harp and Crown (QVC) from the Order of St. Patrick, above a motto scroll *Quis Separabit* all in black. The badge continued in black but with K/C until 1913 when it became a w/m badge, with only a change to Q/C in the 1950s. After 1958 the North Irish Brigade badge was adopted. On the formation of the Irish Free State it became necessary to cut the Irish establishment but the Regiment lived on although restyled **The Royal Ulster Rifles** in 1920.

Princess Victoria's (Royal Irish Fusiliers) wore the brass grenade with, on the body, w/m Prince of Wales's plumes, motto and coronet above an angel harp: above the grenade a w/m coronet. There are sundry myths about the coronet and whether it is affixed to or separate from the grenade but there is no significance to this: badges were issued in two parts but the coronet was often affixed above the grenade under local arrangements purely for personal convenience and security. Plate 19 shows another badge which was worn for a short period during the first decade of this century. It seems to have been worn only in the Brodrick cap, the flat-topped, peakless cap which was worn very briefly in the army from about 1902 to 1906 and by the RMLI and RMA until their merger in 1923. The first, smaller type was worn unchanged until the 1958 upheaval put **The Royal Irish Fusiliers (Princess Victoria's)**, as they became in 1920, into the North Irish Brigade, wearing the Brigade badge with their own green feather hackle. (See also notes on pipers).

The Connaught Rangers was not a new title. It was held by the old 88th before they were linked in 1881 with the 94th. The Harp and Crown of the badge came from the 88th but, as can be seen, this was the Harp of Erin and not the Angel Harp which appeared on their shoulder-belt plates. Below the Harp was a title scroll and the badge was in brass. After 1901, a K/C version appeared and was worn until 1922 when the Regiment was disbanded on the inception of the Irish Free State.

The Princess Louise's (Argyll and Sutherland Highlanders) were formed from the 91st (Princess Louise's Argyllshire) Highlanders and the 93rd Sutherland Highlanders in 1881. The first title in May of that year was The Sutherland and Argyll Highlanders (Princess Louise's). In July, they became Princess Louise's (Sutherland and Argyll Highlanders) but in July the next year the title altered again to the Princess Louise's (Argyll and Sutherland Highlanders) which they kept until 1920 when a further reshuffle made them **The Argyll and Sutherland Highlanders (Princess Louise's).** The badge is probably the largest one in the army and Jocks are accustomed to snide remarks about wearing mess tins in their bonnets. Basically, it is a circle, inscribed 'Argyll and Sutherland'. In the centre, the 'L' cypher of the late Princess Louise is reversed and inter-laced; to one side is the Argylls' boar's head and, to the other, the cat of the Sutherlands. Above the cypher, in the upper part of the circle, the Princess's coronet and, around the circle, a wreath of thistles, all in w/m. Until about 1908 the centre of the badge was solid but, thereafter, the cen-tral devices were fretted and voided. In the earlier badges, the cat's tail curled up behind in the fashion affected by heraldic lions but some real-ist, or cat fancier, pointed out that comfortable cats did not wave their tails but tucked them quietly around their feet: as a result, subsequent issues did not show the tail. The wreath contains ten thistles but it was common practice in the old army for barrack-room NCOs, when questioning recruits on Regimental traditions, honours and badge to ask how many thistles the badge carried. The response 'Ten' drew a barked 'Eleven'. When the puzzled recruit, after a deferential pause, sought enlightenment he was told that the cat was sitting on the eleventh. Perhaps this explains the raised tail. The Regiment took the Highland Brigade badge in 1958 but discarded it in disgust while in Aden in 1967. On return home the Brigade badge was reluctantly reassumed but in early 1969 the Regiment again took its own badge into use.

The Prince of Wales's Leinster Regiment (Royal Canadians) were so styled on linking the 100th (Prince of Wales's Royal Canadians) Regiment of Foot and the 109th (Bombay Infantry) Regiment in 1881. The 100th were raised in 1858 in Canada as an expression of loyalty at the time of the Indian Mutiny and, appropriately enough, the 109th were one of the old Honourable East India Company's European regiments. The Prince of Wales's plumes in w/m had two rather angular scrolls carrying the *Ich Dien* motto in Old English lettering, with a brass coronet superimposed and brass scroll 'The Leinster' below. During the First World War it would appear that the plumes used in The Welsh Regiment badge were utilized so that The Leinster badge is also sometimes seen with the more common curved scrolls (Plate 19). Like the other Irish regiments recruited in the South they were disbanded in 1922.

The Royal Munster Fusiliers were formed by linking two of the old Honourable East India Company's European regiments, the 101st (Royal Bengal Fusiliers) and the 104th (Bengal Fusiliers). The badge was basically the brass grenade with, on the body, a w/m Royal Tiger over a scroll 'Royal Munster'. The Regiment was disbanded in 1922.

The Royal Dublin Fusiliers were another result of linking two old Honourable East India Company's European regiments. The badge was a brass grenade with, on the body, a w/m Royal Tiger brought by the 102nd (Royal Madras Fusiliers) above a w/m Elephant furnished by the 103rd (Royal Bombay Fusiliers). Both these devices clearly echoed the Indian past and only the w/m scroll 'Royal Dublin Fusiliers' below indicated its Irish renaissance. The Regiment was disbanded in 1922.

The Rifle Brigade (The Prince Consort's Own) had borne the Rifle Brigade part of their title from 1816 when they discarded their place in the line as the 95th. In 1881 the title was The Rifle Brigade (Prince Consort's Own), amended in July to The Prince Consort's Own (Rifle Brigade). By 1914 the title had again reshuffled to Rifle Brigade (Prince Consort's Own).

The w/m badge (Plate 15) was taken into use in 1910 and was extremely unpopular. It replaced the w/m pattern (Plate 19) which came in about 1903. The 1910 badge carried fourteen battle-honour scrolls on the wreaths whereas the 1903 badge had only four and the K/C was larger. The four-scroll badge, as it is usually described, was slightly larger than its successor and the four scrolls bore the Crimean honours. The first cap badge (Plate 19) was in blackened brass and also in w/m: it bore the Crimean honours on the wreaths and was surmounted by a Guelphic crown. A smaller version (also shown in Plate 19) existed for wear in the field-service cap. As can be seen, the 1903 badge was simply a K/C version of the same badge. In 1910, critics of the new design complained that the fourteen honour scrolls obscured the wreaths and made them too heavy. Had they still been vocal in 1937 when the badge shown in Plates 15 and 19 came into use there would have been scant consolation: still fourteen scrolls and some of these broader ones bearing cumbersome honours like 'Defence of Ladysmith'. The title around the centre circle became 'The Rifle Brigade' in place of 'Rifle Brigade' as on all previous patterns; two First World War honours appeared at the base in place of the earlier 'Peninsula' which was transferred to the upper arm of the cross, and a new scroll 'Prince Consort's Own' was added. The 1910 badge was still in use and in issue during the Second World War. The final pattern (Plate 19) was authorized in 1956: it reverted to the Guelphic crown and all the honours vanished from the wreath. An innovation was the appearance below the cross of a naval crown superscribed 'Copenhagen 2 April, 1801'. The small crown above the stringed bugle-horn in the centre became Q/C and the title around the band again 'Rifle Brigade'. Although authorized in 1956 the badge was hardly issued to the Regiment as the Green Jackets Brigade absorbed The Rifle Brigade in 1958 and the Brigade badge was assumed. Except for the final pattern, small field-service cap versions existed for all varieties.

The Parachute Regiment is the last of the Infantry of the Line, having been formed officially on 1 August, 1942, as part of the **Army Air Corps** whose w/m badge they wore (Plate 15b) until May 1943 when their own badge (also Plate 15) was authorized. This depicted outstretched wings, in the centre of which was an opened parachute, surmounted by the Royal Crest K/C, all in w/m. During the 1950s a Q/C version appeared. This badge is distinctive but impractical and it is unusual to find a used badge which has not been bent by the wearer to fit his beret. Initially it was hinted that the badge would be replaced after the war by another design but as the same one is still in use in 1994 it now seems unlikely. The Army Air Corps badge continued to be worn by personnel of the Glider Pilot Regiment until 1950. The present Army Air Corps duties are not the same as those of the wartime Corps and are dealt with in the next chapter.

5 *Airborne Forces*

British airborne forces came into being early in the Second World War and at first the **Army Air Corps** embraced glider pilots and parachutists until May 1943 when **The Parachute Regiment** adopted their own badge. The infantry battalions converted to the unattractive role of glider passengers usually wore their own regimental cap badges on the maroon beret of airborne forces. The AAC officially consisted of **The Glider Pilot Regiment, The Special Air Service,** and **The Parachute Regiment.** The last-named had their own badge in May 1943 (Plate 15b) and in August 1949 became a corps of the Infantry of the Line. The officers and NCOs of The Glider Pilot Regiment were therefore the only ones to wear the AAC badge since The Special Air Service, conceived and serving in the Middle East had never been too cognisant of the narrow standards of dress preferred by the War Office. It was not until April 1944 that the SAS became part of the AAC and by then had become used to their own badge when wearing any at all. This consisted of a winged dagger, point down behind a scroll *Who dares wins* (corrupted by long-serving desert soldiers to 'Who cares who wins') and was usually locally made, all in brass. The later, die-struck, official issue gave the dagger a w/m blade. In the beret, originally sand coloured, later maroon to meet War Office preferences as part of the Army Air Corps and then sand coloured again in 1957, a cloth embroidered badge was worn on a black shield (Plate 15b). In 1946 the SAS were disbanded but July 1947 saw them reconstituted as part of the new Territorial Army. In 1950 they became a Regular Corps in their own right since it was in that year that the Army Air Corps was disbanded. The Glider Pilot Regiment then sought their own badge. They took the AAC eagle, turned it around to face the more heraldically acceptable dexter (right) and put it in the middle of an almost circular scroll bearing the Regiment's title and capped it with a K/C, all in w/m. By 1957 the title was a misnomer since gliders had long disappeared as tactical vehicles, all pilots were flying powered aircraft and helicopters were the coming military aviation novelty. So the present Army Air Corps was formed against Army Order 82/57, bringing the new badge shown in Plate 15b, taking the eagle and placing it simply inside a laurel wreath below Q/C, all in a/a (w/m finish). However, a Q/C had been approved for The Glider Pilot Regiment and subsequently appeared.

Infantry of the Line since 1958 6

The changes brought about by the Government White Paper of July 1957 (Cmnd. 230) were as far-reaching and startling in their effects as were the reforms of 1881 on the Infantry of the Line.

In the history of The Royal Hampshire Regiment there is recounted the story of the retired colonel who, invited to a Hampshire Regimental Dinner, wrote 'Damned names mean nothing. Since time immemorial regiments have been numbered according to their precedence in the Line. Nothing can alter the rightness of such a plan and interfering boobies in the War Office can have no effect on my determination to ignore their damned machinery at all costs to myself. I will not come to anything called a Hampshire Regimental Dinner. My compliments, Sir, and be damned.'

In 1958, protests at proposed mergers were even more vocal – due to improved communications media – and officers who might have known better that 'the army can do anything but put you in the family way', raised loud outcries against their regiment being amalgamated with another. All to no avail and the mergers went ahead.

The intention was to group the Infantry into fourteen brigades plus The Parachute Regiment. The brigades, except for the Fusilier, Light Infantry and Green Jacket Brigades were all regionally constituted. Each was to consist of three or four battalions and, to achieve this end, it was necessary to effect a number of mergers, resulting in a reduction of fifteen battalions over the coming three years. The White Paper referred to battalions when it should, more properly, have referred to regiments. Details of the projected Brigades are given on pages 52–6.

The badges (Plate 47) were issued fairly promptly afterwards and the amalgamations began to take effect. As will be seen, many of them were two regiments within the same county, such as North and South Staffordshires, and East and West Surreys and these were accepted with fairly good grace but the most unpalatable appeared to be that of The Royal Scots Fusiliers with The Highland Light Infantry. Nevertheless, by the end of 1961 the mergers were all accomplished and Brigade badges all in use. Exceptions to this were Scottish and Irish pipers and drummers who could retain their regimental pattern. The system meant, for example, that several regiments could be wearing the Lancastrian Brigade cap badge and could only be distinguished from each other by their regimental collar badge. The Fusilier Brigade went one stage further and standardized on a common, Brigade collar badge although they were distinguishable by their coloured hackles.

Over the next ten or twelve years the Brigades fared variously but by 1970 all had effectively ceased to exist. In their place a looser system of groupings under five Divisions embraced the Brigades but this will not affect badges, it is said, so the collector need not be too much concerned. The change meant the disappearance of Brigade cap badges and inevitably the welcome return to the soldier's own regimental badge. Only eight regiments, however, were still left as they were in 1957: the others had either been disbanded or amalgamated or were under sentence of one or the other. (The eight were Royal Scots, Green Howards, Cheshires, Royal Welch Fusiliers, King's Own Scottish Borderers, Duke of Wellington's Regiment, Black Watch and Gordon Highlanders.)

Lowland Brigade

1958 Regiments	Eventual Component Regiments	Badge
Royal Scots	Royal Scots	Saltire, bearing a thistle within circle inscribed *Nemo me impune lacessit.* All w/m (a/a finish).
Royal Scots Fusiliers Highland Light Infantry	Royal Highland Fusiliers (Princess Margaret's Own City of Glasgow & Ayrshire Regt.)	
King's Own Scottish Borderers	King's Own Scottish Borderers	
Cameronians (Scottish Rifles)	Cameronians (Scottish Rifles)	

Home Counties Brigade

1958 Regiments	Eventual Component Regiments	Badge
Queen's Royal Regt. (W. Surrey) East Surrey Regt.	Queen's Royal Surrey Regt.	Sword, point-upwards behind a Saxon crown; below, a scroll 'Home Counties'. All w/m (a/a finish).
The Buffs (R. East Kent Regt.) QO Royal West Kent Regt.	Queen's Own Buffs, Royal Kent Regt.	
Royal Sussex Regt.	Royal Sussex Regt.	
Middlesex Regt.	Middlesex Regt.	

Lancastrian Brigade

1958 Regiments	Eventual Component Regiments	Badge
K.O. Royal Regt. (Lancaster) Border Regt. King's Regt. (Liverpool) Manchester Regt. East Lancashire Regt. South Lancashire Regt. Loyal Regt.	K.O. Royal Border Regt. King's Regt. (Manchester and Liverpool) Lancashire Regt. (Prince of Wales Volunteers) Loyal Regt.	Royal Crest, w/m above Rose of Lancaster within laurel wreath: below, a scroll 'Lancastrian', in brass (a/a finish).

Fusilier Brigade

1958 Regiments	Eventual Component Regiments	Badge
R. Northumberland Fusiliers ·Royal Fusiliers Lancashire Fusiliers	R. Northumberland Fusiliers Royal Fusiliers Lancashire Fusiliers	Brass grenade; on body George & Dragon with laurel wreath, w/m (a/a finish).

Midland Brigade

1958 Regiments	Eventual Component Regiments	Badge
R. Warwickshire Regt. R. Leicestershire Regt. Sherwood Foresters	R. Warwickshire Regt. R. Leicestershire Regt. Sherwood Foresters	Foresters' cross in brass with w/m Garter and motto in centre; within Garter, in w/m, the Warwicks antelope in brass; above the cross, the brass Leicesters' Tiger. Around cross, a w/m oak wreath and below, brass scroll 'Forester Brigade' (a/a finish).

East Anglian Brigade

1958 Regiments	*Eventual* Component Regiments	Badge
R. Norfolk Regt. Suffolk Regt. }	1st East Anglian Regt. (Royal Norfolk & Suffolk)	Eight pointed w/m rayed star; superimposed, the
R. Lincolnshire Regt. Northamptonshire Regt. }	2nd East Anglian Regt. (Duchess of Gloucester's Own R. Lincolnshire & Northamptonshire)	Castle & Key of Gibraltar above scroll 'East Anglian' in brass (a/a finish).
Bedfordshire & Hertfordshire Regt. Essex Regt. }	3rd East Anglian Regt. (16th/44th)	

Wessex Brigade

1958 Regiments	*Eventual* Component Regiments	Badge
Devonshire Regt. Dorset Regt. }	Devonshire & Dorset Regt.	Wessex Wyvern on tablet inscribed 'Wessex', all
Gloucestershire Regt.	Gloucestershire Regt.	brass (a/a finish).
Royal Hampshire Regt.	Royal Hampshire Regt.	
Royal Berkshire Regt. Wiltshire Regt. }	Duke of Edinburgh's Royal Regt.(Berkshire & Wiltshire)	

Light Infantry Brigade

1958 Regiments	*Eventual* Component Regiments	Badge
Somerset L.I. Duke of Cornwall's L.I. }	Somerset & Cornwall L.I.	Stringed L.I. bugle-horn in w/m (a/a finish).
K.O. Yorkshire L.I.	K.O. Yorkshire L.I.	
King's Shropshire L.I.	King's Shropshire L.I.	
Durham L.I.	Durham L.I.	

Yorkshire Brigade

1958 Regiments	Eventual Component Regiments	Badge
West Yorkshire Regt. East Yorkshire Regt. Green Howards Duke of Wellington's Regt. York & Lancaster Regt.	Prince of Wales's Own Regt. of Yorkshire Green Howards Duke of Wellington's Regt. York & Lancaster Regt.	Brass Q/C above w/m Rose of York above brass scroll 'Yorkshire' (a/a finish).

Mercian Brigade

1958 Regiments	Eventual Component Regiments	Badge
Cheshire Regt. Worcestershire Regt. South Staffordshire Regt. North Staffordshire Regt.	Cheshire Regt. Worcestershire Regt. Staffordshire Regt. (Prince of Wales's)	W/m double-headed Eagle surmounted by brass Saxon Crown (a/a finish).

Welsh Brigade

1958 Regiments	Eventual Component Regiments	Badge
Royal Welch Fusiliers South Wales Borderers Welch Regt.	Royal Welch Fusiliers South Wales Borderers Welch Regt.	Prince of Wales's Plumes Motto and Coronet, w/m (a/a finish).

North Irish Brigade

1958 Regiments	Eventual Component Regiments	Badge
Royal Inniskilling Fusiliers Royal Ulster Rifles Royal Irish Fusiliers	Royal Inniskilling Fusiliers Royal Ulster Rifles Royal Irish Fusiliers	W/m Angel harp with brass Q/C above and brass scroll 'North Irish Brigade' below (a/a finish).

Highland Brigade

1958 Regiments	Eventual Component Regiments	Badge
Black Watch	Black Watch	Stag's head above scroll
Seaforth Highlanders	Queen's Own Highlanders	*Cuidich'n Righ* all
Cameron Highlanders	(Seaforth & Cameron)	superimposed on a saltire
Gordon Highlanders	Gordon Highlanders	in w/m (a/a finish).
Argyll & Sutherland Highlanders	Argyll & Sutherland Highlanders	

Green Jackets Brigade

1958 Regiments	Eventual Component Regiments	Badge
Oxfordshire & Buckinghamshire L.I.	1st Green Jackets (43rd/ 52nd)	Maltese Cross with stringed bugle-horn superimposed; above, a tablet 'Peninsula'
King's Royal Rifle Corps	2nd Green Jackets (K.R.R.C.)	with Q/C above that; laurel wreath around the cross, all
Rifle Brigade	3rd Green Jackets (R.B.)	w/m (a/a finish).

On formation the **Lowland Brigade** consisted of five regiments, being reduced to four by amalgamation. In May 1968, The Cameronians (Scottish Rifles) were disbanded, cutting the Brigade to three. The new badge of **The Royal Highland Fusiliers** – brass grenade with w/m Q/C and HLI monogram (in a/a) is shown in Plate 49.

The **Home Counties Brigade** consisted originally of six regiments, later reduced to four by amalgamations. The War Office had urged the formation of Big Regiments, based on the Brigade structure and so on 31 December, 1966 **The Queen's Regiment** was formed, the 1st, 2nd, 3rd and 4th Battalions made up of the four component regiments. The badge chosen is in Plate 49 and embodied ingredients from all four: Queen's title, Buffs Dragon, Royal Sussex Garter and the Middlesex Plumes.

The **Lancastrian Brigade** began with seven regiments, reduced to four by amalgamations. In March 1970, The Loyal Regiment merged with The Lancashire Regiment (PWV) to form **The Queen's Lancashire Regiment.** The badge is the red rose of Lancaster, Q/C above, within an oval carrying the full title; below, a motto scroll *Loyally I serve.* The badge is in brass (a/a finish), with the rose coloured red under local arrangements

(Plate 49). **The King's Regiment** wears a w/m horse upon a brass fleur-de-lys with title scroll below – in a/a finish (Plate 49). In 1970 **The King's Own Royal Border Regiment** received their new badge – a w/m lion within a laurel wreath, surmounted by a Q/C, both in brass (Plate 49).

Shortly after the formation of the **Midland Brigade** the title was changed to the **Forester Brigade** but it was disbanded in 1963. The Royal Warwicks went to the Fusilier Brigade, the Foresters to the Mercian Brigade and the Royal Leicesters to the East Anglian Brigade.

Before the creation of the **Royal Warwickshire Fusiliers** the **Fusilier Brigade** had consisted of three regiments: the Brigade badge embodied the shape and crown of The Royal Fusiliers, the St. George and Dragon of The Royal Northumberland Fusiliers and the laurel wreath of The Lancashire Fusiliers. Since there was no room for an antelope it was decided to use The Royal Warwickshire button which, by a happy chance, did not include a title. On 23 April, 1968 a Big Regiment was formed, using the Brigade badge and standardizing on the red and white hackle for the new **Royal Regiment of Fusiliers.**

The East Anglian Brigade was made up initially of six regiments, reduced to three by amalgamations but augmented in May 1963 by The Royal Leicestershire Regiment. On 1 September, 1964, they formed a Big Regiment and became **The Royal Anglian Regiment.** The badge was basically unchanged except that the title scroll became 'Royal Anglian' and the badge was reduced in size very considerably (Plate 49).

Six regiments went to make up the **Wessex Brigade** but these were reduced to four by amalgamation. In 1969 it was projected that the Gloucestershire and Royal Hampshire Regiments should merge in 1970 to form **The Royal Regiment of Gloucestershire and Hampshire,** but after the return of the Conservative Government in June 1970 it was decided to retain the Gloucesters at Battalion strength and The Royal Hampshires as an independent company. Subsequently, it was increased to battalion strength. Although the new badge was struck it was never issued but is shown in Plate 49. The w/m star comes from the old Royal Hampshire officers' badge and the brass rose bears the w/m Gloucesters' Sphinx. The topmost point of the star is displaced by a brass Q/C. The new **Devonshire & Dorset Regiment** badge, also on Plate 49, had the w/m Exeter Castle with brass Sphinx below and motto scrolls Semper Fidelis above and Primus in Indis below. Another badge which appeared in 1970 was that of **The Duke of Edinburgh's Royal Regiment** (Plate 49) – the Wiltshire cross with the Royal Berkshires' Chinese Dragon in the centre.

The **Light Infantry Brigade** took five regiments and linked two of them to leave four. A Big Regiment was indicated and, on 10 July 1968, some 165 years after the formation of The Light Brigade at Shorncliffe by

Sir John Moore, **The Light Infantry** was formed. The badge remained the same stringed bugle-horn but a red cloth backing was added.

The five regiments of the **Yorkshire Brigade** were early reduced to four by amalgamation and then, in December 1968 The York and Lancaster Regiment was disbanded, leaving three. Plate 49 shows the badge of the combined East and West Yorkshire Regiments – a w/m Horse of Hanover.

The **Mercian Brigade** was constituted initially of four regiments, to be cut to three by amalgamation but, in May 1963 The Sherwood Foresters joined on dissolution of the Forester Brigade. However, early 1970 saw the Worcesters and Foresters amalgamated to form **The Worcestershire and Sherwood Foresters Regiment** (29th/45th) (Plate 49). The new Staffordshire Regiment wears the same badge as the old North Staffords without a title scroll (Plate 49).

The three Welsh regiments went, naturally, to the **Welsh Brigade** but in July 1969 The South Wales Borderers merged with The Welch Regiment to form **The Royal Regiment of Wales.** As The Royal Welch Fusiliers had been among the eight regiments permitted in early 1969 to resume their old badges the new Royal Regiment took the old Brigade badge for its Regimental badge.

A new rendering of this badge, in bi-metal a/a finish was issued in 1975 at the express wish of HRH The Prince of Wales. (Plate 49).

The three Regiments which made up the **North Irish Brigade** converted easily to battalions of **The Royal Irish Rangers** when the Brigade became a Big Regiment on 1 July 1968 and the scroll on the Brigade badge was altered to 'Royal Irish Rangers' (Plate 49).

The five Regiments which made up the **Highland Brigade** were reduced to four by amalgamation. **The Queen's Own Highlanders (Seaforth and Camerons)** use the bonnet badge devised for the 3rd (Territorial) Battalion of the Regiment: the Seaforths' stag's head with the Camerons collar (thistle with Q/C above) between its antlers (Plate 49). It was the verdict of the 1st Argylls in Aden in 1967 that the Highland Brigade badge was nothing but 'a crucified moose' and they reverted unilaterally to their own badge. A silver-plate version of the Brigade badge with the stag's head in relief was used by warrant officers and serjeants.

The three regiments of the **Green Jackets Brigade** could be distinguished only by their shoulder titles, '43/52nd', 'KRRC' and 'RB' as no collar badges were worn. However, on 1 January, 1966 they became a Big Regiment and **The Royal Green Jackets** three battalions wore standard 'RGJ' titles and the new, a/a Rifle Brigade pattern badge in w/m finish shown in Plate 49. This bears the Q/C upon a tablet 'Peninsula', common to all three component regiments with, below the cross, the Rifle Brigade Naval Crown and Copenhagen honour. The central band carries the new title and the arms of the cross bear honours including, on the lowest, three from the Second World War, Calais, El Alamein and Pegasus Bridge.

The Brigade badges were never popular and lasted for barely twelve years. Several of the Brigades fell in with War Office wishes and formed Big Regiments but others proved less cohesive and remained three separate one-battalion regiments.

As a result, the Infantry of the Line in 1971 consisted of twenty-nine regiments (listed in Appendix C) each with its own badge in place of the fourteen Brigades a decade earlier.

7 *Volunteer Battalions*

The Volunteer Force sprang into being in 1859 to combat one of the perennial threats from the Continent. When the 1881 reforms linked two Regular, numbered Regiments to form one territorially-styled Regiment under one badge the Volunteers, previously in loosely defined units, were brought into the family structure, consolidated as battalions, and given a variant of the Regimental badge. These continued in use with appropriate changes of crown until the Territorial Force replaced the Volunteers in 1908.

Plates 24 and 25 depict a representative selection of Volunteer badges. The **5th VB Royal Scots** wore a w/m badge based directly upon the Regimental badge. The **1st VB Royal Warwickshire Regiment** incorporated their own South African battle honour into the badge. Almost invariably the VB's wore w/m badges and buttons with silver lace on full dress to differentiate them from the Regulars who wore brass buttons and gold lace. For example, the **1st VB Royal Fusiliers** wore a w/m grenade with a scroll '1st Volr. Battn' below it. The **5th (Irish) VB King's (Liverpool Regiment)** wore the Irish Angel Harp and a wreath of shamrock above the scroll. The **2nd VB Norfolk Regiment** and the **3rd VB Bedfordshire Regiment** both used the Regimental badge with their own title on the scroll. The **5th VB South Wales Borderers** used an all w/m badge with, simply '5 V.B' at the top of the wreath of immortelles. The Sphinx does not bear the word 'Egypt' on the plinth, as it was felt undesirable at the time to burden the Volunteer with Regular honours. The **2nd VB Worcestershire Regiment** wore their own South Africa scroll below the badge while the **2nd VB East Lancashire Regiment** wore an all w/m badge, again with a blank plinth. On the Cat and Cabbage badge of The Hampshire Regiment the **2nd Volunteer Battalion** had an additional scroll added whilst the **1st VB The Prince of Wales's Volunteers (South Lancashire Regiment)** used the empty plinth below the Sphinx to identify themselves and attached a separate scroll to carry their own South Africa honour. The **2nd VB The Welsh Regiment** wore an all w/m badge with '2nd V.B' on an oval plaque below the coronet while the 1st VB wore their title, '1st Volr. Battn', on a scroll below the plumes.

The first badge shown in Plate 25 is the **4th VB Black Watch** with the double-headed eagle from the Arms of the City of Perth as befitted a battalion whose subsidiary title was '(Perthshire)'. The badges of the **1st** and **2nd VB Essex Regiment** are shown, one with the South Africa honour and the other without. The **1st VBs** of the **Sherwood Foresters** and **Middlesex Regiment** both used their Regimental badges but the Middlesex had the 'Albuhera' scroll blank. The **2nd VB Manchester Regiment** retained the bi-metal badge of Regular pattern and inserted a brass oval plaque above the scroll to identify themselves. When the **3rd VB Durham Light Infantry** attempted to cram their identity between the bugle-strings they found that the tassels would have to be pushed aside, producing the rather curious effect which can be seen.

The next badge is in the traditional form of Scottish clan badges, a device within a Celtic strap. The Gaelic motto translates as 'Highlanders, shoulder to shoulder' and it was worn by the **105th Lanarkshire (Glasgow Highland) Rifle Volunteers**, raised from among the many Highlanders resident in Glasgow in 1868. Renumbered 10th Lanarkshire R,V. in 1880 they had pursued their love affair with the 42nd Highlanders, adopting Black Watch dress and tartan, until in 1887 they were restyled **5th (Glasgow Highland) VB Highland Light Infantry.** The new badge is shown next: the old, anguished-looking St. Andrew reappeared in the neater, military-type saint in the centre of the Black Watch type badge including, it appears, a Black Watch type Sphinx since the HLI did not have this beast among their honours.

General Order No. 12/1884 created the **4th VB Gordon Highlanders** from several corps of Aberdeenshire Rifle Volunteers but it was not until 1893 that they became **4th (Donside Highland) VB.** The badge shows the Cock o' the North inside a band with the unit title and the motto *Watch.* Presumably this was taken from the Regulars' *Bydand.*

The creation in 1884 of the **5th (Deeside Highland) VB Gordon Highlanders** by the same General Order that created the 4th consolidated ten companies of Kincardineshire and Aberdeenshire RV into one battalion which adopted a demi-lion within a Celtic strap bearing the motto *Defence Not Defiance,* a motto much in favour with British Volunteers at that time all over the world.

The final Volunteer badge shown is that of the **1st Dumbartonshire Volunteer Rifle Corps.** It closely resembled in format that of the Argyll and Sutherland Highlanders but in the centre was an elephant and castle with, above, a small scroll *Fortitudo et Fidelitas* with the circle carrying the title 'Dumbartonshire Volunteers'. They resisted all efforts to make them a Volunteer Battalion of the Argylls but the Army List showed them between the 5th and the 7th so that they clearly rated as the 6th. However, in 1908 when the Territorial Force came into being objection was ignored and they became 9th (The Dumbartonshire) Battalion of the Argylls.

8 *Territorial Infantry Badges*

The Territorial Force was created in 1908 when the old Volunteer Battalions were transformed into Territorial Battalions, numbered in sequence with the other battalions of the Regiment. As a general rule, the 1st and 2nd were Regular battalions, the 3rd a Militia battalion and the Territorials were numbered 4th, 5th, 6th, etc. For the most part, Volunteer Battalions were converted en bloc overnight and their special badges discarded. Regular badges were assumed with certain exceptions and these exceptions can be classified as:

i   when the Regular badge carried an honour to which the part-time soldiers were felt not to be entitled,

ii   when the Regular badge, finished in black, was worn by those battalions which, although now part of a 'red-coat' regiment, were raised as 'Rifles',

iii when a special badge of distinctive pattern was worn.

In the case of i and iii these were to be all in w/m when worn in full-dress caps.

Several Volunteer Battalions became Cyclist Battalions of the TF and these are dealt with in another chapter.

The concept behind the first category of exceptions mentioned above was simple but illogical. Tablets inscribed 'Egypt' and 'Marabout' were blanked out, but the Sphinx remained. Even more oddly, the 4th and 5th Battalions Somerset Light Infantry wore a badge from which the Regular honour 'Jellalabad' had been removed, to be replaced with their own 'South Africa 1900–01', worn above the mural crown awarded for the defence of an Afghan stronghold.

Below are listed the special Territorial badges which differed from the patterns worn by the Regular battalions. (I have not illustrated all those variants involving blank plinths below Sphinxes.)

THE ROYAL SCOTS

4th and 5th Battalions (Queen's Edinburgh Rifles) wore the w/m Star of the

Order of the Thistle with K/C above and a stringed bugle-horn below the centre (Plate 21).

THE QUEEN'S (ROYAL WEST SURREY REGIMENT)

5th Battalion wore a black Regular pattern badge as a 'Rifle' battalion.

THE KING'S REGIMENT (LIVERPOOL)

5th Battalion wore black Regular pattern badges of both pre- and post-1920 patterns.

6th Battalion wore a black badge consisting of a stringed bugle-horn bdow a rose, worn on a red cloth oval backing (Plate 21A).

7th Battalion wore a w/m Regular pattern badge still worn by Liverpool University OTC.

8th Battalion continued to wear a badge similar in design to the old 5th (Irish) VB but in black, the scroll reading '8th (Irish) Bn King's Liverpool Regt' (Plate 21A). In 1922 the battalion ceased to exist but was raised again in 1939, the badge being issued in w/m with scroll reading '8th (Irish) Bn. The Kings Regiment, Liverpool' (Plate 21). A Q/C pattern of this appeared in about 1960, also in w/m finish but of a/a.

9th Battalion as the 7th Battalion.

10th Battalion wore the King's White Horse badge upon a saltire within a circle with thistles below the horse and the words 'Liverpool Scottish' above (Plate 21). This was issued all in one piece and also with the Horse superimposed on the saltire (it is said to have been worn by Serjeants). In 1937 the Liverpool Scottish became part of The Queen's Own Cameron Highlanders and their later badge is dealt with under that Regiment.

THE LINCOLNSHIRE REGIMENT

4th and 5th Battalions wore the Regular pattern badge but the plinth below the Sphinx was blank (Plate 21).

THE DEVONSHIRE REGIMENT

4th Battalion wore a black Regular pattern badge.
5th Battalion wore an all w/m Regular pattern badge.

THE SUFFOLK REGIMENT

4th, 5th and 6th Battalions wore the badge shown on Plate 21. The circular band normally carrying the motto was left blank and made narrower whilst the Castle and Key of Gibraltar were replaced by a different castle, popularly said to be that of Bury St. Edmunds. Some years ago, a letter in the *Bulletin of the Military Historical Society* claimed that this badge was worn by the 15th (Suffolk Yeomanry) Bn., using the castle from the badge of the Loyal Suffolk Hussars after they were converted to infantry in 1916 but substantial evidence from pre-war photographs confirms that ⁚ was definitely a 1908 concept.

THE SOMERSET LIGHT INFANTRY

As already mentioned, the 4th and 5th Battalions wore a w/m badge, identical with that of the Regular battalions except that the 'Jellalabad' honour was replaced by 'South Africa 1900–01' (Plate 21). A badge bearing a laurel spray on the scroll was worn by the 3rd (Militia) Bn. of the Regiment until 1908.

THE WEST YORKSHIRE REGIMENT

7th Battalion wore a black 'Rifle Brigade' pattern badge with 'Leeds Rifles' around the central circle, the arms of the cross bare of honours (Plate 21A). The title appeared on the scroll below the cross. This also appeared in w/m, probably for wear on green patrols.

8th Battalion wore a similar black badge to that worn by the 7th but with the numeral '8th' on the scroll (Plate 21A).

7/8th Battalion wore a new black badge (Plate 21A) issued for the combined units after 1922. It embodied the regular West Yorkshire Regiment honours on the arms of the cross plus the Leeds Rifles own honour 'Tardenois' on a scroll below the cross and above the title scroll which was inscribed '7th.8th Bns West Yorkshire Regt P.W.O.' In December 1936, the 7/8th split up, the 7th becoming 45th RTR and the 8th the 66th AA Bde RA TA. The duplicate unit of 45th RTR in 1939 was the 51st RTR. In January 1947, the post-war reconstruction of the TA saw the 7th re-raised as the 45/51st (Leeds Rifles) RTR and the old 8th as 466th (Leeds Rifles) LAA Regt. In October 1956, the 45/51st became the 7th (Leeds Rifles) once more and merged with the 466th LAA Regt in February 1961 to form the Leeds Rifles, The Prince of Wales's Own Regiment of Yorkshire. The projected badge for the 7th was to be the old RB pattern badge with a tank below the cross to record its wartime service. However, this was not issued and the latest Leeds Rifles had a similar badge but without a tank, the arms of the cross bare and 'The Leeds Rifles' on the lower scroll.

THE LEICESTERSHIRE REGIMENT

4th, 5th and 6th Battalions wore the Regular pattern badge but lacking the 'Hindoostan' scroll (Plate 21).

THE LANCASHIRE FUSILIERS

5th, 6th, 7th and 8th Battalions wore the Regular pattern badge but the plinth below the Sphinx was blank.

THE SOUTH WALES BORDERERS

The Regular pattern badge should not be found with a blank plinth below the Sphinx since the TF Battalion of the Regiment was designated The

Brecknockshire Battalion and wore a brass Welsh Dragon above a scroll 'Brecknockshire' (Plate 21). The badge also appears in w/m as well as in brass with a noticeably longer scroll.

THE CAMERONIANS (SCOTTISH RIFLES)

5th Battalion wore the normal pattern badge, substantially smaller, and with a numeral '5' between the bugle strings, a badge which had previously been worn by the 5th VB of the Regiment between 1887 and 1897 (Plate 51).

THE GLOUCESTERSHIRE REGIMENT

5th and 6th Battalions wore the Regular pattern badge but the plinth below the Sphinx was blank.

4th Battalion, a 'Rifles' battalion, wore a blackened version of the badge worn by the 5th and 6th Battalions.

THE EAST LANCASHIRE REGIMENT

4th and 5th Battalions wore the Regular pattern badge (w/m with brass rose) but the plinth below the Sphinx was blank.

THE EAST SURREY REGIMENT

6th Battalion wore a blackened brass Maltese cross with 'South Africa' on the top arm and '1900–02' on the lower. The centre carried a star bearing the arms of Guildford; around the star, a circular band bore the unit title (Plate 21A).

After 1920 the Battalion wore a blackened Regular pattern badge.

THE BORDER REGIMENT

4th Battalion wore the same basic design as the Regular pattern but the arms of the cross carried no honours; in the centre was a numeral '4', surrounded by a circular band bearing the honour 'South Africa 1900–02'. The three-part scroll below read 'Border-Cumberland & Westmorland – Regiment' - all in w/m (Plate 21).

5th Battalion wore a similar pattern to that of the 4th but the South Africa honour surrounding the numeral '5' was dated '1901-02'. The three-part scroll read 'Border–Cumberland–Regiment', all w/m (Plate 21).

THE ROYAL SUSSEX REGIMENT

5th (Cinque Ports) Battalion wore a brass badge consisting of a Maltese Cross backed by the Regulars' plume; superimposed was a circle bearing the shield of the Cinque Ports arms and below, a scroll inscribed 'Cinque Ports' (Plate 21).

THE HAMPSHIRE REGIMENT

6th Battalion wore the badge shown in Plate 21, all w/m except for the title scroll 'Hampshire' and the central rose which were brass. Around the rose was 'Duke of Connaught's Own'. After 1947 it became 383 A/Tk Regiment RA TA and a variant of the badge was worn (Plate 21) which was all in w/m, the 'Hampshire' scroll having been discarded.

7th Battalion wore as the central feature of their brass badge what is usually referred to as a Stirrup but is, in fact, a dog-gauge. This was a device used to measure dogs in the New Forest: any dog which could not get through it was expeditated – that is, the three middle claws were removed from its front paws with a hammer and chisel to prevent it from chasing the deer. This device was worn in the centre of a laurel wreath, with a title scroll below (Plate 21).

8th Battalion (Isle of Wight Rifles) wore the tower of Carisbrooke Castle as the central feature of their badge. The one shown in Plate 21A is in black but it also appeared in w/m, in a/a and chromed. Around the tower on the central circle were the words 'Isle of Wight Rifles', above it the South Africa honour on a scroll below a K/C, and below the centre a scroll bearing the subsidiary title 'Princess Beatrice's'.

Royal Jersey Light Infantry: the Channel Islands Militia units may conveniently be dealt with under The Hampshire Regiment as the R. Jersey L.I. became their 11th Battalion in 1940. The badge shown in Plate 22 was in brass and included three leopards on the central shield facing the viewer's left. A K/C version also existed with leopards facing the viewer's right as did its QVC predecessor. Presumably this was a belated remembrance of heraldic precepts.

Royal Guernsey Light Infantry wore the simple stringed bugle-horn in brass above a scroll 'Royal Guernsey' (Plate 22) but on the outbreak of war in 1939 the other brass pattern shown in Plate 22 was in use, with the Arms of Guernsey in the centre, bearing the title 'Royal Guernsey Militia' on the circle.

The Channel Islands units were not revived in 1947.

THE DORSETSHIRE REGIMENT

4th Battalion wore the Regular pattern badge but the plinth below the Sphinx was blank.

THE SOUTH LANCASHIRE REGIMENT

4th Battalion wore the Regular pattern badge but the plinth below the Sphinx was blank.

5th Battalion followed the 4th, but in blackened brass.

THE BLACK WATCH

4th, 5th, 6th and 7th Battalions wore the Regular pattern badge but without a Sphinx (Plate 22). As usual, this Black Watch variant exists with spellings *Lacessit* and *Lacesset*.

The Tyneside Scottish (see Chapter 14) ceased to exist at the end of the First World War but in 1939 the 9th Battalion DLI was duplicated, another Tyneside Scottish was born and became part of The Black Watch. During the 1914–18 period four badges were worn, the last three basically similar. Two of these are shown in Plate 22: the lion on one paw was the design of late 1915 and the demi-lion pattern came into use in 1916. These two appear to have been those mostly used during the Second World War.

THE OXFORDSHIRE & BUCKINGHAMSHIRE LIGHT INFANTRY

Buckinghamshire Battalion wore a Maltese cross, with K/C above and in the centre, the Swan of Buckinghamshire inside a circle bearing the title, all in black (Plate 21A). This has also been made with Q/C.

THE ESSEX REGIMENT

4th, 5th, 6th and 7th Battalions wore the Regular pattern badge but the plinth below the Sphinx was blank and a small brass scroll below the title scroll read 'South Africa 1900–02' (Plate 22).

THE SHERWOOD FORESTERS

7th (Robin Hoods) Battalion wore a 'Rifle Brigade' type badge with K/C, in blackened brass having the title on the central circle; upon three arms of the cross was the honour 'South Africa 1900–02'. The badge also existed in w/m (Plate 22) and the Q/C issue in a/a.

THE NORTHAMPTONSHIRE REGIMENT

4th Battalion wore the Regular pattern badge but with both upper and lower honour scrolls left blank (Plate 22).

THE MIDDLESEX REGIMENT

7th, 8th and 9th Battalions wore the Regular pattern badge with the honour 'Albuhera' replaced by 'South Africa 1900–02' (Plate 22).

10th Battalion wore the Regular pattern badge with the honour scroll left blank (Plate 22).

THE WILTSHIRE REGIMENT

4th Battalion wore a blackened brass Regular pattern badge.

THE MANCHESTER REGIMENT

7th Battalion wore a brass floriated fleur-de-lys (Plate 22).

THE DURHAM LIGHT INFANTRY

6th Battalion wore a Regular pattern badge in blackened brass.

THE HIGHLAND LIGHT INFANTRY

6th Battalion wore the Regular pattern badge but the 'Assaye' on the honour scroll was replaced by 'South Africa 1900–02' (Plate 22).

5th, 7th and 8th Battalions wore the Regular pattern badge but the 'Assaye' scroll was left empty until 1916 when 5th, 7th and 8th Battalions took into use the badge of the 6th (Plate 22).

(It seems illogical, as all battalions had the South Africa honour, that, initially, only the 6th should display it.)

The 9th (Glasgow Highlanders) Battalion wore the usual pattern Black Watch badge but had 'Glasgow Highlanders' on the upper scrolls and '9th Batn H.L.I.' on the lower (Plate 23). (Another version existed with '9th Bn H.L.I.') As with the Black Watch, a bi-metal badge existed for senior NCOs and with *Lacessit* and *Lacesset* spellings. This badge exists also with 'Black Watch' on the lower scrolls, further evidence of the traditional love-affair maintained with the old 42nd, but at no time have the Glasgow Highlanders ever been part of the Black Watch. In 1939 the TA was doubled in strength and when the 9th Battalion formed another, permission was granted by King George VI for them to be styled respectively 1st and 2nd Battalions The Glasgow Highlanders (HLI). The badge changed to the pattern shown in Plate 23, having a three-part scroll at the bottom inscribed 'Light-Highland-Infantry'. A Q/C version of this pattern has been issued in w/m and also in a/a. It is shown on Plate 51.

The third badge shown has rather blunted points to the Star and was said to have been made in Glasgow and worn by the 2nd Battalion.

THE SEAFORTH HIGHLANDERS

5th (Sutherland & Caithness) Battalion wore a Cat-a-mountain inside a circular Celtic strap bearing the motto *Sans Peur* in w/m (Plate 23). (It is said to have been worn until 1920 but the badge drawings in *Twenty Years After* show the pattern described below for the 4/5th Battalion.)

4/5th (Sutherland & Caithness) Battalion wore a badge similar to the above but after 1920 in a plain circle (Plate 23).

Serjeants of both the 5th and 4/5th Battalions wore the oval badge shown in Plate 23 throughout the period until the 4/5th was disbanded in 1946.

THE QUEEN'S OWN CAMERON HIGHLANDERS

Liverpool Scottish ceased in 1937 to be the 10th Battalion King's Regiment and became part of the Q.O. Cameron Highlanders. The w/m badge (Plate 23) taken was that of the Camerons with the addition of two scrolls flanking St. Andrew inscribed 'Liverpool Scottish'.

THE ARGYLL AND SUTHERLAND HIGHLANDERS

8th Battalion wore the Regular pattern badge with an additional scroll below, reading '8th Bn A. & S.H.' (Plate 51).

Certain other Regular regiments received extra Territorial battalions in 1937 when the London Regiment TA ceased to exist and its battalions were redeployed. Details are given in the next chapter.

Army Order 338 of 1922 ruled that Territorial Army battalions would in future share all the honours of their Regular parents so that the differentiated badges (those with blank plinths, altered scrolls and so on) disappeared, although one may be sure that some of these continued to be worn for many years by proud Territorials insensitive to the honour granted them.

Four new regiments were created in 1908, Cambridgeshire, Herefordshire, Hertfordshire and Monmouthshire.

THE CAMBRIDGESHIRE REGIMENT

A w/m Cambridge Castle with the Arms of Ely in the centre above a brass title scroll (Plate 23). Another stamping of this badge lacked the first 'e' in the county name on the title scroll.

THE HERTFORDSHIRE REGIMENT

A hart in water within a circle bearing the title, surmounted by a K/C, all in brass (Plate 23). A solid brass 'economy strike' also existed as well as a variant of the former with widely-spaced antlers.

THE HEREFORDSHIRE REGIMENT

A w/m lion clutching a dagger standing upon an heraldic wreath over a brass title scroll (Plate 23). This was in use until 1947 when the Regiment became **The Herefordshire Light Infantry** so that it might be seen to be part of the Corps of The King's Shropshire Light Infantry. The badge changed to the w/m design shown in Plate 23, incorporating a stringed bugle-horn and the motto *Manu Forti*.

THE MONMOUTHSHIRE REGIMENT

1st Battalion wore initially, from 1908 to 1922, a w/m Welsh Dragon (Plate 23). In 1922 the Dragon was reduced in size and surrounded by a wreath of laurels and Flanders poppies carrying honour scrolls and topped by K/C, all in w/m (Plate 23).

2nd Battalion wore a brass Welsh Dragon (Plate 23).

In 1958 the Infantry Brigade System took effect and while Regular battalions wore the Brigade badges, Territorial soldiers kept the regimental badges. Those knowing of the 1908 stipulations derived some wry amusement from seeing positions reversed whereby the Territorials of the Somerset Light

Infantry were wearing the 'Jellalabad' honour while the Regulars wore the new (and meaningless) Light Infantry Brigade badge.

In the 1961 reorganizations of the TA several battalions of The Queen's Royal Regiment and The East Surrey Regiment were amalgamated and it was decided to follow the Regular lead and form one regiment for the County, **The Queen's Royal Surrey Regiment TA.** A badge was needed and they took the East Surrey's w/m star and Q/C, placing on it the brass Lamb and Flag (Plate 50). In 1966 the Home Counties Brigade formed a Big Regiment and the Territorials joined them in The Queen's Regiment, discarding their own badge.

Also in 1961 the 4th Battalion The Suffolk Regiment merged with 1st Battalion The Cambridgeshire Regiment to form **The Suffolk and Cambridgeshire Regiment, TA.** The badge showed the Castle and Key of Gibraltar, the Castle carrying the Arms of Ely, in w/m; brass Q/C above and title scroll below (Plate 50).

When the 1st Battalion The Bedfordshire and Hertfordshire Regiment was amalgamated with the 1st Battalion The Essex Regiment in 1958 the Territorial battalion of the former resumed its old title of 5th Battalion The Bedfordshire Regiment and wore the old pre-1920 Bedfords badge but in a/a, w/m. In 1961 they combined with the 1st Battalion The Hertfordshire Regiment to form **The Bedfordshire and Hertfordshire Regiment TA.** The badge chosen is shown in Plate 50, the Eagle and Castle from the arms of the Borough of Bedford (brass eagle, w/m castle), with a brass hart superimposed, in a/a.

The most far-reaching changes that the Territorial soldier had had to face in peacetime since 1908 started in 1966. The TA as it had been was to be changed and stratified into availability layers and was to become the TAVR, Territorial and Army Volunteer Reserve. Classes I and II were on immediate readiness to reinforce Regular units and Class II units were restyled Volunteers, a not unwelcome reversion to an earlier title. With one exception all the Class II units adopted the Regular brigade badges. For example, the Wessex Volunteers, a unit of battalion strength and structure, had companies from Devon, Gloucestershire, Hampshire, Dorset and Wiltshire and wore the Wessex Brigade badge. The exception was the North Irish Militia (another reversion to an older style) which had companies from each of the three Ulster regiments' areas and a fourth company from the London Irish Rifles; the badge chosen was that of the London Irish.

Units classified as TAVR III had no overseas service liability but a lower standard of pay and allowance as well as a reduced annual training commitment and they were generically described as Territorials. The Royal Leicestershire Territorials, for example, wore the badge of the old Regular regiment while Volunteers from the same county furnished a company for the 5th (Volunteer) Battalion The Royal Anglian Regiment and wore the badge of that unit.

Yeomanry units were to be deprived of armoured vehicles and in some cases such as Wiltshire and Somerset both Infantry and Yeomanry were combined in one unit. These units required new badges which were designed and made, but were then put in store as by that time the Government had changed its mind yet again and put the Territorials on a care and maintenance basis, reducing the units to cadre strength of one officer and eight men. The new badges chosen are described below.

The Dorset Territorials were to wear a shield bearing a castle, presumably Dorchester Keep, above a motto *Who's a-fear'd* in a/a (w/m finish) as in Plate 50.

The Hampshire and Isle of Wight Territorials were to wear the brass Hampshire Rose and Q/C with w/m laurel sprays either side and a scroll reading 'Hampshire & Isle of Wight', in a/a finish (Plate 50).

The Royal Berkshire Territorials were to wear a w/m, a/a badge as previously used by the Berkshire Yeomanry, backed by a red plastic oval.

The Royal Wiltshire Territorials were to wear basically the badge of the Wiltshire Regiment in brass with the w/m Prince of Wales's plumes of the Royal Wiltshire Yeomanry in the centre (Plate 50).

The Somerset Yeomanry and Light Infantry (Territorial) were to wear the w/m stringed bugle-horn of the Somerset Light Infantry with, on the strings, a circle carrying the *Arma Pacis Fulcra* motto of the North Somerset Yeomanry surrounding a brass Wyvern of the West Somerset Yeomanry surmounted by a Q/C in w/m.

The 5/6th (Territorial) Battalion The Staffordshire Regiment (Prince of Wales's) were to wear simply the brass Stafford knot, common to both of the old Staffordshire regiments (Plate 50).

The 3rd (Territorial) Battalion Queen's Own Highlanders were to wear the old Seaforth Highlanders badge with the old Cameron Highlanders collar badge within the antlers of the stag (Plate 49). This badge is now worn by the regular Queen's Own Highlanders (Seaforth & Camerons).

The Buckinghamshire Regiment RA were to wear the Swan of the old Royal Bucks Hussars within a circle bearing the title, Q/C above, all in w/m (Plate 50).

The Devonshire Territorials were to wear the Devonshire Regiment Castle within the Garter surmounted by the Royal Crest with laurel wreath and title scroll. (Plate 50).

The Oxfordshire Territorials were to wear the old crown and Royal Cypher 'AR' of Queen Adelaide from the Queen's Own Oxfordshire Hussars above the bugle-horn of the Light Infantry, all in w/m (a/a) as in Plate 50.

The London Yeomanry and Territorials were to wear, in w/m, the saltire within a laurel wreath with Q/C above; in the centre of the saltire the shield from the Arms of the City of London (Plate 50). The constituent elements of this unit were The London Scottish, The Inns of Court and City Yeomanry and a Sapper company.

After effectively demolishing the old Territorial Army the Government raised a new force in Ulster to replace the 'B' Specials of the Royal Ulster Constabulary. Their new badge, as the **Ulster Defence Regiment**, was effectively that of the old Royal Ulster Rifles without the motto scroll – the Angel Harp with Q/C above, all in brass a/a (Plate 50). (See also notes on pipers).

In July, 1992, the Ulster Defence Regiment became part of the new Royal Irish Regiment (see also chapter 20).

The London Regiment 9

For some reason the War Office had always seemed to believe that the County of London did not exist. They knew of the City of London, of course, because The Royal Fusiliers had the subsidiary title 'City of London Regiment'. But one is convinced that they felt that Kent extended to London Bridge, Middlesex to The Temple and Essex to Aldgate Pump.

However, in 1908 The London Regiment was created and consisted of twenty-eight battalions, most of which had previously existed under other titles. The Regiment lasted until 1937 when several of its battalions reverted to their original counties and some were converted to other arms. Of the twenty-eight, only two now remain in their same infantry role.

The 1st, 2nd, 3rd and 4th City of London Battalions all bore the badge of The Royal Fusiliers, with hardly any change since they had all been Volunteer Battalions of that Regiment.

The 5th City of London Battalion – **The London Rifle Brigade**, bore the Royal Arms inside a circle carrying their title and South Africa honour; crossed behind this were the Mace and the Sword of the City Arms and below, a scroll *Primus in Urbe* which referred to their old title of 1st London Rifle Volunteers (doubtless a comment upon their being placed fifth!) and a shield of the City Arms, all surrounded by an oak wreath, the badge being of w/m (Plate 37). After the First World War ten honour scrolls were added (Plate 37). This was worn throughout the Second World War and up to 1956 when the LRB was amalgamated with the 12th London (Rangers). As the London Rifle Brigade/Rangers they wore the badge of the Rifle Brigade with the Guelphic Crown.

The 6th City of London Battalion were known as the 'Cast-iron Sixth' from their black KRRC-type badge (Plate 38). This bore a tablet carrying the City's motto *Domine Dirige Nos* below the K/C, and the top arm of the cross held the honour 'South Africa 1900–2'. In 1935 they became an Anti-Aircraft Battalion RE and adopted the badge of the Royal Engineers.

The 7th City of London Battalion displayed little ingenuity in their choice of badge, simply a w/m '7' on a brass grenade (Plate 37). As the 3rd London RV before 1908 they had borne the numeral '3' on their grenade.

The 8th City of London Battalion (Post Office Rifles) wore a badge of 'Rifle Brigade' pattern in w/m with two unique honours on the laurel wreaths: unique, that is, to Territorial units. The first was 'Egypt 1882' since GPO workers volunteered for service with the RE Cable and Telegraph Corps during that campaign, and the second was 'South Africa 1899–1902'. Other Volunteer units only qualified for the dates '1900–02' (Plate 37). A small version existed for wear in the fs cap.

In 1922 the 7th and 8th merged to form the 7th City of London Battalion (Post Office Rifles) wearing the 7th cap badge and the 8th collar badges until conversion to RE in 1935.

The 9th County of London Battalion (Queen Victoria's Rifles) also wore a black KRRC-type badge: the tablet below the K/C carried the South Africa honour and inside the centre circle was St. George and the Dragon (Plate 38). The Regiment served with distinction as a KRRC Battalion in the Second World War in company with The Queen's Westminsters, so their amalgamation in 1960 was relatively painless.

The 10th County of London Battalion began life in 1908 as The Paddington Rifles and their badge had for a centrepiece the mural crown and crossed swords from the Arms of Paddington within a circle, K/C above, flanked by laurel wreaths carrying 'South Africa 1900–02' on four scrolls (Plate 37). This appeared in w/m, in brass and in black, the centre both voided and solid, a remarkable range for a unit which lasted for only four years. In 1912 because of falling numbers the Paddington Rifles were disbanded and the 10th were re-raised as The Hackney Regiment. Their brass badge was a tower from the Arms of Hackney, within a band carrying the motto *Justitia Turris Nostra*, placed on a star, K/C above, resting upon a laurel wreath, all above a title scroll (Plate 37). During the First World War they acquired the redoubtable nickname of 'The Hackney Gurkhas' (not surprising, perhaps, to those who knew their London). In the changes of 1937 they became the 5th (Hackney) Battalion The Royal Berkshire Regiment (the Royal Berkshire was the nearest regiment to London with just one TA battalion). Became 648 Regt RA (Royal Berks) in 1947.

The 11th County of London Battalion (Finsbury Rifles) became a Royal Artillery unit in 1935 but until then wore a black Maltese Cross for their badge. The South Africa honour appeared on the tablet below the K/C and the motto *Pro Aris et Focis* was borne on the four arms of the cross (Plate 38).

The 12th County of London Battalion (The Rangers) had a variety of black badges. Initially they took the first one shown in Plate 38 in which the motto *Excel* appeared on the tablet below the K/C. (The motto derived from 'XL' as originally in 1860 they were the 40th Middlesex R.V.). The South Africa honour was on the upper arm of the cross and title 'The Rangers' on a scroll below. The central circle bore the title '12th County of London'. A change was made after 1920, ten honours on the arms of the cross being added and the scroll altered to 'Rangers'. The third one, also shown in Plate 38, became necessary in 1937 when the tablet below the K/C disappeared and all reference to the 12th Battalion was removed from the central circle, being replaced by 'King's Royal Rifle Corps' which they had joined that year. In 1949 they transferred from KRRC to the Rifle Brigade but no new badges were issued for other ranks. Upon their subsequent merger with the LRB the combined unit, LRB/Rangers, took into use the last pattern badge of the Rifle Brigade, hardly worn by the regular 1st Battalion since they almost immediately became the 3rd Green Jackets.

The 13th County of London Battalion (Kensington) carried the Arms of Kensington upon an eight-pointed brass star (Plate 37). In 1914 they were granted the title 'Princess Louise's' and in 1937 became Princess Louise's Kensington Regiment (Duke of Cambridge's Own) TA, but still wore the same badge. After 1946 they became a unit of the Royal Signals but kept to the old badge until completely disbanded in the big TA economies of 1968. The last a/a issue was in w/m finish.

The 14th County of London Battalion (London Scottish) wore the w/m badge shown in Plate 37 a Scottish lion upon a saltire carrying the title on upper and lower scrolls, the motto *Strike Sure* and the South Africa honour on an inner circle, flanked by thistles. Also illustrated is a small bronzed badge worn by the 2nd Battalion in the foreign-service helmet in Egypt and Palestine in 1917–18. These were quite unofficial, made by J. R. Gaunt Ltd. and paid for by the CO, Lieutenant-Colonel R. J. L. Ogilby. In 1937 they became The London Scottish (The Gordon Highlanders) TA but they did not wear the Gordon tartan except on their pipe-bags. The original hodden grey, the family tweed of Lord Elcho, was chosen as being a non-partisan 'tartan' when the Regiment was raised in 1859.

The 15th County of London Battalion (Prince of Wales's Own Civil Service Rifles) wore the black Prince of Wales's plumes, motto and coronet (Plate 38) until 1922 when they merged with **The 16th County of London Battalion (Queen's Westminster Rifles)** to form The 16th County of London Battalion (Queen's Westminster and Civil Service Rifles). The black badge of the 16th before 1922 bore as its centrepiece the portcullis from the Arms of the City of Westminster (Plate 38) and on the new one (Plate 38) the plumes of the 15th and the portcullis of the 16th appeared on two ovals in the centre of the familiar Maltese Cross bearing honours on all four arms. In 1938 the title was shortened to The Queen's Westminsters, The King's Royal Rifle Corps and under this title they served with distinction during the Second World War. The Queen Victoria's Rifles amalgamated with them in 1960 when they became **The Queen's Royal Rifles.** The new badge removed the plumes from the oval and put them on the upper arm of the cross, replacing them with St.George and the Dragon. The KRRC motto *Celer et Audax* appeared on a tablet below the Q/C and the battle honours on the arms included a selection from the Second World War (Plate 38).

The 17th County of London Battalion (Poplar and Stepney Rifles) in 1908 took into use a 'Rifle Brigade' type badge (Plate 37) bearing only the South Africa honour on the arms of the cross. It was made in brass and in w/m. After 1926 the w/m badge was changed to include twenty-seven honours on the arms of the cross and on the laurel wreaths and the title 'Tower Hamlets Rifles' appeared on the central circle; the South Africa honour was placed on the previously empty tablet below the K/C. The title dated back to earlier Volunteer units bearing the Tower Hamlets title. As The Tower Hamlets Rifles, The Rifle Brigade they suffered badly in North Africa and were only nominally re-raised in 1947 as a LAA Regiment RA (Rifle Brigade) wearing Royal Artillery badges.

The 18th County of London Battalion (London Irish Rifles) began life as the 16th Middlesex RV and the black Harp of Erin was their first badge. In 1937 they became part of the Royal Ulster Rifles whereupon they changed to a w/m badge (Plate 37) and wore a green feather hackle in the newly-adopted caubeen (hat). Warrant Officers wore the larger badge of slightly different pattern (Plate 37) and in 1962 when a Q/C issue was made the new a/a badges were of the large variety for all other ranks. (See notes on pipers.)

The 19th County of London Battalion (St. Pancras) wore a badge of 'Rifle Brigade' pattern, the motif in the central circle being 'XIX'. The upper and lower arms bore the South Africa honour; one variety carries the correct dates '1900–02' while another, struck in error, is dated '1899–1902'. The badge is generally in brass (Plate 37). In 1935 the 19th became an AA Battalion RE wearing the badges of the Royal Engineers.

The 20th County of London Battalion (Blackheath and Woolwich) was formed in 1908 from two Volunteer battalions of the Queen's Own Royal West Kent Regiment so that their badge of the White Horse of Kent was a natural choice for the new 'London' unit. Below the horse was the motto *Invicta* in Old English lettering, and a lower scroll read '20th The London Regt. Batt', the badge being all w/m (Plate 37). In 1935 they vanished into the Royal Engineers and, subsequently Royal Artillery, but retained their cap-badge until disbandment in 1946.

The 21st County of London Battalion (First Surrey Rifles) wore the ever-popular Maltese Cross in black, a scroll below the K/C reading *Concordia Victrix*. The upper arm of the cross carried the South Africa honour and the lower bore the date '1803', the date of formation of the Surrey Volunteers from which the unit claimed descent. Below the cross a scroll read '21st County of London'. The use of this badge lapsed in 1935 on conversion to a unit of the Royal Engineers and subsequently of Royal Artillery. After 1945, although still a gunner unit, the old badge was brought back into use for a short time (Plate 38).

Both 22nd and 24th County of London Battalions had been Volunteer battalions of the Queen's (Royal West Surrey Regiment) and wore the Regular pattern badges of that Regiment. In the 1937 changes they became respectively the 6th (Bermondsey) Bn and 7th (Southwark) Bn The Queen's Royal Regiment (West Surrey). After the war the 6th continued as infantry but the 7th were reraised as gunners, still wearing Queen's badges. In 1961 the 6th were absorbed into the 3rd Bn The Queen's Royal Surrey Regiment, changing their badge to the star bearing the Paschal Lamb: the same changes saw the old 7th lose its identity in a gunner merger.

The 23rd County of London Battalion carried no further title but its badge indicated its East Surrey origins - the Arms of Guildford inside a circle bearing the honour 'South Africa 1900–2' upon a w/m star with a brass title-scroll below (Plate 37): another pattern had the dates '1900–02'. In 1937 they became the 7th (23rd London) Bn The East Surrey Regiment and, in 1938, heedless of previous allegiances, 42nd Royal Tank Corps, using the Tanks' badge until 1956 when they became once more The 23rd London Regiment TA, wearing a Q/C badge in a/a (with honour 'South Africa 1900–2'), the only unit since 1937 to carry the London Regiment title. At one time they were brigaded with the London Scottish and the London Irish, thus earning for themselves the inevitable title of the 'London English'. After a short revival they joined the 6th East Surreys in 1960 to form the 4th Battalion The Queen's Royal Surrey Regiment TA, changing their badge yet again.

The 25th County of London Battalion (Cyclists) claimed to have been the first Cyclist Battalion in the world, having been raised in 1888 as the 26th Middlesex (Cyclist) Volunteer Rifle Corps. The Battalion HQ of the 25th was in Fulham and F Company came from Harrods, the Knightsbridge store. Their badge was a cycle wheel with '25', inside a band reading 'County of London – Cyclists'. A laurel wreath surrounded the whole; K/C above and a straight motto scroll worded *Tenax et Audax* at the base. The badge was in brass, in bronze and in w/m (Plate 38).

The 28th County of London Battalion (Artists' Rifles) had, as might be expected, a badge devoid of military crudities. It was designed by W. C. Wyon, an original member of the old 38th Middlesex RV raised in 1859, a Queen's Medallist and Engraver to the Signet, who linked the heads of Mars, God of War, and Minerva, Goddess of the Arts. A coarser Regimental rhyme records:

> Mars, he was the God of War
> And didn't stop at trifles.
> Minerva was a bloody whore
> So hence The Artists' Rifles.

Two badges are shown in Plate 37: one has a scroll 'Artists' and this appeared in brass, in w/m and in black, the last for wear on the grey slouch hat worn with grey full dress before 1914. The pattern with 'Artists Rifles' on the scroll was in both brass and w/m and seems to have been the second design. The w/m badge of either pattern seems to have been worn on the green patrol uniform assumed when they became The Artists' Rifles, The Rifle Brigade in 1937. After spending the Second World War as an Officer Cadet Training Unit the Artists were reformed in 1947 as 21st Special Air Service (Artists) but discarded the Mars and Minerva cap badge in 1956 for the SAS badge.

The senior regiment in the Territorial Army is the **Honourable Artillery Company.** It was originally proposed that they become the 26th London Regiment but not surprisingly they refused to step into line and remained unnumbered. However, as a London unit they can rightly be mentioned here. There are two parts of the HAC, infantry and artillery, wearing separate badges.

Infantry: badge was a brass grenade bearing the monogram 'HAC' (Plate 39A), serjeants having the letters superimposed in w/m (Plate 39A). In 1954 badges reverted to w/m in the tradition of the old Volunteers and serjeants had a brass monogram on theirs. The badge had always been difficult to keep in the beret while on training and in 1969 the Regiment had embroidered badges made for wear by other ranks in this head-dress only. The grenade is in white and the monogram gold, all on a black ground (Plate 39A).

Artillery: badge was the gun badge of the Royal Artillery but with the letters 'HAC' on the upper scroll and on the lower scrolls the motto *Arma Pacis Fucra* (Plate 39A). This was in brass, with K/C originally, appearing in the smaller size for the beret and, in both sizes, with Q/C. Oddly enough, for beret wear in training the Gunners had produced at Regimental expense the small w/m badge in Plate 39A, the crest from the Arms of The Company, an armoured right arm grasping an ornamental staff. On each side is a wing bearing St. George's Cross, all on an heraldic wreath.

The unit intended to fill the 27th position was **The Inns of Court Rifle Volunteers.** These will be dealt with in the Yeomanry chapter as that was their ultimate destiny.

Of The London Regiment, only elements of the 14th and 18th still exist recognizably in an infantry role in the Territorial and Army Volunteer Reserve.

Looking at the amalgamations which followed the First World War it is interesting to see that these were the 7th and 8th Battalions and the 15th and 16th Battalions. The 8th were the Post Office Rifles and the 15th the Civil Service Rifles. With their dual responsibilities, these two units were apparently slower in mobilizing than other battalions and it was doubtless felt that to have two battalions consisting wholly of civil servants was not conducive to military efficiency!

Yeomanry 10

The Yeomanry Cavalry as it used to be styled was the mounted counterpart of the Volunteer Force and later was the cavalry of the Territorial Force and of the Territorial Army.

Unlike the infantry, which, in the period under review, was based on Regular infantry regiments mostly using the Regular badges, the Yeomanry were entirely local in concept and wore their own badges. These designs were often based upon County motifs, the arms of their shires and the crests of the landed families responsible for rising them.

Few infantry units could trace their origin back before 1859 but many Yeomanry regiments could look back to an eighteenth century origin. However, because of the many fluctuations in para-military enthusiasm during the nineteenth century, Yeomanry units often lapsed and could not always lay claim to unbroken service. In 1885 the War Office issued a list of precedence and although this created a furore at the time, with counter-claims by various units, it was adhered to and is given below.

Title	Year of Raising	Title	Year of Raising
1. Royal Wiltshire	1794	21. Bucks	1830
2. Warwickshire	1794	22. Derbyshire	1830
3. Yorkshire Hussars	1794	23. Dorset	1830
4. Sherwood Rangers	1794	24. Gloucestershire	1830
5. Staffordshire	1794	25. Herts	1830
6. Shropshire	1795	26. Berks	1831
7. Ayrshire	1803	27. Middlesex	1831
8. Cheshire	1803	28. Royal 1st Devon	1831
9. Yorkshire Dragoons	1803	29. Suffolk	1831
10. Leicestershire	1803	20. North Devon	1831
11. North Somerset	1803	31. Worcestershire	1831
12. Duke of Lancaster's	1819	32. West Kent	1831
13. Lanarkshire	1819	33. West Somerset	1831
14. Northumberland	1819	34. Oxfordshire	1831
15. South Notts	1826	35. Montgomeryshire	1831
16. Denbighshire	1830	36. 2nd West York	1843
17. Westmorland & Cumberland	1830		(disbanded 1894)
18. Pembrokeshire	1830	37. Lothians & Berwick	1846
19. East Kent	1830	38. Glasgow	1848
20. Hampshire	1830	39. Lancshire Hussars	1848

Following the reorganization of 1901 the following additional regiments were raised:

Title	Year of Raising	Title	Year of Raising
39. Surrey	1901 (replacing 2nd West York)	47. 3rd County of London (Sharpshooters)	1901
		48. Bedfordshire	1901
		49. Essex	1901
40. Fife & Forfar	1901	50. King's Colonials	1901
41. Norfolk	1901	51. North of Ireland	1902
42. Sussex	1901	52. South of Ireland	1902
43. Glamorgan	1901	53. Northamptonshire	1902
44. Lincolnshire	1901	54. East Riding of Yorkshire	1902
45. City of London (Rough Riders)	1901	55. Lovat's Scouts	1903
		56. Scottish Horse	1903
46. 2nd County of London (Westminster)	1901		

In 1914 The Welsh Horse were raised in South Wales.

Certain adjustments were made in this table when several regiments became Special Reserve units but this is a technicality outside the scope of this book. The object of the listing is to aid displaying the badges in a recognized sequence and to observe seniority.

It is normal for units formed from a merger to take the precedence of the senior component. The amalgamation of the 13th Hussars and the 18th Hussars for example put the new 13/18th Hussars in place of the old 13th. This chapter deals with amalgamated units *after* the *junior* element of the merger so that the reader may be familiar with the badges of all parties of the union.

The South African War brought about changes in the Yeomanry and in 1901 it was decided to rethink their role. Their training was changed from that of cavalry to mounted infantry, swords were called in and rifles issued. This was unpopular but accepted as was the new title 'Imperial Yeomanry', an honour recognizing their success in South Africa.

So the first cap badges worn by the Yeomanry were the variants generally referred to by collectors as the IY. In 1908, the Territorial Force was formed and the reserve force, Yeomanry and infantry became part of the TF, the Imperial Yeomanry title being dropped. Those badges which had incorporated the title in their designs were changed officially but were often worn on into the First World War by individuals. After the War, the 'cavalry axe' fell on the new Territorial Army as it had fallen on the Regular cavalry. The TA solved the problem of its surplus horsemen by converting them to other arms. Most of these were to RA, some to RE and one to Royal Corps of Signals while others became Armoured Car Companies in the days before the mechanization of the cavalry.

Some kept their own badges, some changed to the badge of their new arm, but almost all retained their Yeomanry title in some way or other.

However, the collector will probably find it easier to ignore the conversions and treat them as Yeomanry regiments throughout their existence.

Plates 28–31 show the Yeomanry of the First World War.

The senior regiment, the **Royal Wiltshire Yeomanry (Prince of Wales's Own)**, was raised in 1794 and was granted its Royal title for service in the riots of 1830. The badge of the Prince of Wales's plumes and motto in w/m with brass coronet commemorated their escort to the Prince of Wales in 1863 when he visited the county. See also The Royal Yeomanry.

The Warwickshire Yeomanry wore the Bear and Ragged Staff of the Earl of Warwick. One of the first earls was said to have killed a giant with an ash tree, hence the ragged trunk as part of the crest. The badge was made in brass and in w/m. In one issue the brass bear appeared to be sitting but this was worn for a short period only and was very unpopular in the Regiment. In 1956 they were amalgamated with the Queen's Own Worcestershire Hussars. See also The Queen's Own Mercian Yeomanry.

The senior of the three Yorkshire regiments was the **Yorkshire Hussars (Alexandra, Princess of Wales's Own)** who wore the w/m White Rose of York below the Prince of Wales's plumes and motto, with brass coronet. This was struck in two sites but the design remained constant. In 1956 the three Yeomanry units in the county merged to form one new regiment, The Queen's Own Yorkshire Yeomanry.

Until 1949 the **Nottinghamshire (Sherwood Rangers) Yeomanry** wore simply a brass stringed bugle-horn but in that year a new design was authorised, the horn within a belt bearing the title 'Notts Sherwood Rangers Yeomanry' with K/C above, all in brass (Plate 33). A Q/C version followed in brass but, inexplicably, its a/a successor had a circle in place of the belt and the title read 'The Sherwood Rangers Yeomanry'. See also The Royal Yeomanry.

The first badge of the **Staffordshire Yeomanry (Queen's Own Royal Regiment)** was that of the Staffordshire IY, the Stafford knot above the letter 'S' above 'IY', all in w/m (Plate 52). The next pattern was the knot with QVC above, all in brass, but it is doubtful if this was ever worn during Queen Victoria's lifetime. The logical successor, the K/C issue, was worn until 1967 although an other-rank quality badge existed in w/m in the officers' pattern. This is shown in Plate 33 and I also have this in Q/C pattern in w/m and in a/a, although this was not in use generally in 1967. See also The Queen's Own Mercian Yeomanry.

The Army List recorded that the badge of the **Shropshire Yeomanry** was 'the arms of Shropshire County Council' although this hardly evokes a vision of martial glory. There is more than a hint of the fierce, however, in the three 'loggerheads', or leopards' faces, of the arms. The badge initially carried them on a shield within a circle bearing the title, surmounted by a K/C, all in brass. The first badge was the IY pattern and the only difference was that the letters also appeared on the circle. Immediately after the Second World War when the Regiment was in Italy some badges were made in which a belt took the place of the circle. In 1950, when the Regiment was back home, in a reconstituted TA, a new badge was authorized (Plate 33) from which the shield was removed so that the three faces might be more clearly seen. A Q/C issue appeared in the late 1950s. See also The Queen's Own Mercian Yeomanry.

The Ayrshire (Earl of Carrick's Own) Yeomanry wore until 1915 the badge in Plate 28, usually referred to as the 'IY pattern', made in brass. It was the crest of the Earl of Carrick, a lion-headed griffin with flaming tongue and eagle's wings. When the Regiment was in the Middle East it was felt that a change in design was called for and the CO, Lieutenant-Colonel Dunlop, asked for ideas. The design chosen was that of Serjeant-Major White and is shown in Plate 33. The beast was set on an heraldic wreath with a three-part scroll below, reading 'Earl of' – 'Ayrshire Yeomanry' - 'Carrick's'. This pattern continued until about 1923 when a change put the ruffled feathers in order and reshuffled the scrolls to read 'Ayrshire' – 'Earl of Carrick's Own' – 'Yeomanry'. This pattern also exists with the word 'of' in smaller letters than the rest of the title but this is without significance. A bi-metal badge was also made, the beast's body and head in w/m, the wings, wreath and scrolls in brass, but I believe this was never issued. The Earl of Carrick is one of the titles held by The Prince of Wales. See also The Queen's Own Yeomanry. (See also p. 98)

The Cheshire Yeomanry was another of the regiments associated with The Prince of Wales as it had the subsidiary title 'Earl of Chester's'. The w/m Prince of Wales's plumes and motto with brass coronet and title scroll reading 'Cheshire (Earl of Chester's) Yeomanry' came into use after 1908 (Plate 28), the previous issue having had the letters 'IY' on the scroll, making it noticeably shorter. See also The Queen's Own Yeomanry.

The Queen's Own Yorkshire Dragoons was the second of the Yeomanry regiments of the county and wore the Rose of York surmounted by a K/C (Plate 28); it appears to have been made in brass, in w/m and also in blackened brass. In 1956 the three Yorkshire regiments formed one.

The Leicestershire Yeomanry (Prince Albert's Own) had the subsidiary title of the Prince Consort but they did not at first take up the Saxe–Coburg device which he had awarded to the 11th Hussars. The first badge (Plate 33) had the letters 'LIY', for Leicestershire Imperial Yeomanry, with K/C above, flanked by laurel wreaths carrying the South Africa honour above a scroll 'Prince Albert's Own', all in w/m. In 1908, when the IY ceased to exist the badge shown in Plate 28 came into use: basically the same design, it carried only the letters 'LY' and was in brass and this continued in use until 1915 when the Saxe–Coburg device was used for the first time (Plate 33), in brass. It bore no South Africa honour and although it might be regarded as an oversight this is scarcely credible among Territorial regiments who had few enough honours that they could afford to discard any. Whatever the explanation, the post-war reformation of the Regiment saw a new brass badge come into use in 1922 with the honour scroll below. In 1952 the same pattern was issued in w/m (Plate 33). In 1957 the Regiment was merged with the Derbyshire Yeomanry.

The North Somerset Yeomanry wore in 1914 a ten-pointed star, the top point displaced by a K/C; in the centre was the Royal Cypher 'GRV' surrounded by a circle bearing the motto *Arma Pacis Fulcra*, all in w/m (Plate 28). This was preceded by the ERVII Cypher. The pre-1908 IY issue bore no crown but the star was surrounded by a blue enamelled belt carrying the full title 'North Somerset Imperial Yeomanry'. In 1937 a GRVI issue was made but when an ERII badge was due it was decided to add a title scroll below, as seen in Plate 33. The 1956 Yeomanry changes amalgamated the NSY with 44 RTR to form the **North Somerset Yeomanry/44th Royal Tank Regiment** and a new design was sought for a badge. The star was retained but surrounded by the RTR's laurel wreath, a tank replacing the central Royal Cypher and the RTR motto *Fear Naught* was added at the foot of the badge. This, bearing a Q/C, was still in w/m finish in a/a (Plate 48). The 44th Royal Tank Regiment had previously been 6th Battalion The Gloucestershire Regiment which was converted to armour in 1938. As Bristol was the HQ of 6 Glosters a change of title was effected in 1965 when the Regiment became **The North Somerset and Bristol Yeomanry.** There was no change in the badge.

The Duke of Lancaster's Own Yeomanry bore the Red Rose of Lancaster within a wreath, laurel on one side and oak on the other, surmounted by a ducal coronet, with the scroll below inscribed 'Duke of Lancaster's Own', all in brass (Plate 28). In about 1954 the design was changed to a more pleasing one (Plate 33), the rose and wreath, all laurel now, in w/m, the coronet, belt and title in brass a/a.

The Lanarkshire Yeomanry bore a brass badge based upon the seal of the Royal Burgh of Lanark. The double-headed eagle clutching a bell was surmounted by a K/C while it balanced upon a title scroll (Plate 28). In about 1953 it was decided to discard the scroll and existing stocks were duly doctored but no Q/C badge was issued. The pre-1908 IY badge is seen in Plate 33, the Eagle within a thistle wreath above a three-part scroll bearing the title in full. In 1956 the Regiment merged with two other Lowland regiments to form The Queen's Own Lowland Yeomanry. (See also p.98)

The Northumberland Hussars dated from 1819 but one of the county's earlier Volunteer cavalry troops bore the splendid title of the Royal Cheviot Legion. The badge (Plate 28) carried a castle, said by Major

Edwards in his *Regimental Badges,* to be from the Arms of Newcastle-upon-Tyne. However, Walter Richards in *His Majesty's Territorial Army* published over sixty years ago, claimed it to be Alnwick Castle, the home of the Dukes of Northumberland, which seems more likely. It was surrounded by a circle bearing the title and carried a K/C above and a South Africa honour scroll below. This initially appeared in brass but early in the 1950s was issued in w/m as was its Q/C successor. See also The Queen's Own Yeomanry.

The South Nottinghamshire Hussars wore simply a slip of oak with an acorn and this can be found in brass, in bronze and in w/m (Plate 28). The symbolism of this is not hard to comprehend.

The Denbighshire Hussars wore simply a bronzed badge of the Prince of Wales's plumes, motto and coronet. After the First World War they were converted into two batteries of the 61st Caernarvon and Denbigh (Yeomanry) Medium Regiment RA and wore Royal Artillery badges until 1949. A new 'Yeomanry' badge was then struck although they kept their artillery role. This consisted of w/m Prince of Wales's plumes and scrolls with brass coronet and scroll below, inscribed **'Caernarvon & Denbigh Yeo'.** A few years later a further merger took place involving a Flintshire unit, and in 1962 another badge was taken into use, identical with the last but, on the scroll, **'Flint, & Denbigh Yeo'** (the last two illustrated in Plate 33).

The Westmorland and Cumberland Yeomanry wore the badge in Plate 29, three sprigs of heather within an oval band carrying the title 'Westmorland & Cumberland Y', surrounded by laurel wreaths, all in brass. Converted to an artillery role after the First World War they wore RA badges until 1962 when a new a/a badge, in w/m finish (Plate 48) came into use. This retained the heather but discarded the laurel wreaths and changed the spelling so that the title read 'Westmoreland & Cumberland Yeo', surmounted by Q/C.

The Pembroke Yeomanry was the only one to bear the honour 'Fishguard', the only honour awarded for service within the British Isles and the first granted to any Volunteer unit of the British Army. In 1797 the French made a landing at Llanwrda near Fishguard. Lord Cawdor, then commanding what was at that time the Castlemartin Yeomanry, roused his men and they went next day to meet the French who surrendered after negotiations. The honour was not granted until 1853, following representations to Queen Victoria. Several apocryphal accounts exist of the 1797 encounter, all of them more exciting and improbable than the truth. One says that the French saw from their ships groups of Welsh women above the town, dressed in their national red cloaks and tall black hats. Thinking these to be reinforcements of Regular British infantry the French turned tail and fled. One cannot deny that this makes a better story than a simple surrender. The badge illustrated in Plate 29 has w/m Prince of Wales's plumes, motto scrolls and scroll below, 'Fishguard', and coronet in brass. Another pattern existed with a brass honour scroll and it was in these metals that the slightly smaller a/a badge was made.

The Royal East Kent Yeomanry (The Duke of Connaught's Own) (Mounted Rifles) was the full title of the older of the two Kentish units. The badge shown in Plate 29 was made in brass and also in bronze, the White Horse of Kent upon a scroll *Invicta* within the Garter, surmounted by K/C. An earlier pattern bore also a scroll inscribed 'Royal East Kent Mounted Rifles'. The two Kent regiments were amalgamated in 1920 and formed a Royal Artillery Regiment, wearing RA badges but KY buttons. They continued as gunners until 1961 when a merger took place with the 3rd/4th County of London Yeomanry (Sharpshooters).

The Hampshire Carabiniers Yeomanry were the only ones to style themselves 'Carabiniers', the result of a new Colonel in 1884, who was a former Regular officer of 6th Dragoon Guards (The Carabiniers). The badge (Plate 29) was a direct copy of that of the Regular regiment except for the insertion of the Hampshire Rose into the centre. The Regiment was converted to RA in 1920 but wore Yeomanry cap badges.

The Royal Buckinghamshire Hussars wore, before 1908, a large w/m Maltese Cross with, in the centre, a belt inscribed 'Royal Bucks Hussars' surrounding an 'ER' Royal Cypher, the top arm of the cross carrying QVC (Plate 33). Correcting this seeming anomaly, the next badge, shown in Plate 29, carried an aggressive looking bird, the White Swan from the Arms of the Dukes of Buckingham, flapping its wings within a circle reading, 'Yeomen of Bucks, strike home', a K/C above and scroll below inscribed 'Royal Bucks Hussars'. This was officially bronzed but is often found in brass; it was also made in w/m and a Q/C issue was made in a/a in w/m finish. Their shoulder titles 'RBH' were construed in the First World War as 'Rothschild's Blood-Hounds' after their colonel at the time.

The Derbyshire Yeomanry wore as its badge a rose with K/C above, flanked by laurel scrolls carrying the South Africa honour, above a three-part scroll inscribed 'Derbyshire' – 'Yeomanry', the words separated by a scroll carrying a laurel spray (Plate 29). This was in w/m. Earlier issues in brass, slightly larger, had borne the word 'Imperial' on the centre laurel-bearing scroll and the next issue had simply a plain scroll before recourse was had to that standard heraldic garnishing. After 163 years of independent existence the Regiment merged in 1957 with the Leicestershire Yeomanry to form the **Leicestershire and Derbyshire (Prince Albert's Own) Yeomanry.** The new badge (Plate 33) has a brass Q/C above a rose which carries a w/m Saxe-Coburg device: below the rose, a brass scroll carries, not without difficulty, the combined title, barely readable to the naked eye.

The Queen's Own Dorsetshire Yeomanry wore a bronzed badge, very similar to that of the Royal Engineers in design: however, as can be seen in Plate 29, the scrolls bore the South Africa honour while inside the Garter, the letters 'QOY' were featured with a scroll 'Dorset'. In 1902 the first Imperial Yeomanry pattern appeared (Plate 34), a broadly similar design but with 'Q.O. Dorset I.Y.' on the solid centre. Honours for South Africa were awarded in 1905 and the new badge carrying honour scrolls (Plate 52) was taken into use briefly, giving way in 1908 to the type in use in 1914. After 1920 another badge appeared but with a three-part scroll below the Garter, inscribed 'The Great War', the only badge I recall to carry such a 'blanket' honour (Plate 34). This was later made in w/m as was a Q/C badge but I believe the latter was never issued. Although a gunner unit after 1922 the Dorsetshire Yeomanry kept their own badges. In 1961 they merged with the West Somerset Yeomanry.

The Royal Gloucestershire Hussars bore as their badge a portcullis surmounted by a ducal coronet and bordered by a title scroll, all in brass (Plate 29). This was the crest from the Arms of the Dukes of Beaufort who were Honorary Colonels of the Regiment. Seen in Plate 34 is the pre-1908 badge, identical except for the letters 'I.Y.' flanking the portcullis.

The Hertfordshire Yeomanry wore a small brass hart, lodged in water (Plate 29). This, in fact, was the collar badge of the old Hertfordshire Imperial Yeomanry who wore in their head-dress the same hart within a circle with the letters 'I.Y.' below the hart (Plate 52). The Regiment became gunners after the First World War. In the early 1950s a new w/m badge was issued, a Q/C above an oval belt carrying the title (Plate 34). The wave of amalgamations in 1961 linked the Regiment with the Bedfordshire Yeomanry.

The Berkshire Yeomanry wore as their badge a device familiar to all railway travellers in the county, the skeletal White Horse of Berkshire, a figure cut into the chalk of the Downs above Uffington. As can be seen in Plate 29 it stood upon a scroll 'Berkshire' and was of brass. A smaller beret badge also existed. Before 1908, the badge was the same except for the addition of the letters 'I.Y.' below the scroll (Plate 34). The Regiment became gunners after the First World War and in 1956 merged with the Royal Bucks Hussars and the Queen's Own Oxfordshire Hussars to form one RA Regiment. In 1961 the Berkshire Yeomanry battery was extricated from the Regiment to be amalgamated with the Westminster Dragoons. Alas, the White Horse, since the reorganisation in 1974, is now in Oxfordshire.

The 1st County of London Yeomanry (Middlesex, The Duke of Cambridge's Hussars) is better known as the Middlesex Yeomanry. The badge (Plate 29) was an eight-pointed star carrying the motto *Pro Aris et Focis* and the words 'Middlesex Yeomanry' on a circle, having in its centre the GRV Royal Cypher, all in w/m. This pattern also existed in brass. Its successor, with GRVI Cypher, was also in w/m. The pre-1908 badge carried the ERVII Cypher and the additional word 'Imperial' on the central band. It was made both in brass and in w/m. Following Queen Elizabeth's accession to the throne in 1952 a new badge became necessary and the pattern previously worn by the officers was adopted by all ranks. It is shown in Plate 34 and consisted of a w/m star and Q/C with a brass centrepiece bearing the motto and the letters 'M.D.C.H' on the circdc with 'ERII' in the centre. The Regiment became a Signals unit in 1920 and remained so throughout the Second World War and after.

The Royal First Devonshire Yeomanry wore as their badge the bronzed Royal Crest (with K/C) as seen in Plate 29. It was also worn in brass. In 1920 the Regiment merged with Royal North Devonshire Hussars.

The Duke of York's Own Loyal Suffolk Hussars wore as their badge a brass castle, said to be that of Bury St. Edmunds with the date of raising '1793' below it; the title 'Loyal Suffolk Hussars' was on a three/part w/m scroll below the date. A smaller a/a version of the badge was issued in the early 1960s. The Regiment was another of those which became gunners in 1920. In 1961 they were merged with the Norfolk Yeomanry. Until 1900 the Loyal Suffolk Hussars were the only Volunteer cavalry in the Eastern Counties although both Essex and Norfolk squadrons existed under the badge of the Suffolks.

The Royal North Devonshire Hussars wore as their badge the monogram 'NDH' surmounted by K/C, made in brass and also bronzed. In 1920 they merged with the Royal First Devonshire Yeomanry and took a new badge: this consisted of the crest of Lord Rolle (who had been responsible for raising both regiments), a hand grasping a parchment roll with coronet above, all within a circle inscribed 'Royal Devon Yeomanry Artillery' and surmounted by a Royal Crest, with K/C. This had a solid centre and was in both bronze and brass. The design was finally approved in December 1924. It also appeared with 'RFA' in place of the word 'Artillery'. Later badges had a voided centre and the first Q/C issue (Plate 34) had a misspelling when the letter 'n' was left out of the word 'Yeomanry'. These were quickly withdrawn and a correct version issued in a/a. In 1976 a new badge (Plate 52) was authorised as D Sqn, The Wessex Yeomanry, a w/m version of the previous badge but with no mention of Artillery.

The Queen's Own Worcestershire Hussars wore as the centrepiece of their badge (Plate 30) a sprig of pear blossom in w/m, surrounded by a brass wreath with K/C above and full title on the scroll below. Before 1908 the badge was all in brass and the scroll read 'Worcestershire Imperial Yeomanry'. The pear blossom had long been associated with the County. Although converted to a gunner role in 1920 the Regiment changed back to its old cavalry role in 1947 on reconstitution of the TA when it became a unit of the Royal Armoured Corps. In 1956 it merged with the Warwickshire Yeomanry to form the **Queen's Own Warwickshire and Worcestershire Yeomanry**: a suitable badge might have been arrived at, one thinks, by having the Warwickshire bear climbing up a Worcestershire pear tree but the College of Heralds is not often disposed to whimsy and so the end product (Plate 48), depicts the Warwickshire device within a wreath of pear blossom. This may be an equable solution but it left a singularly unfinished looking badge. See also The Queen's Own Mercian Yeomanry.

The West Kent Yeomanry (Queen's Own) wore as their badge the w/m White Horse of Kent above a scroll *Invicta* (Plate 30). The Regiment merged with the Royal East Kent Yeomanry, as it was more generally called, in 1920 to form a gunner unit and then, in 1961, the combined Kent Yeomanries merged with the 3rd/4th County of London Yeomanry (Sharpshooters) to form The Kent and County of London Yeomanry.

The West Somerset Yeomanry wore the Wyvern, the emblem of the ancient Kings of Wessex within an oval carrying the title, and, below, a scroll inscribed 'S. Africa 1900–01', all in brass. Before 1908 the IY had worn the same badge but with the title suitably amended. They were converted to a Royal Artillery role after the First World War and remained so throughout the Second. In 1961 they were amalgamated with the Q.O. Dorset Yeomanry to form the **Queen's Own Dorset and West Somerset Yeomanry.** The new badge (Plate 48) was basically that of the West Somerset, backed by the crossed rifle and sword previously worn by the Dorset on their collars. The Garter motto replaced the West Somerset title and the new title appeared on scrolls at the base; it was in a/a all in w/m finish except for the Wyvern which was in brass.

The Queen's Own Oxfordshire Hussars were the first Yeomanry regiment to go on active service in the First World War. Their badge was basically the Royal Cypher of Queen Adelaide, wife of King William IV and the crown shown on the badge in Plate 30 was appropriate to the period of the Cypher. The Queen visited Oxford in 1835 and the Regiment furnished guards of honour which led to her conferring on them the title 'Queen's Own Royal Oxfordshire Yeomanry Cavalry'. This was later shortened and the title adopted in 1881, 'Queen's Own Oxfordshire Hussars', appeared on the scrolls below the Cypher. This badge is in w/m, in brass and also bronzed. It is found with K/C but these were not accepted by the Regiment as it was incorrect to be worn above the 'AR' Royal Cypher.

The Montgomeryshire Yeomanry, like many of the others, had broken service during the nineteenth century. They were first formed in 1803. The w/m badge (Plate 30) was a Welsh dragon above a scroll lettered 'M.Y.' Before 1908 the only difference was that the scroll read 'M.I.Y'. After the First World War it was converted to infantry and subsequently to artillery. In any event, all reference to a Yeomanry function ceased in 1918.

The Lothians and Border Horse wore in 1914 one of the most simple badges, a brass garb, or wheatsheaf (Plate 30), symbolic of the Border farmlands where they recruited. It remained unchanged until 1956 when they merged with the Lanarkshire and Q.O. Royal Glasgow Yeomanry. Prior to 1908 the brass badge shown in Plate 34 was worn. It consisted of the same garb with a long scroll reading 'Lothians and Berwickshire Imperial Yeomanry'. A similar badge followed with the new title 'Lothians and Border Horse' (Plate 52) on a scroll but was not worn for long before replacement by the plain brass garb. (See notes on pipers). (See also p.98)

The Queen's Own Royal Glasgow Yeomanry also suffered several fluctuations in fortune in the early years of the last century but in 1849 the Regiment provided the escort to Queen Victoria and the Prince Consort on a visit to Glasgow. This led to their being styled The Queen's own Royal Regiment of Glasgow Yeomanry. Their badge was the Royal Crest (K/C) of Scotland over a wreath of thistles, in brass (Plate 30); it appeared in two sizes. Converted to Field Artillery after the First World War they continued as gunners until 1947 when they became a unit of the Royal Armoured Corps on the reconstitution of the TA. During the Second World War the collar badge was worn in the field-service cap: a lion sitting up inside a circle bearing the full title, with K/C above, all in brass (Plate 34). After nine years as an armoured cavalry unit the Regiment was merged with the Lanarkshire Yeomanry and the Lothians and Border Horse to form the **Queen's Own Lowland Yeomanry.** It was clearly impossible to achieve a satisfactory badge for the new regiment by equal representation from the three constituent elements and so a completely new design was chosen (Plate 48). The Scottish Royal Unicorn was superimposed upon a pair of crossed swords, points upwards, all in w/m, with a brass scroll inscribed 'The Queen's Own Lowland Yeo' below the unicorn (made in a/a). (See notes on pipers). (See also p.98)

The Lancashire Hussars wore simply the Red Rose of Lancaster above a scroll inscribed 'Lancashire Hussars', all in brass (Plate 30). Prior to 1908 the badge was the same except that the scroll read 'Lancashire Hussars IY.'. The post-1908 badge was also made in w/m. After 1920 the Regiment became Royal Horse Artillery and lost their badges.

The Surrey Yeomanry (Queen Mary's Regiment) were a 1901 creation although Yeomanry regiments had existed in the county early in the last century. Styled at first the Surrey Imperial Yeomanry, the w/m badge was the crest of the Earl of Midleton, then Colonel of the Regiment (better known as Mr. Brodrick when, as Secretary of State for War, he was nominally responsible for the introduction of the unpopular 'Brodrick cap'), a w/m coronet with spearhead issuing therefrom (Plate 52). In 1910 on the death of King Edward VII the Regiment received the subsidiary title 'Queen Mary's Regiment' and the badge shown in Plate 30 was adopted: the Royal Cypher 'MR' was set inside the Garter, a K/C above and two scrolls below, bearing the full title 'Queen Mary's Regiment Surrey Yeomanry'. This appeared in both brass and in w/m and also in two sizes: a small brass variety also had a red enamelled backing to the Royal Cypher. The small Q/C badge was issued in a/a and w/m and the large in w/m only.

The Fife and Forfar Yeomanry wore as a badge a w/m armoured knight, normally referred to as the Thain of Fife (Plate 30). This was issued in brass also and after 1947 in a smaller size, more suitable for the beret. Another strike is also found in which the horse armour is different but this is not significant. Before 1908 the same armoured horseman appeared in an oval band carrying the full title 'Fife & Forfar Imperial Yeomanry', all in w/m (Plate 52). In 1956 the Regiment merged with the Scottish Horse.

The Norfolk Yeomanry, The King's Own Royal Regiment only formed in 1901 when the Norfolk Squadron of the Loyal Suffolk Hussars was expanded into a Norfolk unit. The first badge, worn on the slouch hat was a brass Royal Arms with title scroll below but in 1908 they took simply the brass Royal Cypher ERVII until 1911 when it changed to GRV (Plate 30), then to GRVI and ERII. King Edward VII had been a staunch patron of the Regiment and in 1906 had become Colonel-in-Chief of the 'King's Own Royal Regiment of Imperial Norfolk Yeomanry'. They became gunners after the First World War but continued to wear the Yeomanry badges until 1960 when they were merged with the Loyal Suffolk Hussars to form **The Suffolk and Norfolk Yeomanry.** The brass Castle was kept in the new badge but the Q/C, the superimposed 'ERII' Royal Cypher and the title scrolls 'Suffolk and Norfolk Yeomanry' were in w/m (a/a finish) shown in Plate 48. The date '1793' was discarded.

The Sussex Yeomanry wore a brass badge (Plate 30) in which a central shield bearing six martlets (from the Arms of the ancient Kingdom of the South Saxons) was set on an ornamental ground surmounted by a K/C, all above a title scroll. Before 1908 the badge was worn without the scroll. A Q/C issue was made in the 1960s in a/a and, in fact, the Regiment had the doubtful distinction of being perhaps the first to have an a/a badge – a K/C version exists.

The Glamorgan Yeomanry wore the familiar Prince of Wales's plumes and scrolls in w/m with a brass coronet but the scrolls were mysteriously blank (Plate 30) and did not carry their usual *Ich Dien* motto. Below was a three-part scroll bearing the title 'Glamorgan' – 'Yeomanry'. Before 1908, the blank central portion was inscribed 'Imperial' (Plate 52).

The Lincolnshire Yeomanry wore as the centrepiece of their badge a shield from the Arms of the City of Lincoln, surmounted by a K/C and flanked by laurel wreaths carrying a three-part scroll inscribed 'Lincolnshire' – 'Yeomanry', all in brass (Plate 30). The badge before 1908 had been of w/m with 'Imperial' inscribed on the part of the scroll which bears a laurel spray in the badge illustrated (Plate 52).

The City of London Yeomanry (Rough Riders) were habitually referred to as 'The Roughs' by the other London Yeomen. Their 1914 badge (Plate 30), was a large one and carried the City Arms in w/m inside a brass circle inscribed 'The City of London Yeomanry', flanked by a laurel wreath carrying the South Africa honour, topped by a K/C. This badge was far too large to be worn in the field-service cap and the small badge shown in Plate 34, a brass spur with w/m letters 'RR', one of the collar-badges, was worn. This continued in use until 1950 when the final badge, also shown in Plate 34, was issued: w/m Arms of the City of London on a brass backing, surrounded by a circle bearing the title as in the earlier badge, topped by a K/C and all above a small w/m double scroll reading 'Rough Riders'. A Q/C version of this was also made. During the IY period the first pattern was similar to the 1914 type but with title 'The City of London Imperial Yeomanry' and no honour scroll: after 1905 a version appeared with the newly-granted battle-honour. In the slouch hat a larger version of the spur badge was worn before 1908. In 1960 the Rough Riders amalgamated with The Inns of Court Regiment.

The 2nd County of London Yeomanry (Westminster Dragoons) wore simply the Arms of the City of Westminster in brass above a three-part scroll 'Westminster TY Dragoons' (TY for Territorial Yeomanry). This changed to a w/m badge in 1938. The pre-1908 badge was also in brass and carried the title 'Westminster Dragoons IY'. In 1961 the Berkshire Yeomanry battery was amalgamated with the Regiment, forming the **Berkshire and Westminster Dragoons.** The new badge (Plate 48) showed the w/m Berkshire Horse above a brass portcullis and scrolls bearing the full title. See also The Royal Yeomanry.

The 3rd County of London Yeomanry (Sharpshooters) were usually referred to by other London Yeomen as 'The Sharps' and had a range of badges for a unit which dated only from 1901. The first (Plate 34) was all in brass: generally in the format of the Royal Engineers badge it was lettered 'SS' in the centre and around the band was the title '3rd County of London Imperial Yeomanry'. The regimental history records that another badge – crossed rifles, K/C above and title scroll 'Sharpshooters' below – was worn as 'an alternative badge' during this period (Plate 52). After 1908 came the badge in Plate 31 showing the numeral '3' backed by crossed rifles, the circle inscribed 'County of London Yeomanry' with the scroll below carrying the South Africa honour. Following the First World War the 3rd CLY became **23rd London Armoured Car Company** and adopted first the badge shown (Plate 34): the numeral was replaced by w/m 'XXIII', the brass circle was inscribed 'London Armoured Car Company' and the honour scroll changed to carry the old title 'Sharp-shooters'. In about 1938 the design was again changed; w/m letters 'CLY' replaced the roman numerals and the full title appeared on the circle. The threat of war then permitted expansion once more to regimental strength and eventual duplication necessitated a further change of badge as shown, simply a change of title on the circle to read 'County of London Yeomanry'. The duplicated regiment was at first to be designated the 2/3rd, but independent counsels prevailed and they became the **4th County of London Yeomanry (Sharpshooters).** Their badge was similar to the old 3rd badge but the 4th used a w/m numeral and, having no South Africa honour, kept the 'Sharpshooters' scroll (Plate 34). War losses made it necessary to merge both regiments in 1944 to form the **3rd/4th County of London Yeomanry (Sharpshooters),** whereupon the badge of the 3rd was used. Finally, in 1961 the Kent Yeomanry joined the Sharpshooters to become the **Kent and County of London Yeomanry.** The final badge was basically the Sharpshooters badge with a w/m White Horse of Kent superimposed and the new title around the circle (Plate 34), in a/a. See also The Royal Yeomanry.

The Bedfordshire Yeomanry wore the brass badge shown in Plate 31. The eagle featured in the Arms of the Beauchamp family while the Castle on its breast is said to be the old Bedford Castle which once stood on the north bank of the River Ouse. In 1961 the Regiment, gunners since 1920, merged with the Hertfordshire Yeomanry forming the **Hertfordshire and Bedfordshire Yeomanry.** The badge chosen was simply a brass a/a hart (Plate 48).

The Essex Yeomanry wore as the principal feature of all its badges the shield from the Arms of the County of Essex. The first badge, worn 1901–05, was a shield with the three seaxes, surmounted by K/C, in brass (Plate 35). The next badge, similar to the 1914 pattern, had a different motto, *Audacter et Sincere* that of Lieutenant-Colonel R. B. Colvin C.B. who raised the Essex Imperial Yeomanry. In 1909 it was ruled that personal mottoes should not be used and the next badge (Plate 31) had the motto *Decus et Tutamen* which was that of the old West Essex Yeomanry, in existence 1830–77. This badge was worn 1909–16 and also in the field-service cap, general-service cap and beret during and after the Second World War. In 1916 a new badge was issued (Plate 35). Only the war can explain this singularly ill-favoured badge: the crown closely resembled the flat-topped QVC and the circle, carrying two words, was clearly divided into two halves, the word 'Essex' being spread out comfortably while 'Yeomanry' was crammed into the other half. The motto *Decus et Tutamen* was on a scroll below. This was shortly after replaced by a badge with correct Crown and proportions. About 1954 a miniature version of this (Plate 35) was issued for the beret and in 1963 a Q/C beret badge made its appearance, followed shortly after by a large version for the service-dress cap.

King Edward's Horse (The King's Oversea Dominions Regiment) ought to have a chapter of their own. The many badges in their short history are shown in Plate 32. It was felt during the South African War that there was room in the Home Defence Forces for a Yeomanry-type unit raised from overseas volunteers in the U.K. and sanction was given in November 1901 for The King's Colonials to be raised. The first headdress was the slouch hat with a high crown and a scarlet plume issuing from it at the front. On the front of the hat were two badges, the Regimental badge with the coat of arms (inexplicably with QVC, although the unit was raised after Queen Victoria's death) above the Squadron badge, and at the side the monogram 'KC' badge. The Regiment was officially styled **4th County of London (King's Colonials) Imperial Yeomanry** until 1905 when they became simply **King's Colonials, Imperial Yeomanry.** It consisted of four squadrons: A Sqn., British Asian, who wore the elephant badge; B Sqn., Canadian, who wore the beaver over a scroll 'British American'; C Sqn., Australasian, who wore the kangaroo and tree fern against a rising sun; and D Sqn., South African, who wore the ostrich above a scroll 'British African'. A fifth, New Zealand, Squadron was formed when it was felt that the number of New Zealand recruits justified it and the N.Z. fern badge was produced for them. Correspondingly, C Sqn.'s badge changed to the plain kangaroo above a scroll 'Australian'. All badges were in brass. In 1905 the hat was changed for one with a lower crown having a bunch of black cock feathers worn on the left-hand side. This had one badge only although the Regimental history does not say which one. In fact, the Regiment was among the first wearers of the khaki service-dress cap on which personnel of the squadrons wore their squadron badge while HQ staff wore the 'KC' monogram. In 1909 'colony squadrons' were abolished and all ranks dropped the squadron badges, adopting the brass monogram. On the death of King Edward VII, King George V assumed the title of Colonel-in-Chief. As the self-governing dominions were then becoming sensitive to being called colonials it was decided to style the Regiment, **King Edward's Horse (The King's Oversea Dominions Regiment).** The new badge is shown at the foot of Plate 32: wreaths of oak and laurel carry scrolls 'Canada', 'Australia', 'New Zealand', 'S. Africa' and 'India' with, at the base 'Regi Adsumus Coloni' – the old King's Colonials tag. Below the 'India' scroll is another, 'KODR'. During the First World War the Regiment was broken up, serving in France and Italy in a variety of roles. Some of the men became mounted orderlies and KODR became 'King's Own Despatch Riders', to the jeers of the infantry.

In 1914 a unit bearing the title 2nd King Edwards' Horse made its appearance and produced a badge (Plate 35) slightly larger than the KEH but with the additional scrolls 'Crown Colonies', '1914 and 'Empire and Liberty' plus '2nd' in the title. There was no connection between the two units and certainly no love. King Edward's Horse never called themselves the 1st simply because they preferred to believe that the 2nd never existed. The 2nd did not survive the war and the KEH was disbanded in March 1924.

The North Irish Horse was the title taken in 1908 when the Territorial Force was raised. Before that, the cap badge of the North of Ireland Imperial Yeomanry had been a w/m Angel Harp with K/C above and three-part scroll below, reading 'North' – 'of Ireland' – 'IY' (Plate 52). No Territorial units were formed in Ireland and the North Irish became Special Reserve, changing their title to North Irish Horse. The badge was identical with the IY pattern but in brass and with the new title (Plate 31). In about 1952 the K/C badge became w/m once more and it was in this metal that the Q/C badge appeared. See also The Royal Yeomanry.

The South Irish Horse, like the North Irish Horse, had been Yeomanry before the formation of the Territorial Force and the earlier badge had borne the letters 'SIY' (Plate 52) against the 'SIH' of the post-1908 brass badge (Plate 31). In common with Southern Irish infantry regiments the South Irish Horse was disbanded on the formation of the Irish Free State.

The Northamptonshire Yeomanry wore the w/m White Horse of Hanover (Plate 31), probably dating from an earlier unit, since the Regiment was raised only in 1902. The original Northamptonshire Imperial Yeomanry badge was as shown in Plate 35 but after 1908 the plain White Horse was worn. In 1939 when the TA was duplicated the newly-raised 2nd Northamptonshire Yeomanry chose to revert to the old badge in some measure and so the badge of the 2nd, all in w/m, showed the horse within an oval simply inscribed 'Northamptonshire Yeomanry' (Plate 35). After the War the 2nd ceased to exist. In 1956 the Regiment became a squadron of the Inns of Court Regiment but this ceased to be in 1960 when that unit itself merged with the City of London Yeomanry (Rough Riders).

The East Riding of Yorkshire Yeomanry was the third and by far the youngest of the three Yeomanry regiments in the county, having been raised only in 1903. The first badge chosen was simply a brass fox (Plate 31). After about 1920 the same animal, looking now a little better fed, was worn above a w/m scroll *Forrard*, from the hunting term 'Hark Forrard' (Plate 35). In 1956 the Yorkshire Dragoons, the Yorkshire Hussars and the East Riding Yeomanry were merged to form **The Queen's Own Yorkshire Yeomanry.** In the days when these things were important it was normal to dress the Yeomanry as either Dragoons, Hussars or Lancers. Yorkshire had three Yeomanry regiments and the East Riding were dressed as Lancers. The badge chosen (Plate 35) included the rose common to both Dragoons and the Hussars while the crossed lances and the motto *Forrard* on the scroll represented the junior unit. The badge was all in w/m. See also The Queen's Own Yeomanry.

Lovat's Scouts, as they were known in 1914, wore a range of badges. Basically, the crest in the centre of the circle or strap was that of Clan Fraser, whose chief, Lord Lovat, raised the unit in South Africa. From 1900 to 1903, a w/m Celtic strap was worn bearing the motto *Je suis prest* with the stag's head and shoulders in the centre, all in w/m (Plate 35). From 1903 to 1922 they wore the w/m pattern shown in Plate 31, a circle carrying the title 'Lovat's Scouts' with stag in centre. It was in 1922 that the possessive disappeared from the Army List and the Regiment was known thereafter as **Lovat Scouts.** There is some inconsistency however, as the Imperial Yeomanry variant was in brass – a solid brass badge, about one inch in diameter bearing 'Lovat Scouts' on the circle and lettered 'IY' at the bottom. The successor to this badge is shown in Plate 31: of brass, it has a voided centre and only the letter 'Y' at the base. This smaller pattern appears to have been worn in the coloured field-service cap. The pattern worn from 1900 to 1903 seems to have been taken into use again after 1922 and worn even after the Scouts became gunners in 1949.

The Scottish Horse had a w/m badge (Plate 31), basically an oval carrying the words 'Scottish Horse' and '1900', the date of raising in South Africa, with a saltire superimposed and KIC above; on one side was a spray of bay leaves, on the other, a spray of juniper, the badge of Clan Murray. Below, on scrolls, was inscribed 'South Africa 1900 1901 1902'. Although raised in 1900 the Regiment was not brought on to the Home Establishment until 1903 at the same time as Lovat's Scouts. The badge described above was also struck in brass and the predecessor with a Scots crown was also produced in both metals (Plate 52). The first badge of the Scottish Horse in South Africa was cut from brass and was the same as that described above except for the crown and the honour scrolls. Subsequently, a w/m badge in this format was made (Plate 35). In 1956 the Regiment merged with the Fife and Forfar Yeomanry; neither partner was prepared to yield a syllable of its title which necessitated the unwieldy style of **Fife and Forfar Yeomanry/Scottish Horse.** The badge was a happier choice, however. It showed the Thane of Fife superimposed upon a saltire, the arms of which bore sprigs of bay and juniper, surmounted by a Q/C, all in w/m (Plate 35). Some twelve years after its creation the new regiment yielded to its polysyllabic title to be restyled The Highlands Yeomanry, resisting, for some reason, any temptation to call themselves Highland Horse, the title of an earlier unit. (See also page 98)

The Welsh Horse were raised only in 1914 and took as their badge a brass leek, flanked by the letters 'W–H' (Plate 31). This was also made in bronze. The Regiment was disbanded in 1921.

The Inns of Court OTC were so styled in 1909 after only a year as the 27th London Regt. Their badge was the brass one shown in Plate 31. This appeared to be a badge of Rifle Brigade pattern but was in fact made up of four shields, all pointing to the centre; each shield bore the Arms of the following Inns: at the top, Lincoln's Inn; on the right, Inner Temple; at the bottom, Gray's Inn; on the left, Middle Temple. The laurel wreaths carried the South African honour and the scroll reads 'Inns of Court OTC'. Before incorporation into the Territorial Force in 1908 a similar badge was in use but in black, without a crown and bearing a scroll inscribed 'Inns of Court VRC'. In 1932 the 'OTC' part of the title was discarded and they became **The Inns of Court Regiment** (Plate 35). But the old badges continued in use for many years and many were still being worn well after the Second World War by which time badges carrying the new title had long been available. In 1961 they were amalgamated with the City of London Yeomanry (Rough Riders) to form **The Inns of Court and City Yeomanry.** The new badge (Plate 48) was basically a Q/C version of the Inns of Court badge with a w/m shield from the Arms of the City of London superimposed in the centre while the scroll bore simply 'IC & CY' and the wreath was without honour scrolls. An Inns of Court Regt badge with Q/C was produced but not worn.

The Royal Yeomanry Regiment was created in 1967, made up of:

HQ	(Berkshire & Westminster Dragoons) Sqn
A	(Royal Wiltshire Yeomanry) Sqn
B	(Sherwood Rangers Yeomanry) Sqn
C	(Kent & County of London Yeomanry) Sqn
D	(North Irish Horse) Sqn
Band	(Inns of Court & City Yeomanry)

The squadrons each wore their regimental badges and there was no Royal Yeomanry Regimental Badge as such.

In 1984, the Berkshire element left the Regiment and the Westminster Dragoons regained their old badge, without the 'T.Y.' scroll and now in silver-plate. In 1992, the Sherwood Rangers left for **The Queen's Own Yeomanry** whilst the North Irish Horse became an independent squadron in Ulster. At the same time, the Leicester & Derbyshire Yeomanry was reactivated and joined the Regiment as its B Sqn and, in the meantime, the Kent & County of London Yeomanry had been restyled the Kent & Sharpshooters Yeomanry. The present structure of **The Royal Yeomanry** is as follows:

HQ	(Westminster Dragoons) Sqn
A	(Royal Wiltshire Yeomanry) Sqn
B	(Leicester & Derbyshire Yeomanry) Sqn
C	(Kent & Sharpshooters Yeomanry) Sqn
Band	(Inns of Court & City Yeomanry)

Four North Country regiments went to form **The Queen's Own Yeomanry** in 1971 and a new badge was struck for the new regiment, a brass fox with w/m title-scroll below (Plate 52) for wear on collective regimental training. In squadron locations, the old badges were worn as under:

NH	(Northumberland Hussars) Sqn
Y	(QO Yorkshire Yeomanry) Sqn
A	(Ayrshire Yeomanry) Sqn
C	(Cheshire Yeomanry) Sqn

In 1992, the Ayrshire Yeomanry squadron went to form part of the new **Scottish Yeomanry** and, in its place, the Regiment received a squadron of Sherwood Rangers Yeomanry from The Royal Yeomanry. The present line-up is as follows:

HQ & D	(Northumberland Hussars) Sqns
B	(Sherwood Rangers Yeomanry) Sqn
C	(Cheshire Yeomanry) Sqn
Y	(QO Yorkshire Yeomanry) Sqn

Two other regiments, nominally yeomanry were created in 1971 to operate in an infantry role. **The Queen's Own Mercian Yeomanry** badge (plate 52), had the w/m Mercian Eagle with a brass coronet, set inside a brass circle bearing the full title, surmounted by a Q/C in a/a finish. The constituent squadrons were:

A	(QO Warwickshire & Worcestershire Yeomanry) Sqn
B	(Staffordshire Yeomanry) Sqn
C	(Shropshire Yeomanry) Sqn

In 1992, the Regiment amalgamated with The Duke of Lancaster's Own Yeomanry to form **The Royal Mercian & Lancastrian Yeomanry** and 1994 saw their new badge, a splendid extravagance – a red enamelled rose with green petals, surmounted by a gilt ducal coronet: on the rose is placed a silvered Mercian eagle topped by a gilt Saxon crown (Plate 57). The current structure of the Regiment is as follows:

HQ	(Shropshire Yeomanry) Sqn
A	(QO Warwickshire & Worcestershire Yeomanry) Sqn
B	(Staffordshire Yeomanry) Sqn
D	(Duke of Lancaster's Own Yeomanry) Sqn

The second such regiment was **The Royal Wessex Yeomanry,** made Royal in 1979. Its various squadrons wear their own badges as under:

HQ & A	(Royal Gloucestershire Hussars) Sqns
B	(Royal Wiltshire Yeomanry) Sqn
D	(Royal Devon Yeomanry) Sqn
Band	(Royal Gloucestershire Hussars)

The badge for D Sqn is shown on Plate 52.

The Scottish Yeomanry was formed on 1 Nov 92, the only yeomanry regiment now north of the Border and the Ayrshire Yeomanry squadron was retreived from The Queen's Own Yeomanry to become A Sqn of the new regiment. The new all-ranks badge shows crossed lances with Scots crown above and title scroll 'Scottish Yeomanry' across the lance-butts: on the interssection of the lances, a Scottish lion. All is in silver-plate except for the upper half of the lance-pennons and the lion which are in gilt (Plate 57). Pending manufacture, a woven badge was worn on the grey beret. The constituent squadrons, which will wear the old regimental collar-badges are as follows:

HQ	(Lothians & Border Horse) Sqn
A	(Ayrshire Yeomanry) Sqn
B	(Lanarkshire & QO Royal Glasgow Yeomanry) Sqn
C	(Fife & Forfar Yeomanry/Scottish Horse) Sqn

After the TA reorganisation in 1967–68, many other yeomanry regiments were either disbanded or cut to cadre strength of one officer and eight men on which, it was claimed, the regiments could again be built if the need arose. As has been seen, some of them have, indeed, been born again, even if only in squadron strength.

Arms and Services 11

The arms are the cavalry and infantry (both dealt with elsewhere), the Royal Artillery, the Royal Engineers, Royal Signals, Army Air Corps and Intelligence Corps; the remaining corps constitute the services.

The brass badge of **The Royal Regiment of Artillery** (Plate 40) is probably the best-known badge in the Army, embodying an old field gun, often with a revolving wheel. Above the wheel is a scroll *Ubique* (Everywhere). The Royal Artillery carry no battle honours as such, as they take part in almost all engagements, so the motto is particularly suitable. Below the gun is a three-part scroll *Quo fas et gloria ducunt* an amplification of the first motto. The badge did not appear with QVC but came into use in 1902, changing after the Second World War to a smaller pattern for the beret; in 1954 the crown changed to Q/C for both sizes. There are innumerable canteen stories to account for badges with or without a moving wheel but there is apparently no distinction in having this. Territorial gunners wore the badge but the *Ubique* scroll carried a spray of laurel (Plate 40) until 1917 when the Regular honour was granted to Territorial Force Artillery. The latter badge appeared in w/m and also in brass whereas the earlier Volunteer Force badge, worn 1902 – 08, was only issued in w/m with 'Volunteers' on the *Ubique* scroll (Plate 40). Five Volunteer/Territorial variations are shown on Plate 51. The 3rd Middlesex RGA Volunteers became the 5th London RFA Brigade in 1908 and, of course, insisted on having their own distinctive badge once more. The gun badge was worn by Horse, Field, Garrison and Coast Artillery but the RHA had a distinctive badge of their own for certain head-dress and this is shown in Plate 40 in four different Cyphers. The first two, GRV and ERVIII, both in w/m, were believed to have been worn in the foreign-service helmet and were apparently produced under Regimental arrangements. In 1948 an official GRVI pattern appeared in brass and also in w/m as did its ERII successor in 1954. These last two were worn in the beret. When the blue forage cap or the khaki service-dress cap are worn the gun badge is used. In 1941 it was felt that the gun was too large for the field-service cap and authority was given for the grenade collar badge to be worn in its place (Plate 40). During the 1915–18 period a solid brass gun badge appeared as an economy measure in common with several Corps.

The **Corps of Royal Engineers** have worn basically the same badge for years. The VR pattern cypher shown first in Plate 40 was an all-brass badge but the title surrounded the Cypher. In the ERVII issue the motto of the Order of the Garter replaced the title which appeared on a lower scroll; this was succeeded by the GRV, ERVIII and GRVI Cyphers in brass, the GRV also appearing in a solid 'economy strike'. The ERVII badges and GRV are found in w/m for Volunteer Force sappers and the title on the scroll of this is 'Royal Engineers (Volunteers)' shown in Plate 40. Following the Second World War the GRVI badge was issued in a bi-metal finish, the laurel wreaths w/m and the rest of the badge brass (Plate 40). The ERII badge is also in bi-metal with, of course, the Q/C. The next badge shown is that of the **Royal Monmouthshire Royal Engineers (Militia) TA** who at one time boasted the longest title in the Army List. They began life in 1660 as infantry and in 1832 were known as the Royal Monmouthshire (Light Infantry) Militia. They were reconstituted in 1877 as the Royal Monmouthshire Engineers Militia. In 1925 they became the Royal Monmouthshire Royal Engineers (Militia) (Supplementary Reserve). The badge had w/m plumes, brass coronet, K/C, letters 'RE' and title scroll 'Royal Monmouthshire' with the numeral '1' above the scroll (Plate 40). A Q/C badge appeared in a/a finish and also in bi-metal.

Born in 1920 from the Royal Engineers the **Royal Corps of Signals** had a badge depicting Mercury, the Messenger of the Gods, in w/m upon a globe within an oval band carrying the full title and K/C above in brass. It was worn until 1947 when 'Jimmy', as he has come to be known by all signalmen, stepped out and now stands upon a globe flanked by two brass scrolls carrying the Corps motto *Certa Cito*. The K/C was separate, connected to Jimmy by a back-plate inside the cap. A Q/C version followed (Plate 40).

Three badges in Plate 40 serve to represent the old **Royal Army Service Corps.** The first carried QVC and in the centre the fretted monogram 'ASC'; the star had rather prominent points. A K/C pattern followed and in 1915 a solid brass 'economy strike'. The K/C badge was also issued in w/m for Volunteer Force personnel of the Corps. In 1918 the Royal title was granted and in due course a new badge appeared in which the Royal Cypher GRV replaced the monogram; the full title was featured on a scroll outside and below the Garter. The sequence of Cyphers, ERVIII, GRVI and ERII followed, the last with a Q/C, of course. One should examine closely any ASC/RASC badges as there were numerous issues which had slight differences in size and position of crown, but the basic design stayed constant.

In July 1965 the **Royal Corps of Transport** was created taking over transport duties of the RE and RASC. Stores and clerical responsibilities were transferred to the RAOC. The badge chosen is also shown in Plate 40, a w/m star and Q/C, with centrepiece and title scroll in brass (a/a finish), clearly taken from the RASC. (See also Chapter 20)

Another Corps bearing a classical device is the **Royal Army Medical Corps** (Plate 40). The rod and serpent of Aesculapius, the Greek God of medicine, are universally accepted as indicative of the medical service. The first badge shown is the brass one issued in 1902: the Corps was formed in 1898 and a QVC pattern was issued first. Both had the title on the scroll. Another pattern bearing QVC was in w/m, the scroll inscribed 'Volr. Medical Staff Corps'. After the Second World War a brass badge was issued with a w/m scroll *In arduis fidelis*, replacing the title. A Q/C badge followed shortly after.

One of the oldest military motifs is the badge of the Arms of the Board of Ordnance and this is appropriately borne by the **Royal Army Ordnance Corps.** The brass shield with its three guns and three balls (Plate 41) was worn by the old AOC during the First World War but when the Corps was awarded the Royal title for its 1914–18 services, a more elaborate badge was designed with the shield in the centre of the Garter, K/C above and title scrolls below, still in brass (Plate 41). In March 1947 the same basic pattern badge was kept but the scrolls carried instead the motto *Sua Tela Tonanti.* This was worn until November 1949 when the badge was reduced in size and the central shield was in w/m. The K/C dropped to rest on the lower edge of the Garter (Plate 41), but this was only in use for a short time before a Q/C issue replaced it. The motto describes Jupiter and denotes the Corps' duties, the supply of stores, arms and ammunition to the fighting arms. (See also Chapter 20)

Springing from the RAOC in 1942 the **Royal Electrical and Mechanical Engineers**, adopted as their badge a pair of calipers indicative of their trade, surrounded by four shields lettered respectively 'R-E-M-E' and topped by a K/C, all in brass. The design (Plate 41), was not impressive and in the post-war reorganization it was decided to give them something more heraldically pleasing. In consequence, the new badge featured a w/m horse suggesting horse-power, chained to emphasize that it was under control, poised upon a globe; the brass lightning flash behind illustrated the electrical part of the title while a scroll above was lettered 'R.E.M.E', with a K/C resting upon it. A Q/C version appeared in the mid-1950s.

The **Corps of Military Police** badge in brass (Plate 41) bears the Royal Cypher of King Edward VII. Issues followed carrying the Royal Cyphers GRV, ERVIII and GRVI. The Corps was one of those made 'Royal' in 1946 in recognition of services in the Second World War and they merely added the word to their title scroll (Plate 41). An ERII badge was issued in about 1955. (See also Chapter 20)

During the First World War the **Army Pay Corps** wore simply the brass monogram 'APC' with K/C above (Plate 41) similar to its QVC predecessor, but in 1920 they became a Royal Corps and the letter 'R' was added. In place of the K/C, the Royal Crest was placed above the monogram (Plate 41) as this was the badge of the old Army Pay Department, incorporated into the Corps in that year. In 1929 the motto *Fide et Fiducia* was awarded and the badge changed yet again, the Royal Crest being in brass and the motto scroll in w/m (Plate 41). After 1950 a smaller badge was struck for beret wear and later, of course, a Q/C version was issued. Briefly, from 1898 to 1900, the very large and ugly brass badge shown in Plate 41 was worn. (See also Chapter 20)

No longer in existence but shown in Plate 41 is the **Corps of Military Accountants** badge, all in brass, the oval band carrying the full title. It spent the post-war years in sorting out the financial profligacies of the years 1914–19 and was quietly closed down in 1927. The remaining personnel were transferred to the RAPC.

Formed in 1903, the **Army Veterinary Corps** had as its badge the w/m monogram 'AVC' inside a brass laurel wreath with K/C above (Plate 41). In 1918 they received the 'Royal' title and recourse was again had to that storehouse of ideas and precedents, Greek mythology. The result was the w/m figure of Chiron, a centaur (half-horse, half-man), within a brass laurel wreath with full title below and K/C above. A Q/C badge was issued about 1957.

The crossed rifles with K/C above, all in brass (Plate 41) was the badge worn by the **School of Musketry** and later, when redesignated the Small Arms School, Hythe. In 1923 it combined with the Machine Gun School, Netheravon. In 1929 the **Small Arms School Corps** was born, the new brass badge (Plate 41) embodying the Vickers machine gun and the crossed rifles to which bayonets had been added. The K/C appeared inside the wreath and the title scrolls read simply 'Small Arms School'. The subsequent Q/C issue was in w/m (a/a finish).

The **Military Prison Staff Corps** was raised in 1901 and changed its title to **Military Provost Staff Corps** in 1906 but the badge remained, the Royal Cypher surmounted by K/C, in brass. The official task of the Corps is to make good soldiers out of bad. When a badge was issued bearing the Q/C and the new Royal Cypher a title scroll was added below, for a more distinctive design (Plate 41). (See also Chapter 20)

Raised only in 1920, the **Army Educational Corps** succeeded a series of other systems and establishments traceable back to the eighteenth century. A higher standard of military education was demanded by the increasing complexity of modern warfare and the Corps of Army Schoolmasters gave way to the AEC. Their first badge (Plate 41) was an open book resting on crossed lances and rifles all in brass and this was both interesting and attractive. Made 'Royal' in 1946 the Corps sought a new badge and a w/m torch of learning came into use with a brass K/C superimposed mid-way rather than above, the scroll below the crown being lettered 'RAEC' (Plate 41). A Q/C badge was issued subsequently. (See also Chapter 20)

The **Army Dental Corps** was formed in 1921 under Army Order 4/21 and the first, simple brass badge was the monogram 'ADC' within a laurel wreath, surmounted by a K/C (Plate 41). Army Order 167/46 awarded the Corps the Royal title and a new badge became necessary. Recourse was had to mythology and once again the Greeks had a sign for it. A dragon once slew the friends of Cadmus, the son of a King of Phoenicia. Cadmus killed the dragon and sowed its teeth in the ground whereupon armed men sprang forth. The Chinese emblem of dentistry is the dragon and other stories, too, serve to indicate that dragons and dentists have something in common. The dragon shown in the badge in Plate 41 is in w/m and has a sword in its teeth. The K/C, laurel wreath, sword hilt and scroll are in brass; the scroll reads *Ex dentibus ensis*. A Q/C issue was made in the mid-1950s.

Raised in 1939 under the cumbersome title of the **Auxiliary Military Pioneer Corps**, the Pioneer Corps had had a previous existence during the First World War as the **Labour Corps** but in that war they were not rated as a combatant unit. The 1939 title was short-lived and in late 1940 it was shortened to Pioneer Corps. Its badge continued to be the brass piled pick, rifle and shovel, K/C above, all standing on a motto scroll *Labor Omnia Vincit* shown in Plate 42. Around the intersection of the pick, rifle and shovel, is a circular laurel wreath. After the Second World War the Corps became 'Royal' but no change took place in the badge except for the issue of a small one for the beret: the Q/C issue appears only in this size. In February, 1985, a new badge was approved (Plate 56). It embodied crossed pioneer axes behind an upright pioneer sword, Q/C above, laurel wreaths, all above a title scroll 'Royal Pioneers', all in w/m (See also Chapter 20).

Authority was given by Army Order 112/40 for the **Intelligence Corps** to be raised although one had previously existed by name during the First World War. The badge (Plate 42), was sometimes irreverently described as 'a pansy resting on its laurels' but it was based on the rose as the emblem of secrecy while the laurel sprays are standard garnishing for military insignia. The badge is all in brass and a Q/C issue was made about 1956.

Crossed swords with K/C above, all in brass, was the badge of the **Army Physical Training Staff.** In 1940 the **Army Physical Training Corps** was formed and the badge for the Corps reappeared in w/m. The only change since is the Q/C variety appearing in the 1950s (Plate 42).

The Army School of Cookery had long been established at Aldershot for the training of regimental cooks but the **Army Catering Corps** was not formed until 1941. The badge, all in brass at first, was a Grecian brazier, supposedly symbolic of the art of cookery, set in a circle carrying the

Corps title, with K/C above. This was popularly seen as a bowl of porridge undergoing the Corps' special treatment but one Scottish cook-corporal of my acquaintance, armed with half of the truth, asserted that it was 'a Greek brassière'. After the war the basis of the badge remained brass but the brazier was made of w/m. In due course a Q/C version was issued. In 1973 a new badge was issued: a scroll was added below the badge with the motto 'We sustain'. (Plate 42). (See also Chapter 20)

The **Army Legal Service** came into being in 1948 when it was part of the Military Staff of the Judge Advocate-General and officers serving with it wore the badges of the regiment or corps to which they were formerly badged. In 1958, however, a badge was designed – the blindfolded figure of Justice, a sword in her right hand and the scales in her left, behind her a globe showing the Eastern Hemisphere. Behind the globe were crossed swords, points upwards, the Royal Crest above all. A circlet bearing the title enclosed everything whilst a scroll below carried the motto 'Justitia in armis', all in frosted silver, the cushion of the crown red and the inner background black-enamelled. On becoming the Army Legal Corps in 1978, a change of badge became necessary and an inspired designer transferred the new title to the former motto-scroll and the motto to the circlet (Plate 57).

Raised in 1955 the **Mobile Defence Corps** was disbanded in 1959. It was to be responsible for all aspects of Civil Defence training within the army and was largely composed of Territorial soldiers. Its badge (Plate 42) was a brass phoenix rising from the flames of destruction, backed by w/m crossed swords, Q/C above and three-part title scroll below.

The badges of the **Royal Defence Corps** underwent a series of changes. During the First World War the GRV Royal Cypher with K/C above and title below (Plate 42) was worn in brass but Plate 42 also shows subsequent issues, a solid brass disc with Cypher and K/C in the centre and the title around the circle. The Corps changed its title in 1936 to **National Defence Company** and this is seen on the ERVIII badge, also shown. The design was not popular and when the time came to change the Royal Cypher again the third pattern illustrated was brought into use: GRVI Cypher in a voided centre, K/C above, in a circular band carrying the title, all in brass. The Corps was formed of men too old for the Territorial Army who were mobilized for guard and security duties in August 1939. After three or four years the companies linked up to form battalions of line infantry regiments, usually designated the 30th Battalion. And so the NDC ceased to exist.

The **Non-Combatant Labour Corps** was raised on 12 July, 1939 and changed title simply to the **Non-Combatant Corps** in April 1940. The two badges shown in Plate 42 are the cap badges, in brass, and not shoulder titles as might be thought. Many conscientious objectors served in its unarmed ranks. In the post-war reorganization the Corps ceased to exist.

A Non-Combatant Corps had also existed during the First World War wearing the same badge.

Properly speaking, the **Royal Army Chaplains' Department** takes precedence over the Royal Corps of Transport but I have left it to the end because it is an 'Officers Only' corps without other ranks. It has two badges, one for Christian denominations and one for Jewish padres: the centrepiece is a quatrefoil in each case and in the Jewish badge it is in the centre of the Star of David. The Christian one is surrounded by a circle *In this Sign Conquer*, in the centre of a Maltese Cross. Both badges are surmounted by the appropriate crown, K/C or Q/C, surrounded by an oak and laurel wreath, and both are in black (Plate 42). These designs were authorized in 1940; before that the designs had been simply a cross pattern and a Star of David, both with K/C, and both in black.

The **Royal Flying Corps** was formed in 1912 from personnel of the Royal Engineers and the simple badge shown in Plate 42 was worn: the letters 'RFC' in a wreath, with K/C above, in brass. At some time after 1915 a solid 'economy strike' badge was issued. When the Corps became The Royal Air Force in 1917 only the letters were changed.

12 *Women's Units*

For generations women served with the army in the field but always on a domestic or subtler basis. It was not until early 1917 that the War Office raised the **Women's Army Auxiliary Corps** for duties other than nursing and they wore the brass or bronze badge shown in Plate 42, simply the letters 'WAAC' within a laurel wreath. In May 1918 Queen Mary became Colonel-in-Chief of the Corps, the title became **Queen Mary's Army Auxiliary Corps** and the badge was changed to include a K/C above a scroll 'Queen Mary's' above the letters 'AAC', all in brass (Plate 42). With peace came dissolution of the Corps and women were not recruited again until 1938 when the **Auxiliary Territorial Service** was formed. They wore the plain, rather uninspired brass badge shown in Plate 42, the initial letters 'ATS' within a laurel wreath with K/C above. After the Second World War the ATS was put on a firmer footing and reborn on 1 February, 1949 as **The Women's Royal Army Corps**, now a part of the Regular Army. The badge chosen is shown in Plate 42. The beast in the centre is a w/m lioness, the counterpart of the masculine military lion, within a brass laurel wreath, topped by a K/C. In due course a Q/C badge was issued. (See also Chapter 20)

   The First Aid Nursing Yeomanry was formed in 1909, initially as a corps of horsewomen who would ride into action, succouring the wounded and carrying them back for further treatment. When war broke out in 1914 it was decided that the intended activity of the FANY would not be practicable and personnel were used in hospitals and as ambulance drivers. Their badge was in bronze, a cross within a circle carrying the full title. The Corps continued to exist between the wars and in 1933 its title was changed to the **Women's Transport Service (FANY)**, the personnel being inducted after 1939 into the ATS. The new badge was similar to the last but was in bronze, bearing the new title.

   Before 1949 military nursing had been done by male nursing orderlies of the Royal Army Medical Corps and by commissioned female State Registered Nurses of the **Queen Alexandra's Imperial Military Nursing Service.** On 1 February that year **Queen Alexandra's Royal Army Nursing Corps** was formed as a corps of the Regular Army as successor to the QAIMNS and recruiting other ranks. The badge (Plate 42) consisted of the Dannebrog lettered 'A' for Alexandra in the centre within a brass wreath; above was a K/C and below a scroll initialled 'QARANC' and motto scrolls inscribed *Sub Cruce Candida.* A Q/C issue was produced in the 1950s.

I 3 *Pipers*

From the very earliest times in Scotland's history pipers have been persons of note in the clan structure, subject only to their chieftain.

Although not so well known in England as the Scottish bagpipe, the Irish warpipe has a long and honourable record. It has only two drones against the three of the Scottish instrument. King Edward III, concerned to pacify Ireland, forbade the practice of pipe music. Oliver Cromwell held similar views and threatened any player with banishment to Barbados. There is no apparent record of any piper being caught.

The unpopularity of the Scottish bagpipe is better known. It was felt to inspire militant nationalism and when the second Jacobite Rebellion in 1745 brought about the proscription of the tartan at least one piper was executed, his pipes being regarded as an instrument of war.

Distinctive pipers' badges are believed to have come into use about a century ago. They are normally worn in the glengarry together with black cock feathers in Scottish regiments and in the caubeen with a regimental hackle in the Irish.

From a collector's view, pipers' badges are not easy to come by since very few are made and they are normally regimental property. A number of them are shown in Plates 26 and 27.

The Queen's Royal Irish Hussars had badges made for their regimental pipers in about 1985 and these were a larger, all-gilt version of the regimental badge, worn with a white over red feather hackle (Plate 57).

After the Second World War the **Lothians and Border Horse** raised pipes and drums and the badge illustrated, in silver plate, was worn for the short period 1955-58. During the war two Regiments were raised and the numerals '1/2' are included in the title on the strap. The central device is the garb of the Regimental badge.

In 1956 the Lothians merged with the Lanarkshire Yeomanry and the Queen's Own Royal Glasgow Yeomanry to form the **Queen's Own Lowland Yeomanry** and the combined pipes and drums continued to wear the Lothians' badge. In 1958 a new badge was struck: the unicorn on crossed swords within a Celtic strap, all in silver plate with full title on the strap.

The **Scots Guards** pipers wear the badge shown: the Star of the Order of the Thistle within a Celtic strap. From photographs it would appear that this has been in use for almost a century. For pipers the badge is in frosted silver but Serjeant-pipers wear the Bi-m version of the cap-star within the strap and the Pipe Major wears a superior badge with a Warrant Officer's cap-star as the centrepiece.

Fourth in seniority in the Brigade of Guards, the **Irish Guards** were raised in 1900 but the pipes and drums were not raised until 1916 when they were trained by the London Irish Rifles. Their badge is a large w/m version of the Star of the Order of St. Patrick. Here again, the Pipe-Major wears a similar badge but the centre-piece is in gilt with red, white, blue and green enamels.

The Royal Scots, after many years during which their old pipers' badges were very rarely seen, recently produced a new supply and one can be seen on Plate 26. It is basically the Regimental badge with a diamond-cut saltire and a solid brass centrepiece.

The pipers of the **1st Battalion The Royal Scots Fusiliers** wore the heavy silver plate Star of the Order of the Thistle from 1881 until 1960. Across the base of the Star is a title scroll 'Royal Scots Fusiliers' and above it a tablet '1678', the date of the raising of the Regiment. The 2nd Battalion wore the thistle within a Celtic strap and the title included the old '21st'. This badge was worn until the 2nd Battalion was placed in suspended animation in 1948. The badge can be found with two leaves and with four leaves. Another variant bore the title 'The Royal Scots Fusiliers' around the strap and had two leaves to the thistle.

In 1959 the Regiment joined The Highland Light Infantry to form **The Royal Highland Fusiliers** and in 1960 a new badge came into use for pipers, drummers and military bandsmen. It embodies the Star of the HLI and the grenade of the Fusiliers and the motto scroll *Nemo nos impune lacesset*. The badge is in w/m and a/a.

The Mullet of the Douglas family arms looms large in the badge worn by pipers of the **1st Battalion The Cameronians (Scottish Rifles).** The badge shown is two-and-three-eighths inches high and was worn 1921–1968. An identical badge, also in wtm, but one-and-seven-eighths inches high was worn 1860–1921. The pipers of the 2nd Battalion wore simply a larger variety of the Jocks' badge (three inches wide).

Both badges at the foot of Plate 26 were worn by **The Royal Inniskilling Fusiliers.** I saw the two-piece badge in use during the Second World War but the one-piece badge was worn afterwards until the Regiment entered the North Irish Brigade. Both are in silver-plate.

From 1960 the three regiments of the **North Irish Brigade** wore the badge shown at the top of Plate 27: it had a heavy silver-plate angel harp with gilt Q/C and title scroll. In 1968, on the creation of **The Royal Irish Rangers** the same badge was issued but with the new title on the scroll.

The 87th Foot were among those who once captured a French Eagle, that of the 8th Regiment, and this is commemorated in the very handsome **Royal**

Irish Fusiliers pipers' badge shown. The w/m coronet is attached to the flames of the brass grenade while the eagle is in w/m. This was in use from just after the First World War until 1960 when they adopted the badge of the North Irish Brigade.

The **London Irish Rifles** formed their pipe band in about 1906 and wore until 1961 the silver-plate badge shown. The back has a tube to take a St. Patrick's green hackle which to a layman looks blue. Riflemen in the Regiment wear an ordinary green hackle, which looks green. In 1961 a new badge appeared with Q/C but with the South Africa battle honour added on a scroll below the harp; this is likewise tubed to take a hackle.

The badge of **the Liverpool Irish** was in use only for a short time after 1957 but it is actually a copy of that worn by the old Irish Rifle Volunteers, hence the monogram 'IRV' above the harp. The badge is in w/m and was worn with a two-coloured hackle, red above and blue below, an agreeable coincidence since the Liverpool Irish were latterly a gunner battery.

At the bottom centre of Plate 27 is the a/a badge, in w/m finish, worn from 1961 by pipers of **The Queen's Own Highlanders.** The Celtic strap carried the subsidiary title 'Seaforth and Camerons' and the badge was worn until June 1970 when the whole Regiment, pipers included, adopted the 'new' Queen's Own Highlanders badge (Plate 49).

The part-time Ulster Defence Regiment, once the largest regiment in the British Army, had pipers who wore the badge shown on Plate 27, a larger version of the regimental badge in gilt. The Royal Irish Regiment, formed 1 Jul 92, the anniversary of the Battle of the Somme, and embodying The Royal Irish Rangers and The Ulster Defence Regiment, has its pipers wearing the old UDR pipers' badge but in silver-plate.

The last two badges in this Plate are those of Corps units. The silver-plate star was worn by **123 (Scottish) Transport Column RASC (TA)** and was simply a large Corps badge. In common with several other medical units the **2nd Scottish General Hospital RAMC (TA)** wore the Corps badge within a Celtic strap which carried its identity.

It is surprising that some of the oldest and best-known Scottish regiments such as The Black Watch and The King's Own Scottish Borderers did not have distinctive pipers' badges.

During 1914–18 several of the Service Battalions had badges for their own pipers but these are extremely scarce and for the most part pipers wore the badge of the Regiment.

Kitchener's Army 14

Lord Kitchener, Secretary of State for War in August 1914, made an appeal on the 7th of that month for 100,000 volunteers for the Regular Army.

These volunteers were initially to constitute an extra battalion to every pair of line battalions. Certain regiments at that time, however, had four Regular battalions, Royal Fusiliers, Middlesex Regiment, Rifle Brigade, and they were to have three each of these so-called 'service battalions'. Many regiments, of course, raised more than the statutory requirement and the end of the war found the Middlesex Regiment with 49 and the Northumberland Fusiliers with 51 battalions.

For the most part these volunteers wore the normal cap badge of their county regiment. The exceptions are mentioned here.

Most of these battalions were raised by standard recruiting practice, not difficult in the patriotic fervour of the time, but others were sponsored by municipalities and by local notables, being gifted then to the War Office.

The **Northumberland Fusiliers** raised five Scottish battalions (20th to 23rd and 29th) and their first badge was the small circular device, the first badge in Plate 36, in w/m. This included a Scottish lion amid thistle sprays with the title **Tyneside Scottish**, all within a circle carrying the Fusiliers' *Quo Fata Vocant* motto. But something more impressive was wanted and the larger badge shown was designed by a subaltern of the Regiment in January, 1915. The same ingredients were present but the constraining circular band disappeared. The 24th to 27th Battalions were raised as the **Tyneside Irish** and their brass badge was identical with that of the Connaught Rangers but with 'Tyneside Irish' on the scroll.

The 14th to 16th Battalions **Royal Warwickshire Regiment** were raised as the 'Birmingham Pals' (these 'Pals' battalions began with Lord Derby's raising of the Liverpool Pals mentioned below) and were known as the 1st, 2nd and 3rd Birmingham Battalions. As can be seen from the badge of the 1st, which is illustrated, the normal pattern was worn with an additional brass scroll below inscribed '1st (or 2nd or 3rd) Birmingham Battalion'.

The **Royal Fusiliers** had a variety of volunteers including the 23rd

Battalion (1st Sportsmen's) but they wore the normal cap badge. However, the 25th Battalion (Frontiersmen), raised from the Legion of Frontiersmen (a non-military organization of ex-soldiers who volunteered for service as a body immediately war broke out but whose services were at first declined) wore the splendid badge shown. The grenade bore the numerals '25' while the flames carried the Union Jack motif of the Legion in coloured enamel, with the scroll 'Frontiersmen' below. The Battalion also wore one or two other patterns but these were all locally made and this one is probably the most common. In 1917 the 38th, 40th and 42nd Jewish Battalions were raised and their cap badge was the Menorah, the ceremonial seven-branched candlestick, with the Hebrew motto *Kadimah* below, all in brass.

Lord Derby raised the 17th to 20th Battalions of the **King's (Liverpool) Regiment** as the Liverpool Pals and being known as the King of Lancashire he gave his crest to them as a badge. His motto *Sans changer* was fortunately apposite for a military device. All volunteers who joined before 16 October, 1914 received the badge in silver as his personal gift but later issues, as the one shown, were in brass. I understand that bronzed badges in 'other-rank' quality also exist.

The 15th and 17th (Leeds) Battalions of the **West Yorkshire Regiment** known as the Leeds Pals, wore a brass replica of the Arms of the City. This embodied a golden fleece, symbolic of Leeds' importance in the wool trade.

The central device of the **East Surrey Regiment** badge, the Arms of Guildford, was replaced by the Arms of Wandsworth for wear by the 13th (Wandsworth) Battalion. In all other respects it was an East Surreys' badge (Plate 36). This battalion was raised in June 1915 by the Mayor, Lieutenant-Colonel Sir Archibald Dawnay.

Like Lord Derby, Lord Lonsdale also gave silver badges to the first volunteers for the 11th (Lonsdale) Battalion of the **Border Regiment**, but most of these were lost during a raid on the battalion lines by a neighbouring unit while under canvas on Salisbury Plain. Subsequent issues were in brass as is the one shown.

The Cardiff Pals, the 16th (Cardiff City) Battalion The **Welsh Regiment** wore the Arms of the City of Cardiff. The brass badge carried two mottoes in Welsh: the upper one, *Deffro mae'n Dydd* translates as 'Awake! It is day', and the lower *Y ddraig goch ddyry gychwyn* as 'The Red Dragon will lead'.

Most **Middlesex Regiment** service battalions wore the standard badge except for the 18th Battalion. This was styled the '1st Public Works, Pioneers' and their bi-metal badge carried an additional brass scroll below, reading 'Public Works Pioneer Battalion'.

Formed from the Young Citizens' Volunteer Corps, the 14th Battalion **The Royal Irish Rifles** continued to wear YCV badges and buttons.

Their badge was the shamrock bearing the Red Hand of Ulster and a K/C above, found in brass and also in w/m.

There were other service battalions, of course, such as the Manchester Pals and the Sheffield Pals, but they wore distinctive shoulder-titles only. With the single exception of the Tyneside Scottish, the badges did not survive the war and nor, sad to say, did most of the wearers, thousands of whom perished in the Somme and other offensives.

I5 *Military Cyclists*

It was the Volunteers of 1885 who first used cyclists in the Easter manoeuvres that year, forming sections from various Rifle Volunteer Corps. In 1888
the first completely cyclist unit was formed, the 26th Middlesex (Cyclist)
Volunteer Corps, and it remained the only unit wholly dedicated to the cyclist
role until 1908 when it became the 25th London Regiment (see chapter on
the London Regiment). But many other Volunteer Rifle Corps formed cyclist
sections in that period.

When the Territorial Force was created in 1908 it was considered that
cyclists had a military role and a further nine battalions were formed. Of these,
three were made up from existing Volunteer battalions and six were new units.

The new units were:

> 6th Battalion The Norfolk Regiment
> 7th Battalion The Devonshire Regiment
> 7th Battalion The Welsh Regiment
> The Northern Cyclist Battalion
> The Kent Cyclist Battalion
> The Essex and Suffolk Cyclist Battalion

The Volunteer Battalions concerned were:

> 8th VB to form 10th Battalion The Royal Scots TF
> 2nd VB to form 5th Battalion The East Yorkshire Regiment TF
> 5th VB The Black Watch to form Highland Cyclist Battalion TF

In 1911 the Essex and Suffolk Cyclist Battalion was divided and formed
6th Battalion The Suffolk Regiment and 8th Battalion The Essex Regiment.
Also that year the 6th Battalion The Royal Sussex Regiment and 9th Battalion
The Hampshire Regiment were raised as cyclists and early in 1914 The
Huntingdonshire Cyclist Battalion was raised. With fourteen battalions,
the star of the military cyclists might have been thought to have been in the
ascendant and in November 1914 The Army Cyclist Corps was formed.

The Army Cyclist Corps badge is shown in Plate 39B. The badge was in brass and embodied a cycle wheel in front of crossed rifles, a K/C above and a three-part title scroll below. It can be found with either sixteen or eighteen spokes to the wheel.

The Highland Cyclist Battalion wore, appropriately enough, a w/m badge of Black Watch format (Plate 39B), the upper scrolls inscribed 'Highland' – 'Cyclist' and the lower scrolls 'Battalion' - 'TF'. As with all other badges in this pattern, the spelling of the motto is a vexed question and *Lacessit* and *Lacesset* appear. In keeping with the unit's TP status, the Sphinx is missing from the foot of the badge. Serjeants wore a w/m star with brass scrolls and centrepiece.

The Northern Cyclist Battalion for administrative purposes was a part of The Northumberland Fusiliers but wore as their badge a cycle wheel in front of crossed rifles below a K/C, all in brass (Plate 39B).

The Huntingdonshire Cyclist Battalion wore the stag from the seal of the County Council above a scroll 'Huntingdonshire', all in brass (Plate 39B). This badge was used in the Second World War by the county's Home Guard.

The Kent Cyclist Battalion wore the w/m White Horse of Kent above a scroll carrying the motto *Invicta* – the same badge as worn by the West Kent Yeomanry (Plate 30).

The Essex and Suffolk Cyclist Battalion existed for only three years, 1908–11 and wore the badge shown in Plate 39B. It shows the shield from the Arms of Essex above a castle (presumably not the Suffolks' Gibraltar Castle because it has no Key), probably that of Bury St. Edmunds, all sur-mounted by a K/C and surrounded by an oak wreath. This was all in brass and had a w/m scroll below the castle, inscribed 'Essex & Suffolk Cyclist Battn'.

8th (Cyclist) Battalion The Essex Regiment, formed in 1911, wore the Regular pattern badge but the tablet below the Sphinx was blank (Plate 39B).

9th (Cyclist) Battalion The Hampshire Regiment wore a cycle wheel with K/C above and in place of the wheel hub a Hampshire rose; below was a scroll, inscribed 'Hampshire Cyclist Battalion', all in brass (Plate 39B). For use in blue patrols, a badge existed with 'solid' wheel, a red enamelled rose and a blue enamelled scroll.

5th (Cyclist) Battalion The East Yorkshire Regiment and **7th (Cyclist) Battalion The Welsh Regiment** both wore blackened Regular pattern badges since both of them had previously been 'Rifles'.

25th London Regiment (Cyclists) is dealt with and the badge illustrated in the chapter on the London Regiment.

1/1st London Divisional Cyclist Company was very short-lived indeed. It was formed in early 1916 and ceased after only three months. The badge worn was based upon that of the 25th London Regiment but a shield from the Arms of the City of London, surmounted by the city crest, was placed in the centre of the wheel. A laurel wreath surrounded the wheel and it was surmounted by a K/C, all being placed upon crossed rifles above a three-part scroll, inscribed 'City of – London – Cyclists', all in brass (Plate 39B).

The Army Cyclist Corps ceased after 1919 and military cyclists as such ceased even in name, after 1922. In the Second World War, however, battalions in Malta were using bicycles for tactical movement across the island but I understand that these were not popular and no badge commemorates them.

The Home Guard 16

The Home Guard was raised in May 1940 as the LDV or Local Defence Volunteers and was renamed in June at Churchill's suggestion. At first an arm-band was supplied and most units wore the cap badge of the County regiment since the force was raised on the structure of the local TA Associations. Paradoxically, the smaller the contingent, the more likely it was to have a distinctive badge. In these cases, no county regiment existed bearing that name.

In December 1951 the Home Guard, disbanded in 1945, was again raised, to be finally stood down in July 1957.

One of the most unusual units was the **Upper Thames Patrol** raised initially from personnel of the Thames Conservancy whose badge was worn with the letters 'UTP' below (Plate 46). Many of the personnel were lock-keepers and the launches used belonged to volunteers who had loaned their services for the duration of the war. The UTPs responsibilities stretched from Teddington Lock up-river to Lechlade and, administratively, these banks were covered by Middlesex and Berkshire battalions. The Patrol was commanded by the late Lord Glyn, an old Rifle Brigade officer but was not re-raised during the second, 1951–57 phase.

The **Windsor Castle Company** of the Crown Lands Battalion of the Berkshire Home Guard should normally have borne the badge of the Royal Berkshire Regiment but permission was granted for them to wear that of the Grenadier Guards.

The small horse shoe badge worn by the **1st Rutlandshire Battalion Home Guard** is interesting. It can hardly be said to have been designed by the unit but the then CO, Wing Commander J. Ogilvy Dalgleish, pressed for its adoption and the War Office graciously agreed, provided that no charge fell upon public funds in its production. The horse shoe was taken from the Arms of Oakham, the County Town. When Queen Elizabeth I was riding through the town her horse is said to have cast a shoe and the town thereby acquired the right to claim a horse shoe from any royal or noble personage passing through.

During the second phase the use of this badge was not resumed and the volunteers of Rutland wore that of the Royal Leicestershire Regiment.

The old badge of the Huntingdonshire Cyclist Battalion was revived for the **Huntingdonshire Home Guard** during both phases. This was a brass leaping stag which also appears in the County Seal.

Another badge produced at unit expense was that of the **Radnor Home Guard**. The county was in the South Wales Borderers' recruiting area but permission was sought and granted for the old badge of the Royal Radnor Militia to be adopted. In brass, this was a Rifle Brigade-type badge with a Guelphic crown and around the central band the word 'Radnor'. During the second phase another pattern was issued having a Q/C and with 'H.G.' added in the central circle. A K/C badge has been seen but this was never authorised and would appear to have been a manufacturer's error as it was disowned by the unit.

Also without a County Regiment as such was the **Isle of Man** and they took into use the old Manx device, the three legs pointing one each to England, Scotland and Ireland. During the first phase the motif was inside a Celtic strap carrying the motto *Quocunque Jeceris Stabit* with K/C above, all brass. In the second phase the same device and motto were used, with Q/C, plus a scroll below, inscribed 'Home Guard', all in w/m.

Home Guard units in **Caithness and Sutherland** during the second phase wore the old badge of the 4/5th (Caithness and Sutherland) Battalion Seaforth Highlanders TA which was disbanded on 3 September, 1946. This already had a long volunteer connection and was the badge of the Duke of Sutherland. The animal within the circle was a Cat-a-mountain sejant, rampant, guardant, with the motto *Sans Peur* on the band, all w/m.

In the Six Counties of **Northern Ireland** during the War the Home Guard used the badge of the Royal Ulster Constabulary, itself a paramilitary force: a black Harp of Erin with K/C above, a piece of red felt showing through the strings of the harp. In 1951 they reverted to more common practice and wore the badges either of the Royal Iniskilling Fusiliers, the Royal Ulster Rifles or the Royal Irish Fusiliers.

The British Army is full of oddities and the **1st American Squadron**, Home Guard, must surely rate as one. Its formation in London in 1940 required a special Order in Council, signed by King George VI in September, to permit its incorporation in the Armed Forces of the Crown. It actually began life on 4 July (Independence Day), 1940 when the Squadron moved into 58 Buckingham Gate the HQ of the Queen's Westminster's TA which was the Squadron HQ for the remainder of its life. American arms, privately purchased, were supplied to the personnel and their cars were either donated or loaned for the duration of the war in the Squadron's service. The only expense to fall on the British taxpayer was the supply of khaki battle dress. The cap badge (Plate 46) was the normal US Army officer's cap badge but lacking the usual constellation above the eagle's head.

Miscellaneous Schools and Training Establishments 17

Probably the best known of the training establishments is that referred to as 'Sandhurst' within the Army and as the RMC or the RMA by the residents of Camberley, dependent upon their age. Officially its designation is **The Royal Military Academy Sandhurst.** Before the Second World War the training of officers was carried out at two establishments: cadets for the Royal Artillery, the Royal Engineers and the Royal Corps of Signals went to the **Royal Military Academy**, Woolwich, usually called 'The Shop' because of its preoccupation with tradesmen. Future officers of Cavalry, Infantry and other arms went to the **Royal Military College**, Sandhurst. The brass badge of 'The Shop' is shown in Plate 43, a field gun inside a circle bearing the title and surmounted by a K/C. The brass RMC badge, also in Plate 43, had the Royal Cypher of the reigning monarch inside a circle bearing the motto *Vires Acquirit Eundo* surmounted by a K/C. For cadet under-officers the Cypher was in w/m on a brass badge and the two patterns exist with ERVII, GRV and GRVI Cyphers. The RMC Band and Staff wore the brass badge shown in Plate 43, the letters 'RMC' finished as if in gold embroidery. A picture in *The Navy and Army Illustrated* shows this badge in use in 1897. It was still being worn in the 1920s and perhaps up until 1939 although records at Sandhurst cannot confirm this.

In 1947 the two establishments became one and the resultant badge is seen in Plate 43. The GRVI Cypher was placed in the centre of a circle bearing the new combined title 'Royal Military Academy Sandhurst' with K/C above. Below the circle was a motto scroll *Serve to Lead* and the entire badge was in w/m. Subsequently, the badge was reissued with Q/C and ERII Royal Cypher.

The Royal Military School of Music is another of the establishments better known by its location than its title. Kneller Hall at Twickenham, Middlesex, was built for Sir Godfrey Kneller, court painter to Charles II. The Duke of Cambridge, then Commander-in-Chief of the Army, established it as the 'Military Music Class' in 1857 for the training of Army boys and soldiers to become band NCOs and, later, Bandmasters. In 1887 it received its present title but the badge in Plate 43 was not brought into

use until 1907. It is simply the brass monogram 'RMSM' with K/C above and is worn by Student-Bandmasters who cease wearing their own regimental insignia for the duration of their stay. The badge has appeared also with Q/C.

With the closure of the infantry divisional schools of music, it became necessary to raise two Army Junior Schools of Music. One was at Bovington, serving cavalry and infantry bands whilst the other was at Pirbright serving the staff bands. Both were raised in March 1987, but, with the end of Junior Entry for the Army in 1992, the two AJSMs ceased to exist. Their badge was a lyre, surmounted by a Q/C, with a scroll below, reading 'AJSM' all in silver a/a. (Plate 57)

Officer-cadets not receiving Regular commissions but who were on Short Service terms used to undergo their training at **Mons Officer Cadet School**, Aldershot. National Service officers also trained there until 1961. The badge (Plate 43) shows the w/m Royal Crest, with Q/C, above a scroll inscribed *Leadership* within a brass wreath carrying a tablet 'Mons' at the top, all in a/a.

The badge of the **Army Apprentices' School** (Plate 43) is no longer worn since all Junior Tradesmen now wear the cap badge of their particular arm. The principal feature was the cog wheel, superimposed on which were a cross, crossed swords and the torch of learning, all surmounted by a K/C; below, a scroll reading 'Army Apprentices School'. For apprentices it was in brass, and for pipers in chrome. A Q/C version was issued before the badge became obsolete.

Welbeck College is the Army's pre-Sandhurst public school for boys who are to go into one of the technical Corps. The badge is a brass circle inscribed 'Welbeck College' with a w/m cross-moliné in the centre; behind the circle are crossed swords, the blades in w/m and the hilts brass (Plate 43), in bi-metal and in a/a.

The next three badges in Plate 43 are those of boys' schools which are or were maintained by the Army although military service afterwards is not mandatory. The first is the **Duke of York's Royal Military School** at Dover although it only moved there in 1909 from Chelsea where it was founded in 1801. The badge consists of the current Royal Cypher in w/m set inside a brass circle inscribed 'Royal Military School' with the appropriate crown above. It appears with ERVII, GRV, GRVI and ERII Cyphers.

The Scottish equivalent is **Queen Victoria's School**, Dunblane, founded in 1903 as a memorial to the late Queen. The badge is in w/m and consists of the Scottish Royal Crest, with the appropriate crown, above a three-part scroll inscribed 'Queen Victoria School' within a wreath of oak and thistles.

The third no longer exists. It is the **Royal Hibernian Military School**, situated in Dublin and dating from 1769. As expected, the brass badge had the Harp of Erin as its central feature within an oval carrying the title and date, all above a scroll inscribed *Fear God, Honour the King.*

When the Irish Free State came into being the staff and pupils were transferred to the Duke of York's Royal Military School.

Belonging in this category also are the school units of OTC and CCF but coverage of their badges would require another book.

The final item shown under this chapter heading is that in Plate 43. The vast majority of Officer Cadet Battalions during the First World War either wore no special badge or had cloth devices on the upper arm. Illustrated is the cap badge, in w/m, of the **21st Officer Cadet Battalion**, the numerals 'XXI' superimposed upon the letters 'OCB'. No trace of a sealed pattern exists for this and it must have been made as a private enterprise.

18 *War-raised Units*

Every war has brought new units: some proved to be more durable than others and became part of the Army, others did not survive their own particular conflict. Needless to say, such badges as may have been produced for war-raised units were few in number and correspondingly hard to locate.

SOUTH AFRICA 1899–1902

The first 'Fifty thousand horse and foot, going to Table Bay' proved insufficient and because of the Boers' mobile warfare tactics more mounted men were essential. **The Imperial Yeomanry** was raised from volunteers at home, both from the established Yeomanry Cavalry and from civilians. The IY Companies, even if raised from existing Yeomanry at home, generally did not wear their parent badge but often had company badges of their own. One of these was **13th Duke of Cambridge's Own Company**, Imperial Yeomanry, which wore the brass badge shown in Plate 44, the letters 'DCO' above the numerals '13'. The 13th was 120 strong and the men supplied their own equipment and horses, so keen were they to get to the front. **Fincastle's Horse** was the 31st Imperial Yeomanry, raised by Lord Fincastle vc of the 16th Lancers. Their badge, the five-pointed star, is shown in Plate 44. They did not reach South Africa until early 1902 and the unit did not survive the war. Not surprisingly, the Irish were not slow to volunteer for mounted service and the small brass shamrock above the letters 'I.H' is that of the **29th Battalion Irish Horse IY** (Plate 44). Those units which did not have a badge of their own usually wore a Prince of Wales's plumes above the letters 'IY' on a coloured rosette (Plate 44). These rosettes were reported to be of different colours but I have only seen the one shown, centre purple, the outer ring red.

The Scottish Horse and Lovat's Scouts, of course, were born in this war but lived on afterwards in the U.K.

As the Imperial garrisons were emptied of first-line troops to serve in South Africa there was a need to replace them and this was filled by raising the **Royal Reserve Regiments** in March 1900. The Dragoons, Dragoon Guards and Hussars wore the letters 'HMRR' with QVC above, all over a scroll, reading

'Dragoons' etc. The Lancers wore brass crossed lances lettered 'RR' on the intersection, QVC above and scroll 'Lancers' below.

In the Infantry the Guards wore their own badges while the Home Counties, Northern, Southern and Eastern Regiments wore the Royal Arms in brass. Rifles wore a bronzed French horn, Scottish a w/m thistle, Irish a brass Harp of Erin with the flat-topped QVC and the Lancashire wore a brass rose. The Irish Fusiliers Reserve Regiment wore a brass grenade with pointed flames and a w/m shamrock on the body of the bomb. This was raised from reservists of all four Irish Fusilier regiments, Fogs, Skins, Munsters and Dublins. It was originally intended that Regular reservists could elect to serve in the Royal Reserve Regiments for one year. Most of the units ceased to exist at the war's end. (These are shown in Plate 53).

The City Imperial Volunteers, raised from London Volunteers wore on the upturned left-hand side of their slouch hat the separate letters 'CIV' in brass or bronzed finish.

Careful scrutiny of contemporary photographs will reveal other badges worn by wartime units and identification of these makes an interesting study.

FIRST WORLD WAR 1914–18

This war produced the Royal Corps of Signals and the Royal Tank Corps, dealt with elsewhere as they later became Regular corps. However the Tanks sprang from **The Machine Gun Corps** in 1917. The Corps badge (Plate 44), showed brass crossed Vickers machine guns with KIC above. Connoisseurs of this very long-lived weapon may like to know that different Marks of the gun were used on successive dies for the badge. The **Motor Branch** of the Corps wore this same badge but with w/m letters 'MMG' below the guns (Plate 44).

The Household Battalion was not raised, as was once explained to me, from surplus male staff at Buckingham Palace and other royal residences but was an infantry battalion formed from reservists of the Household Cavalry. Its badge was an oval Garter with K/C above; in the solid centre was the Royal Cypher of King George V, all in brass (Plate 44).

Also raised from reservists were the battalions of the **Royal Naval Division.** Although still officially sailors they served as soldiers and wore khaki in France. Until May 1916, when they arrived in France, they had worn either sailor caps or foreign-service helmets without badges. Originally there were eight named battalions but Benbow and Collingwood were disbanded before badges were produced. The remaining six wore the brass badges shown in Plate 44: **Anson Battalion** a coronet; **Drake Battalion** a ship on top of the world; **Hawke Battalion** and **Hood Battalion** birds from the ships' badges; **Howe Battalion** a naval crown and **Nelson Battalion** a head-on view of a ship.

Also in the 63rd Royal Naval Division was the **Machine Gun Battalion** which wore the badge of the Machine Gun Corps with the letters 'RND', a brass shoulder title, below the guns (Plate 44).

The **Remounts Service** came into its own during the war with the heavy demands of cavalry, transport horses and pack-animals and two badges were in use. One was all in brass and showed a horse within a horseshoe against a background of crossed whips above a scroll 'Remounts'. The other was a w/m prancing horse within an oval brass band, 'Army Remount Service'; above the oval was a K/C over a Royal Cypher (Plate 45).

Not strictly speaking a wartime unit but formed and serving in the immediate post-war Arab Rebellion in Mesopotamia was the **1st Armoured Motor Battery.** Its badge, bearing a period armoured car, title scroll, etc., all in brass, is shown in Plate 45. I have not seen a 2nd or subsequently numbered unit and can only presume that either they were not formed or that they served under a Regular unit's badge.

SECOND WORLD WAR 1939–45

Several of the units raised in this war continued in the post-war army: Parachute Regiment, REME, Intelligence Corps, Pioneer Corps, Army Catering Corps, SAS and Army Air Corps. These are dealt with elsewhere as are the six wartime cavalry regiments, covered in the chapter on Cavalry as being the most logical place for them.

The Reconnaissance Corps was raised in January 1941 and its badge is shown in Plate 45. The central feature was a spear, flanked by forked lightning above a scroll 'Reconnaissance Corps', all in brass. The badge was also struck in w/m and this was said to have been worn by Scottish units. I am assured that the very first pattern badge for the Corps was struck in w/m, changing later to brass. The Reconnaissance Regiment of the 49th (West Riding) Division wore a w/m badge with a w/m rose of York superimposed half-way up the spear (Plate 45). The Corps was disbanded in August 1946.

The Highland Regiment and **The Lowland Regiment** were both formed in January 1942 as Young Soldiers' Battalions but both units were shortlived and were disbanded the following year. Both wore large w/m badges of distinctive Scottish character: the Highland was a Celtic strap carrying the title, placed upon a saltire bearing two broadswords and a targe (shield); the Lowland wore the saltire with a thistle in the centre above a two-part title scroll (Plate 45).

The **General Service Corps** was formed in February 1942 as a 'Reception Corps', receiving trainees before posting to field force units and wore the Royal Arms in brass. In 1944 a special badge (Plate 45) was authorized for training battalions which were responsible for training officer-cadets before going on to OCTU. It was the British Army badge in brass, crossed swords carrying the Royal Crest with K/C above a union spray of rose, thistle, shamrock and leek with scroll below *Deus Vult.* This badge was later to appear with Q/C, it having been used by Infantry Boys Regiments, later styled Junior

Leaders Regiments, under the War Office adaptation of the familiar adage that 'Boys will be Junior Leaders'.

The Second World War was perhaps as prolific as the Boer War in its raising of special units but not all their badges were authorized.

The Commandos began life in 1940 and for the most part did not wear distinctive head-dress badges. However, **No. 2 Commando** was wearing a w/m dagger, point down, made I am told, from NAAFI spoons. In Plate 45 is a variant of this which was actually worn in the unit. **No. 6 Commando** wore an embroidered 'VI' on a black patch on their khaki bonnet while **No. 9 Commando wore** a black feather hackle. **Nos. 50, 51 and 52 Commandos** were raised in the Middle East and wore the brass knuckle-duster knife shown in Plate 45. There would appear to have been some independence of thought in wearing this. I have seen a photograph of an officer wearing the badge in the horizontal way shown here, and in the field-service cap this seemed ideal. Another wearer told me that it was worn in the beret beside the wearer's own regimental badge and in his case the dagger pointed down to 'seven o'clock'.

The Long Range Desert Group was officially recognized in June 1940 and badges were issued in Cairo. Initial badges were in brass but subsequent strikes were made bronzed and in w/m. It shows (Plate 45) a scorpion above the letters 'L.R.D.G.' within a circle. The Group served with great success in the North African desert until 1943 when it moved to the Adriatic and the Greek islands, being disbanded in late 1945.

Another Middle East unit was the **Raiding Support Regiment** whose cloth badge is shown in Plate 45. It was raised in 1943 and served principally in the Balkans before disbandment in 1945. The badge shows a winged gaunt-let grasping the bare hand outstretched from the fortress of Europe, with the initials 'RSR' above and a scroll below reading *Quit you like men.*

Probably the most curiously named of these special forces units was No. 1 Demolition Squadron, better known as **Popski's Private Army.** It was raised in the Middle East in 1942 by Vladimir Peniakoff, an Anglophile Pole living in Egypt, and later served in Italy and through to Austria. The badge shown (Plate 45) is engraved in brass but other issues appeared in a rough w/m casting.

Ideal though the Western Desert was for the strategist – plenty of space, normally good weather conditions, no women and children and few man-made hazards – the war rolled inconsiderately on and Special Forces reached South East Asia Command. The locally made, blackened badge worn by personnel of **V Force** (Plate 45) shows crossed Commando daggers with letter 'V' on the intersection and a scroll inscribed 'Force' below. The Force's objective was to arm insurgent natives and to persuade them to harry the Japanese lines of communication.

An aftermath of the war was the **Control Commission, Germany.** Its uninspired brass badge was not worn by anyone who had the slightest claim to any other and the initial letters (Plate 45) were rapidly identified as 'Charlie Chaplin's Grenadiers'.

CYPRUS 1960s

Not a regimental, nor yet a British badge but one worn by British troops is that of the **United Nations Emergency Force**. It is in gilt and white enamel, showing the globe within a laurel wreath (Plate 45) and is being worn now in the sky blue U.N. beret by units serving the U.N. Organisation on the island in place of their regimental badge, as it is in former Yugoslavia, Somalia and elsewhere.

Although not new badges in themselves, plastic issues were made in 1941 and continued for the rest of the war. Not all badges were of a suitable design to be made in this material but the finish achieved was remarkably good. They were not popular and at one Highland Infantry Training Centre of which I heard, recruits were given plastic badges only to be told that they should 'forget about those things and get a metal one from the canteen for 9d'.

A list of known plastic issues is given in *Appendix E*.

NORTHERN IRELAND

Most units serving in Northern Ireland since the beginning of the emergency in the province in 1969 have worn blackened cap-bages. Usually, these have been simply ordinary badges, blackened under unit arrangements but, in at least one case, special badges have been produced: this is the Royal Regiment of Fusiliers who had them made in black plastic.

Brigade of Gurkhas 19

Throughout its long history the British Army has made a habit of recruiting its old enemies following a campaign and using them to serve the Crown thereafter. In the eighteenth century they enlisted highlanders to subdue the Highlands of Scotland, in the nineteenth it was Sikhs, Gurkhas and Maoris and, in the twentieth, Boers and Italians.

It was in 1814 that Britain, keen to prevent further depredations by Nepal upon its neighbouring territories, sent an expeditionary force to subdue the Nepalese. The campaign was a particularly gruelling one although conducted along chivalrous lines with more than one instance of Gurkha soldiers coming to British medical officers before returning to their own lines to resume the action after the necessary treatment. In 1815 it was decided to recruit some of the now unemployed Gurkhas for the British service and this became a jealously-guarded privilege – more potential recruits existed than we were able to take. Despite the fierce Gurkha pride, there was no reluctance to accept mercenary service for, as one remarked in later years after the battle of Bhurtpore, 'The English are as brave as lions; they are splendid sepoys, very nearly equal to us.'

Further recruitment was undertaken over the ensuing century, especially after the splendid record of Gurkhas in the Indian Mutiny in 1857. When war broke out in 1914 ten regiments of Gurkha Rifles, each of two battalions, were in the order of battle of the Indian Army. Wartime expansion followed as did the subsequent rundown but ten regiments were again ready in 1939, the Gurkha Brigade, an independent-minded, non-tactical grouping, proud of its Rifle traditions, in the Indian Army yet not of it. Scornful of the Indian plains-soldier, the Gurkha spent most of his service on one frontier or the other and he enjoyed an acceptance by the British soldier granted to no others.

Plate 54 shows the badges of the ten regiments in 1939. **The 1st King George's Own Gurkha Rifles (The Malaun Regiment)** wore crossed kukris with a Rifles stringed bugle-horn and numeral '1' below and the Prince of Wales's plumes above. Before 1910, of course, they had been the 1st Prince of Wales's Own Gurkha Rifles (The Malaun Regiment) and their title was changed on the accession of HM King George V.

Almost all Gurkha units used the kukri as the principal feature of their badge but the **2nd King Edward VII's Own Gurkha Rifles (The Sirmoor Rifles)** did not, but then, the 2nd were always different. In the first place, they insisted upon being referred to as the 2nd Goorkhas colloquially: they have a diced band to their pill-box cap to recall a one-time Scottish colonel yet, paradoxically, only the 2nd did not have pipes and drums. Their badge was the black Prince of Wales's plumes shown on a red backing. Like the 1st, they also had been styled 'Prince of Wales's' before 1906, but referring to an earlier monarch – HM King Edward VII.

The wife of Edward VII gave her name to the 3rd. In fact, as can be seen, she also gave her Cypher, two 'A's entwined above a figure '3', over crossed kukris with a K/C above, all in w/m. Styled **3rd The Queen's Own Gurkha Rifles** in 1907, they changed the following year to 3rd Queen Alexandra's Own Gurkha Rifles.

Readers of John Masters' *Bugles and a Tiger* will be familiar with the immediate pre-1939 activities of the **4th Prince of Wales's Own Gurkha Rifles**. Before 1924 they were simply the 4th Gurkha Rifles and 'their' Prince of Wales was to become HM King Edward VIII which would have brought them another title-change had he not abdicated in 1936. Their badge was an unusual one in that the kukris were not symmetrically placed: the Prince of Wales's plumes feature above and the numerals 'IV' below, all in w/m except for the kukri-hilts which were in black. In the Gurkha hat they wore simply the black metal numerals shown.

Following the First World War, in 1921, the **5th Gurkha Rifles (Frontier Force)** became the 5th Royal Gurkha Rifles (Frontier Force) for their services in the war and their w/m badge shown bores the Royal Crest over the numeral '5' above crossed kukris. On the occasion of the Victory Parade in London in 1946 the pipers of the 5th wore the same design badge but larger.

The remaining five regiments had titles devoid of regal or princely styles and their badges were similarly bare, functional permutations of numerals and kukris. The 9th had a K/C but no regal association. Only the 10th broke away and incorporated a Rifles stringed bugle-horn with a single kukri and its numeral.

The Second World War ended with fifty Gurkha battalions under arms. Then came the partition of India. Of the ten regiments, six were allocated to the new India and four to the British Army. Surprisingly, the latter were not the four senior regiments but were selected because most of them were already serving outside India. They were the 2nd, 6th, 7th and 10th, which came to constitute the infantry element of the British Brigade of Gurkhas whose badges are shown in Plate 55.

The 2nd Goorkhas continued to wear their own old badge but in 1959 the 6th and 7th were granted Royal titles in recognition of their war records and, more especially, for their recent services in Malaya. The 6th became the **6th Queen Elizabeth's Own Gurkha Rifles** and a Q/C was added to their previous badge. The 7th became the **7th Duke of Edinburgh's Own Gurkha Rifles** and their badge was retained with the addition of the coronet and Cypher of HRH The Duke of Edinburgh. Earlier, in 1949, the 10th had become the **10th Princess Mary's Own Gurkha Rifles**; their badge had been implemented by the Cypher of the Princess Royal with her coronet and the addition of the title scroll below. As can be seen, the 10th also had a smaller badge, less the scroll, for use in the beret.

The decision was taken in 1948 to form a Gurkha Division, based on the old 17th Indian Division and it became necessary to raise, train or convert gunners, sappers, signalmen and other arms. Both battalions of the 7th Gurkha Rifles were converted to become 101 and 102 Field Regiments RA (7th Gurkha Rifles) but after about a year the Malayan emergency demanded more infantry and the 7th reverted to their old role. In 1948 67 Gurkha Field Squadron RE was formed, wearing Royal Engineers' badges until 1955 when the **Gurkha Engineers** were formed. Their first badge was all in w/m, crossed kukris with grenade above and a scroll *Ubique* below. Later, the badge was reissued with w/m kukris and a brass grenade and scroll. In the same way, the **Gurkha Signals** was formed in 1955 from Gurkha squadrons of the Royal Signals, the first of which was raised in 1949. Their badge is the familiar Jimmy – the figure of Mercury – between crossed kukris in w/m, with brass Q/C above and brass scrolls *Certa Cito* below.

The Gurkha Army Service Corps was formed in July, 1958, and took a badge based naturally on that of the RASC in that they assumed an eight-pointed star; this was in w/m, with, superimposed upon it, a brass wreath, crossed kukris, Royal Cypher, Q/C and title scroll, all in a/a finish. When the parent Corps became the Royal Corps of Transport in July, 1965, its offspring became the **Gurkha Transport Regiment** and the badge changed minimally to take the new title. A change of title took place on 30 Sep 92 and the now **Queen's Own Gurkha Transport Regiment** changed its badge minimally to incorporate a small scroll 'Queen's Own' above the title scroll (see Plate 57).

The Gurkha Divisional Provost Company was raised in June, 1949, as part of the Royal Military Police until January, 1957, when their title changed to the **Gurkha Military Police**. Their first distinctive badge was manufactured locally in Malaya, crossed kukris with Royal Cypher and Q/C above and title scroll below reading 'Gurkha Military Police', all in w/m. The badge was not officially approved and a new issue was made, based on that of the RMP, crossed kukris with Royal Cypher inside a circle of laurel sprays, Q/C above and title scroll below. This was made in brass and in a/a. It ceased to be used in 1966 and the Gurkha Military Police was formally disbanded in January, 1970. The popular story is that the Gurkhas were too good-humoured to make good policemen.

With the formation of their own division Gurkha soldiers were trained in RAMC, RAOC and REME duties but no units were formed to wear distinctive Gurkha badges.

However, in 1961, a platoon each from the 1/7th and from 1/10th and 2/10th combined to form the Gurkha Parachute Company and the small badge shown – a w/m parachute above crossed kukris, all in w/m - was made locally in Malaya. On 1 January, 1963, the Gurkha Independent Company was formed as a unit of The Parachute Regiment. The parent regiment's badge was worn on a rectangular rifle-green patch with a strip of Brigade of Gurkhas ribbon at each vertical edge. The Company was disbanded in December, 1971.

The Brigade Staff Band wore crossed kukris in w/m and the Boys' Company a similar badge with a scroll reading 'Boys' between the handles of the kukris.

On the 21st April 1977 the Gurkha Engineers and the Gurkha Signals were honoured by HM The Queen and became respectively **The Queen's Gurkha Engineers** and **The Queen's Gurkha Signals**. There have, however, been no changes in the badges worn to date (see also Chapter 20).

Options for Change 20

This was the infelicitous title chosen to introduce 1990's Defence Review. Even the most naive student of British Parliament-speak is well aware that a Defence Review means Defence Cuts and 1990's was no exception.

One of the declared aims of the Review was to make many of the cuts from the supporting services but, notwithstanding, the cavalry reductions have meant the disappearance of nine cap-badges from the Cavalry of the Line: only eight cavalry regiments remain in addition to the now one Household Cavalry Regiment, a composite unit made up of men from both The Life Guards and The Blues and Royals. To these reductions must be added the mergers of 1 & 4 Royal Tank Regiments and 2 & 3 Royal Tank Regiments although this, of course, is not a cap-badge issue.

Twelve infantry regiments were to be linked in pairs to form six but the Threat from the East having been seen to vanish, a Threat from Elsewhere mainfested itself in Somalia, in the Balkans and who-knows-where-else: hence, a policy U-turn was executed and four regiments were saved to fight another day. Britain's professional soldiers were eagerly sought after by the United Nations Organization faced with the alternatives of short-service continental conscripts and undependable third-world contingents.

Within the Corps, ten were to lose their separate identities with the formation of two new corps. **The Adjutant General's Corps** was formed on 6 Apr 92, embodying the staff-clerks of the RAOC and personnel of the RMP, RAPC, MPSC, RAEC, ALC and personnel of the WRAC not otherwise badged. Women-soldiers were henceforth to be badged as for the unit with which they were serving, be it cavalry, RA, RE, R Signals, infantry or Corps. Thus it was that the 6 Apr 92 saw the effective disbandment of the Women's Royal Army Corps. **The Royal Logistic Corps** was formed on the 5 Apr 93, embracing the Postal and Courier elements of the RE, the RCT, the remainder of the RAOC, the RPC and the ACC. Despite provision of two new badges for the new Corps, personnel of the RMP, MPSC and the ALC will continue to wear their old cap-badges although training and administration will go on under the AGC umbrella.

The 4/7th Royal Dragoon Guards merged with the 5th Royal

Inniskilling Dragoon Guards on 1 Aug 92. Their new badge is basically the eight-pointed star of the 4/7 RDG: in the centre, a circular band carries the new title **'Royal Dragoon Guards'** and the date 'MCMXCII: within the circle one is pleased to see the return of the Castle with 'Inniskilling' below. Behind the castle, one can just see the St George's Cross within the circle. Made in W/m, the badge is in two sizes, the smaller for wear by senior NCOs. However, a superior badge is worn by soldiers in the coloured forage-cap – a dead-burnished silver star, gilt castle and scroll, the title-band and St George's Cross in coloured enamels (see Plate 56).

The Queen's Own Hussars and The Queen's Royal Irish Hussars amalgamated on 1 Sep 93 to form **The Queen's Royal Hussars (Queen's Own and Royal Irish)**. Their new badge is the W/m monogram 'QO' of the QOH, surmounted by the gilt Royal Crest with, superimposed upon the monogram, the gilt Angel Harp of the QRIH above a gilt title-scroll with blue inlay (see Plate 56).

Two more Hussar regiments went to form **The King's Royal Hussars** on 1 Dec 92. These were The Royal Hussars and the 14/20th King's Hussars. The new badge is The Hawk of the 14/20H but larger and with the letters 'FR' on the bird's chest: the eagle is black but the letters are in gilt as are the crown, the orb, the sceptre and the tiny shamrocks below the wings. The Prince of Wales's Plumes of The Royal Hussars are used as collar-badges (see Plate 56).

The third pair of Hussar regiments required to merge were the 13/18th Royal Hussars and the 15/19th King's Royal Hussars. Their problem was to find a suitable title and recourse was had to history. On 1 Dec 92, they became **The Light Dragoons**, a title which they felt had 'bite' and would be even-handed to both partners of the merger. Basically, the badge is a reversion to the Maltese Cross once worn on the old light dragoon helmet, in W/m with a brass border: in the centre, a W/m disc bears the letters 'LD' in brass within a circle which carries two mottoes – 'Viret in aeternum' (of the 13H) and 'Merebimur' (of the 15H) – surrounded by a laurel wreath and surmounted by a brass Royal Crest (see Plate 56).

The final cavalry merger was on 25 Jun 93, that of the 16/5th Queen's Royal Lancers and the 17/21st Lancers to form **The Queen's Royal Lancers**. The decision was made to assume the 'motto' of the junior element of the merger: it was well-known, distinctive and bore no compromising numbers but the collar-badges of the 16/5L are to be retained for the new regiment.

The Foot Guards were not to be spared and the Grenadier, Coldstream and Scots Guards each lost their 2nd Battalion (the Irish and Welsh Guards were already down to one battalion each).

The amalgamation of The Royal Scots and The King's Own Scottish Borderers, planned for October 1994 and that of The Cheshire Regiment and The Staffordshire Regiment, planned for September 1993 were both stood down in February 1993 when the army's over-stretch was realised.

However, the merger of The Queen's Regiment and The Royal Hampshire Regiment to form **The Princess of Wales's Royal Regiment (Queen's and Royal Hampshires)** took place on 9 Sep 92. The new badge is based largely upon that of the Queen's but with a Hampshire Rose below the Dragon and the bottom scroll reading 'Princess of Wales's'. This design is in bronze for soldiers for wear in the beret on a patch of blue-yellow-blue regimental ribbon: the badge worn on the coloured forage-cap is identical but the Garter and the title-scroll are in gilt with a blue inlay whilst the Plumes, Dragon and Rose are in silver-plate (see Plate 56).

On 1 Jul 92, the anniversary of the Battle of the Somme, The Royal Irish Rangers joined with The Ulster Defence Regiment to form **The Royal Irish Regiment**, making it the largest in the army with one regular and seven part-time battalions. The badge is simply the Angel Harp with Q/C above, the same as was worn by the UDR but in W/m.

The 27 Apr 94 saw the amalgamation of The Gloucestershire Regiment and The Duke of Edinburgh's Royal Regiment (Berkshire and Wiltshire) to form **The Royal Gloucestershire, Berkshire and Wiltshire Regiment**. The new badge is the cross pattée of the DERR and the old Wiltshires in W/m with, superimposed thereon, a brass Sphinx above a tablet 'Egypt'. No trace of the old Berkshires remains except for the red felt Brandywine Flash backing, adopted following an incident in the American War of Independence in 1777. The Regiment will continue to wear the old Gloucesters' back-badge and the US Presidential Unit Citation (see Plate 56).

Finally, in the infantry line, The Queen's Own Highlanders (Seaforth and Cameron), merged with The Gordon Highlanders on 17 Sep 94 to form **The Highlanders (Seaforth, Gordons and Camerons)**, retaining the badge of the QO Hdrs with the Jocks of the rifle companies wearing Gordon tartan. However, the badge is to be the three-dimensional badge, the stag's head in high-relief (Plate 56), as previously worn by senior NCOs.

The Royal Regiment of Fusiliers, The Royal Anglian Regiment and The Royal Green Jackets all reduced to two battalions each in 1992.

Within the Brigade of Gurkhas, there existed one battalion each of the 2nd King Edward VII's Own Gurkha Rifles, the 6th Queen Elizabeth's Own Gurkha Rifles, the 7th Duke of Edinburgh's Own Gurkha Rifles and the 10th Princess Mary's Own Gurkha Rifles. These four were to be reduced initially to three battalions. Rather than disband any one, it was agreed that a three-battalion Royal Gurkha Rifles should be formed on 1 Jul 94. On that day, 2GR and 6GR amalgamated to form the 1st Battalion **Royal Gurkha Rifles**, whilst 7GR became the 2nd Battalion and 10GR became the 3rd Battalion. After withdrawal of Gurkha troops from Hong Kong in 1996, 2RGR and 3RGR will merge to form 2RGR, remaining in Brunei whilst 1RGR will move to the UK. Their new badge will be simply crossed kukris (left over right) with cutting edges down, surmounted by Q/C, all in silver-plate (Plate 57). The existing engineer, signals and transport regiments will reduce to squadron strengths, so forming, with the three battalions, an effective Gurkha brigade, in tactical terms.

The new badge for the Adjutant General's Corps consists of the Royal Crest in brass within a laurel wreath surmounted by a Q/C, all in brass, above a W/m scroll 'Animo et Fide' (Plate 57). That of the Royal Logistic Corps is rather more inspired, taking elements from the badges of the constituent corps: the basic format is the RCT star and Q/C in brass, with the RPC crossed axes superimposed: upon these is the brass Garter enclosing a W/m shield of the Board of Ordnance, all above a scroll ('We sustain', taken from the last ACC badge and an appropriate motto for a logistical body (see Plate 57). A smaller pattern of the AGC badge exists for wear in the beret.

Appendices

A *Order of precedence – 1971*

The Life Guards
The Blues and Royals
Royal Armoured Corps (as in Chapter 2)
Royal Horse Artillery
Royal Artillery
Royal Engineers
Royal Signals
Brigade of Guards (as in Chapter 3)
Infantry of the Line (as in Chapters 4 and 6)
Special Air Service
Army Air Corps
Royal Army Chaplains Dept.
Royal Corps of Transport (and Royal Army Service Corps)
Royal Army Medical Corps
Royal Army Ordnance Corps
Royal Electrical and Mechanical Engineers
Royal Military Police
Royal Army Pay Corps
Royal Army Veterinary Corps
Small Arms School Corps
Royal Army Educational Corps
Royal Army Dental Corps
Royal Pioneer Corps
Intelligence Corps
Army Physical Training Corps
Armny Catering Corps
General Service Corps
Queen Alexandra's Royal Army Nursing Corps
Women's Royal Army Corps
Royal Monmouthshire Royal Engineers (Militia)
Mobile Defence Corps
Honourable Artillery Company
Territorial Army (as for Regular regiments and corps)
The Home Guard

B The Formation of Territorial Regiments 1881

Below are the names allocated in 1881 to the 109 previously numbered regiments of infantry. In several cases the title given under General Order 41 of 1 May was reversed under General Order 70 of 1 July. In 1920 many of them reverted to their first title. It is of passing interest that the 30/59th Foot in May were The West Lancashire Regt. but in July became The East Lancashire Regt. yet both Orders listed their Depot as Burnley.

	G.O. 41 of 1 May 1881	*G.O. 70 of 1 July 1881*
1st	The Lothian Regt. (Royal Scots)	The Royal Scots (Lothian Regt.)
2nd	The Royal West Surrey Regt. (The Queen's)	The Queen's (Royal West Surrey Regt.)
3rd	The Kentish Regt. (The Buffs)	The Buffs (East Kent Regt.)
4th	The Royal Lancaster Regt. (King's Own)	The King's Own (Royal Lancaster Regt.)
5th	The Northumberland Fusiliers	The Northurnberland Fusiliers
6th	The Royal Warwickshire Regt.	The Royal Warwickshire Regt.
7th	The City of London Regt. (Royal Fusiliers)	The Royal Fusiliers (City of London Regt.)
8th	The Liverpool Regt. (The King's)	The King's (Liverpool Regt.)
9th	The Norfolk Regt.	The Norfolk Regt.
10th	The Lincolnshire Regt.	The Lincolnshire Regt.
11th	The Devonshire Regt.	The Devonshire Regt.
12th	The Suffolk Regt.	The Suffolk Regt
13th	The Somersetshire Regt, (Prince Albert's L.I.)	Prince Albert's L I. (Somersetshire Regt.)
14th	The West Yorkshire Regt. (Prince of Wales's Own)	The Prince of Wales's Own (West Yorkshire Regt.)
15th	The East Yorkshire Regt.	The East Yorkshire Regt.
16th	The Bedfordshire Regt.	The Bedfordshire Regt
17th	The Leicestershire Regt.	The Leicestershire Regt.
18th	The Royal Irish Regt.	The Royal Irish Regt.
19th	The North Yorkshire Regt. (Princess of Wales's Own)	The Princess of Wales's Own (Yorkshire Regt.)
20th	The Lancashire Fusiliers	The Lancashire Fusiliers
21st	The Royal Scots Fusiliers	The Royal Scots Fusiliers
22nd	The Cheshire Regt.	The Cheshire Regt.
23rd	The Royal Welsh Fusiliers	The Royal Welsh Fusiliers
24th	The South Wales Borderers	The South Wales Borderers
25th	The York Regt. (King's Own Borderers)	The King's Own Borderers
26th and 90th	The Scotch Rifles (Cameronian)	The Cameronians (Scotch Rifles)
27th and 108th	The Royal Inniskilling Fusiliers	The Royal Inniskilling Fusiliers

	G.O. 41 of 1 May 1881	G.O. 70 of 1 July 1881
28th and 61st	The Gloucestershire Regt.	The Gloucestershire Regt.
29th and 36th	The Worcestershire Regt.	The Worcestershire Regt.
30th and 59th	The West Lancashire Regt.	The East Lancashire Regt.
31st and 70th	The East Surrey Regt.	The East Surrey Regt.
32nd and 46th	The Duke of Cornwall's L.I.	The Duke of Cornwall's L.I.
33rd and 76th	The Halifax Regt. (Duke of Wellington's)	The Duke of Wellington's (West Riding Regt.)
34th and 55th	The Cumberland Regt.	The Border Regt.
35th and 107th	The Royal Sussex Regt.	The Royal Sussex Regt.
37th and 67th	The Hampshire Regt.	The Hampshire Regt.
38th and 80th	The South Staffordshire Regt.	The South Staffordshire Regt.
39th and 54th	The Dorsetshire Regt.	The Dorsetshire Regt.
40th and 82nd	The South Lancashire Regt. (Prince of Wales's Volunteers)	The Prince of Wales's Volunteers (South Lancashire Regt.)
41st and 69th	The Welsh Regt.	The Welsh Regt.
42nd and 73rd	The Royal Highlanders (Black Watch)	The Black Watch (Royal Highlanders)
43rd and 52nd	The Oxfordshire L.I.	The Oxfordshire L.I.
44th and 56th	The Essex Regt.	The Essex Regt.
45th and 95th	The Derbyshire Regt. (Sherwood Foresters)	The Sherwood Foresters (Derbyshire Regt.)
47th and 81st	The North Lancashire Regt.	The Loyal North Lancashire Regt.
48th and 58th	The Northamptonshire Regt.	The Northamptonshire Regt.
49th and 66th	The Berkshire Regt. (Princess Charlotte of Wales's)	The Princess Charlotte of Wales's (Berkshire Regt.)
50th and 97th	The Royal West Kent Regt. (Queen's Own)	The Queen's Own (Royal West Kent Regt,)
51st and 105th	The South Yorkshire Regt. (King's Own L.I.)	The King's Own L.I. (South Yorkshire Regt.)
53rd and 85th	The Shropshire Regt. (King's L.I.)	The King's L.I. (Shropshire Regt,)
57th and 77th	The Middlesex Regt. (Duke of Cambridge's Own)	The (Duke of Cambridge's Own) Middlesex Regt.
60th	The King's Royal Rifle Corps	The King's Royal Rifle Corps
62nd and 99th	The Wiltshire Regt. (Duke of Edinburgh's)	The (Duke of Edinburgh's) Wiltshire Regt.
63rd and 96th	The Manchester Regt.	The Manchester Regt.
64th and 98th	The North Staffordshire Regt. (Prince of Wales's)	The (Prince of Wales's) North Staffordshire Regt.
65th and 84th	The York and Lancaster Regt.	The York and Lancaster Regt.
68th and 106th	The Durham L.I.	The Durham L.I.
71st and 74th	The Highland L.I.	The Highland L.I.
72nd and 78th	The Seaforth Highlanders	Seaforth Highlanders (Ross-shire Buffs)
75th and 92nd	The Gordon Highlanders	The Gordon Highlanders
79th	The Queen's Own Cameron Highlanders	The Queen's Own Cameron Highlanders
83rd and 86th	The Royal Irish Rifles	The Royal Irish Rifles
87th and 89th	The Royal Irish Fusiliers (Princess Victoria's)	Princess Victoria's (Royal Irish Fusiliers)
88th and 94th	The Connaught Rangers	The Connaught Rangers
91st and 93rd	The Sutherland & Argyll Highlanders (Princess Louise's)	Princess Louise's (Sutherland & Argyll Highlanders)
100th and 109th	The Prince of Wales's Royal Canadian Regt.	The Prince of Wales's Leinster Regt. (Royal Canadians)
101st and 104	The Royal Munster Fusiliers	The Royal Munster Fusiliers
102nd and 103rd	The Royal Dublin Fusiliers	The Royal Dublin Fusiliers
Unnumbered	The Rifle Brigade (Prince Consort's Own)	The Prince Consort's Own (Rifle Brigade)

C *The 1971 Infantry Line-up*

Following the break-up of the Brigade system and final disbandments and amalgamations, the Infantry of the Line on 1 January 1971 was as follows:

Royal Scots
Queen's Regt.
King's Own Royal Border Regt.
Royal Regt. of Fusiliers
King's Regt.
Royal Anglian Regt.
Devonshire and Dorset Regt.
Light Infantry
Prince of Wales's Own Regt. of Yorkshire
Green Howards
Royal Highland Fusiliers
Cheshire Regt.
Royal Welch Fusiliers
Royal Regt. of Wales
King's Own Scottish Borderers
Royal Irish Rangers
Gloucestershire Regt.
Worcestershire and Sherwood Foresters Regt.
Queen's Lancashire Regt.
Duke of Wellington's Regt.
Royal Hampshire Regt.
Staffordshire Regt.
Black Watch
Duke of Edinburgh's Royal Regt.
Queen's Own Highlanders (Seaforth & Camerons)
Gordon Highlanders
Argyll and Sutherland Highlanders
Parachute Regt.
Brigade of Gurkhas
Royal Green Jackets

All-Brass Issue Badges **D**

Because of the shortage of nickel in 1916 badges previously made in bi-metal finish, i.e. brass and white-metal (nickel), were struck in all brass. This also had the advantage of speeding up production of badges at a time when they were needed in large numbers.

The following is a non-official list, compiled in 1965 by a group of collectors and based on badges held by them. Badges such as The Buffs, normally only in brass, of course, are not included. Shortened titles have been used.

Cavalry

1st King's Dragoon Guards (star pattern)
3rd Dragoon Guards
5th Dragoon Guards
6th Carabiniers
5th Lancers
7th Hussars
8th Hussars
9th Lancers
10th Hussars
12th Lancers
15th Hussars
16th Lancers
17th Lancers
19th Hussars
21st Lancers

Infantry

Royal Scots
Queen's
King's
Norfolk Regt.
Lincolnshire Regt.
Devonshire Regt.
Suffolk Regt.
Somerset L.I.
West Yorkshire Regt.
East Yorkshire Regt.
Bedfordshire Regt.
Leicestershire Regt.
Green Howards

Cheshire Regt.
Royal Welsh Fusiliers
South Wales Borderers
Royal Inniskilling Fusiliers
Gloucestershire Regt.
East Lancashire Regt.
East Surrey Regt.
Duke of Cornwall's L.I.
Duke of Wellington's Regt.
Border Regt.
Royal Sussex Regt.
Hampshire Regt.
South Staffordshire Regt
Dorsetshire Regt.
South Lancashire Regt.
Welsh Regt.
Black Watch
Essex Regt.
Sherwood Foresters
Northamptonshire Regt.
Royal West Kent Regt.
King's Own Yorkshire L.I.
King's Shropshire L.I.
Middlesex Regt.
Manchester Regt.
North Staffordshire Regt.
York & Lancaster Regt.
Durham L.I.
Highland L.I.
Gordon Highlanders
Cameron Highlanders
Leicester Regt.
Royal Munster Fusiliers
Royal Dublin Fusiliers

Corps

Army Veterinary Corps

Yeomanry

Yorkshire Hussars
Yorkshire Dragoons
Pembrokeshire
Worcestershire
Glamorgan
East Riding

Territorial Infantry

Suffolk Regt. (plain circle and two tower castle)
Leicestershire Regt. (no 'Hindoostan' scroll)
East Lancashire Regt. (blank plinth)
South Lancashire Regt. (blank plinth)
Essex Regt. (blank plinth)
Northamptonshire Regt. (blank scrolls)
Middlesex Regt. (plain 'Albuhera' scroll)
Highland L.I. (with short and long blank scroll)
Cambridgeshire Regt.
Herefordshire Regt.
23rd London Regt. (both '1900–2 and '1900–02')

Plastic Cap Badges E

In 1941 an Army Council Instruction announced that certain cap-badges would be made of plastic because of the metal shortage. Further ACIs made it clear that the practice, unpopular though it was, would be extended to include as many regiments and corps as possible. It was pointed out, however, that both plastic and metal badges could be worn within a unit and that excessive orders should not be placed for plastic badges merely to ensure uniformity.

The badges were made in three colours: grey, pale fawn and chocolate brown. Most of the infantry were covered except those with badges whose reproduction in plastic would be impractical on the score of fragility, such as the Royal Norfolk Regiment, Seaforth Highlanders and Gordon Highlanders. The cavalry were not provided for at all, probably due to the small quantities required of each.

So far as is possible, I have compiled a list of those known to exist but this is not necessarily complete as no official list appears to have survived:

Royal Armoured Corps
Royal Tank Regt.
Reconnaissance Corps

Royal Artillery (gun)
Royal Artillery (grenade)
Royal Engineers
Royal Corps of Signals

Grenadier Guards
Scots Guards
Royal Scots
Queen's Royal Regt.
Buffs
King's Own Royal Regt.
Royal Northumberland Fusiliers
Royal Fusiliers
King's Regt.
Lincolnshire Regt.
Devonshire Regt.
Suffolk Regt.

Lancashire Fusiliers
Cheshire Regt.
Royal Welch Fusiliers
South Wales Borderers
Royal Inniskilling Fusiliers
Gloucestershire Regt. (both front and back)
East Lancashire Regt.
East Surrey Regt.
Duke of Cornwall's L.I.
Duke of Wellington's Regt.
Border Regt.
Royal Sussex Regt.
Hampshire Regt.
South Staffordshire Regt.
Dorsetshire Regt.
South Lancashire Regt.
Welch Regt.
Black Watch
Essex Regt.
Sherwood Foresters
Loyal Regt.

West Yorkshire Regt.
East Yorkshire Regt.
Bedfordshire & Hertfordshire Regt.
Leicestershire Regt.
Green Howards
Middlesex Regt.
King's Royal Rifle Corps★
Manchester Regt.
North Staffordshire Regt.
York and Lancaster Regt.
Durham L.I.
Highland L.I.
Cameron Highlanders
Royal Ulster Rifles
Royal Irish Fusiliers (two-part badge)
Argyll and Sutherland Highlanders
Rifle Brigade
Parachute Regt.
Army Air Corps
Cambridgeshire Regt.
Hertfordshire Regt

Northamptonshire Regt.
Royal Marines
Royal West Kent Regt.
King's Own Yorkshire L.I.
King's Shropshire L.I.
Bucks Bn.
Highland Regt.
RASC
RAMC
RAOC
REME
CMP
AEC
Pioneer Corps
Intelligence Corps
APTC
ACC
General Service Corps
ATS

These badges were not popular with collectors either and for many years were ignored by them. About 1958 I saw them for sale in a London market at a penny each. At an auction in October 1994, a collection of these badges was sold: the average price was about £9 each but a Royal Irish Fusiliers reached £310 whilst the AEC raised £440.

★ The KRRC badge was also made in black plastic with a Q/C in the 1950s.

Mounting and Displaying Badges F

This is a matter on which there is much divergent opinion but it can generally be resolved by reference to your individual circumstances. One friend of mine had some forty to fifty glazed frames of badges hanging in his home. They made a splendid display. But even putting everything on show has its limitations. There is the problem of either making a symmetrical and artistically pleasing display or abandoning any attempt to preserve the order of precedence.

Another disadvantage of frames is that when the 'card full' stage is reached and after the glass is fixed and sealed, an interesting badge variation turns up which should have gone into the frame. But the prospect of displayed frames with gaps awaiting scarce specimens is not a pleasing one. There is no simple solution.

I have seen at sales large albums with stout card 'pages' on which badges were mounted. Such books can then go on bookshelves, but it is a rarely used method nowadays.

One will sometimes also find at sales a wooden shield or board bearing badges. The badges have had their prongs or loop fasteners removed and then been nailed to the wood. This method is beyond the pale for serious collectors. It may serve to account for the odd badge which one finds with small holes in the face and no apparent means of fastening. I have had several of these but take the earliest opportunity to replace them with unblemished specimens. I might make the point here that the 'good soldier' who polishes his badge until he obliterates part of the design or the lettering is not popular with the collector, although, as with the holed ones, better that than none at all.

Possibly the best solution is to look for a coin or medal cabinet having a number of shallow drawers. An office stationery cabinet with open-fronted drawers has suited me. Cards on which about thirty badges can be fixed in order of precedence are easily put in and taken out of the compartments. With such a cabinet gaps can always be left on the cards. Safety is ensured by locks usually fitted to these cabinets.

In mounting badges in sequence, say, of The Middlesex Regiment, I allow space for the following:

  i)   the normal bi-metal badge
 ii)   the all-brass 1915 economy issue
iii)   the T.F. badge on which 'Albuhera' is replaced by 'South Africa 1900–02'

iv)   the 10th Bn. TF badge with the 'Albuhcra' scroll blank
v)   the w/m versions of iii and iv
vi)   the pre-1908 Volunteer Bn. badges
vii) the 18th Bn. forming part of Kitchener's Army
viii) the plastic WWII badge
ix)   the post–1945, all w/m version of i, worn by Warrant Officers of the 1st Bn.
x)   the last, a/a version of i
xi)   two or three spaces for unsuspected variations

Not all infantry regiments had such a plenitude of badges but there are several with at least as many. It is better to leave too many spaces than too few, since the unexpected, the inexplicable and the unknown will always be turning up.

The beginner will now ask how he is to know that such varieties even exist. The answer is that the system outlined is the ultimate arrangement, arrived at after several tentative starts.

Non-collectors have often asked me if I have the 'complete set' but this is not something to which anyone can justifiably lay claim. Regimental historians have not given the full coverage to badges and insignia that they might have done. A little research or effort of memory, undertaken fifty years ago by the chronicler, would have saved many hours of discussion and correspondence for their readers now. Even Depot Museums are fallible and I have on several occasions found items which were unknown to the officer in charge. If this is so for Infantry how much more so it must be for Cavalry who have no depots other than a Home HQ which practically consists of their Regimental Secretary. It is fairly safe to say that there is more information on badges in the hands of collectors than in the military museums.

Several collectors whom I know have lately based their infantry badges on the Brigade groupings authorized in 1957. This means, for example, that if one mounts the badge of the Home Counties Brigade at the head of a card then the badges of the Queen's, Buffs, East Surreys, Royal Sussex, Royal West Kent and Middlesex can be assembled below it. As the Brigade system proved ephemeral it seems more desirable to adhere to the old 1881 titles and precedence.

In the case of merged cavalry and Yeomanry regiments, the official ruling is that the new combined unit takes the precedence of the senior partner of the amalgamation. Thus, in 1956, the Queen's Own Yorkshire Yeomanry took third place in the Yeomanry seniority list since it embodied the Yorkshire Hussars (3rd on the official list), the Yorkshire Dragoons (9th) and the East Riding Yeomanry (54th).

Even if you choose the cupboard or cabinet for your main collection, locked away out of sight, there is much to be said for having a representative frame of badges hanging in the hall for casual callers to see. A visitor, or even the milkman, may have served with an interesting wartime unit not so far represented in your collection.

The best way to mount your collection is the one that best suits you. My only plea is that you do not opt for a wooden plaque and a bag of nails!

Translation of Foreign-Language Mottoes G

Animo et Fide	With spirit and faith
Arma pacis fulcra	Arms, the mainstay of peace
Audacter et sincere	Boldly and truly
Bydand	Watchful
Cede nullis	Yield to none
Celer et audax	Swift and bold
Certa cito	Swift and sure
Concordia victrix	Unity is victorious
Cuidich'n righ	Help to the king
Cymru am byth	Wales for ever
Decus et tutamen	An ornament and a safeguard
Deffro mae'n dydd	Awake, it is day
Deus vult	God wills
Dieu et mon droit	God and my right
Diex aie	With God's help
Domine dirige nos	Lord direct us
Ex dentibus ensis	From the teeth of the sword
Fide et fiducia	In faith and trust
Fortitudo et Fidelitas	Strength and trust
Gwell angau na chywilydd ⎱ *Gwell angau neu chywilydd* ⎰	Death before dishonour
Honi soit qui mal y pense (the motto of the Order of the Garter)	Evil to him who evil thinks
Ich dien	I serve
In arduis fidelis	Faithful in adversity
In veritate religionis confido	I trust in the truth of my conscience
Invicta	Unconquered
Je suis prest	I am ready
Justitia in armis	Justice in arms
Justitia turris nostra	Justice is our fortress
Kadimah	Eastward
Labor omnia vincit	Work conquers all

Manu forti	With a strong hand
Mente et manu	With heart and hand
Merebimur	We shall be worthy
Montis insignia calpe	The badge of the Rock of Gibraltar
Nemo menos impune lacessit (lacesset) (The motto of the Order of the Thistle)	{ None may touch me/us with impunity
Nemo nos impnue lacesset	
Nisi dominus frustra	Unless the Lord be with us all is in vain
Primus in Indis	First in India
Primus in urbe	First in the City
Pro aris et focis	For hearth and home
Pro patria conamur	For our country we strive
Pro rege, pro lege, pro patria conamur	For king, for law and for country we strive
Quinque juncta in uno	Five joined in one
Quis separabit?	Who shall separate us?
Quocunque jeceris stabit	Whichever way you throw him he will stand
Quo fas et gloria ducunt	Wherever right and glory lead
Quo fata vocant	Wherever fate calls
Regi adsumus coloni	As Colonials we stand by the King
Sans changer	Constant
Sans peur	Without fear
Semper fidelis	Ever faithful
Sua tela tonanti	Thundering forth his weapons (Said of Jupiter)
Sub cruce candida	Under the white cross
Treu und fest	Loyal and steadfast
Ubique	Everywhere
Vires aquirit eundo	Strength through progress
Viret in aeternum	It flourishes for ever
Virtutis fortuna comes	Fortune favours the brave
Y ddraig goch ddyry gychwyn	The Red Dragon will lead

Plumes and Hackles H

During the Second World War and immediately afterwards, in the National Service era, all the fusilier regiments seized the opportunity to readopt the distinctive coloured plumes worn originally in the fusilier fur-cap until 1914. In the between-wars period the khaki service-dress cap was not felt to be a suitable headdress for embellishment but the g.s. cap and the beret were improved by the addition of feather hackles in the colours of the old brush-plumes. In addition to the fusiliers, of course, other regiments wore feather hackles and details are given below of all those in use since 1939:

White	Royal Fusiliers
	Royal Scots Fusiliers
	Royal Welch Fusiliers
	Royal Highland Fusiliers (in the khaki bonnet this is now worn without a badge, tucked behind the tartan patch).
Red (uppermost) and White	Royal Northumberland Fusiliers
	Royal Regiment of Fusiliers
Blue (uppermost) and Orange	Royal Warwickshire Fusiliers
Primrose	Lancashire Fusiliers
Black	Cameronians
	Royal Ulster Rifles
	No 9 Commando
Grey	Royal Inniskilling Fusiliers
Red	Black Watch ⎫ (worn instead of a
	Tyneside Scottish ⎬ badge in the
	⎭ khaki bonnet)
White (uppermost) and Red	1 Bn Highland LI 1948 to 1959
	2 Bn Highland LI until 1948
	Pipers, Queen's Royal Irish Hussars

Green	1 Bn Highland LI 1944 to 1948 (un-officially)
	Royal Irish Fusiliers
	London Irish Rifles (Pipers – St Patrick's green)
Blue	Cameron Highlanders
	Queen's Own Highlanders
	Liverpool Scottish
Blue (uppermost) and Red	Liverpool Irish
Red, brown and green (equally spaced left to right)	Royal Tank Regt.

If the collector aims to mount the badges complete with their respective hackle it is a good plan to ensure that the glazed cabinet has a depth of at least one inch so that the plume is not crushed and distorted.

Volunteer Battalions *I*

With the proliferation of forged badges there has, naturally, been a tendency to concentrate on production of the more expensive varieties. Among these fall the badges of the volunteer battalions of infantry and whilst I can offer no foolproof method of identifying these forgeries it may be of some help to list below the full details of those battalions in being at the beginning of 1908 the year in which they were converted to units of the new Territorial Force. Recently, a member of the Military Historical Society purchased the badge of the 3rd Volunteer Bn, The Duke of Cornwall's Light Infantry: suspicious of this, he approached the Regimental Museum which confirmed his suspicions – there was no 3 VB and the badge was the result of over-zealous production.

Against each battalion listed below is indicated in brackets the location of its headquarters.

This listing should enable you to plan the necessary spaces in mounting your collection. However, additional complications arise and you should remember that as the Volunteer Battalions existed from 1881 until 1908 those badges which bore a crown can be found in both QVC and K/C varieties. Also, when the Boer War honour was granted in 1905 this was usually added below the badge on a separate scroll, thus making yet a further variant.

Royal Scots

1 VB ⎤	Queens Rifle
2 VB ⎬	Vol Bde
3 VB ⎦	(Edinburgh)
4 VB (Edinburgh)	
5 VB (Leith)	
6 VB (Peebles)	
7 VB (Haddington)	
8 VB (Linlithgow)	
9 VB (Edinburgh)	

Queen's (R W Surrey)

1 VB (Croydon)
2 VB (Guildford)
3 VB (Bermondsey)
4 VB (Kennington Park)

Buffs

1 VB (Dover)
2 VB (Cranbrook)

King's Own

1 VB (Ulverston)
2 VB (Lancaster)

Northumberland Fusiliers

1 VB (Hexham)
2 VB (Newcastle-on-Tyne)
3 VB (Newcastle-on-Tyne)

R Warwickshire

1 VB (Birmingham)
2 VB (Coventry)

Royal Fusiliers

(all in London)
1 VB (33 Fitzroy Sq, W)
2 VB (9 Tufton St, SW1)
3 VB (Edward St, NW)
4 VB (112 Shaftesbury St, EC1)

King's (Liverpool)

(all in L'pool except 3 & 7 VBs)
1 VB (65 St Anne St)
2 VB (Upper Warwick St)
3 VB (Southport)
4 VB (77 Shaw St)
5 VB (50/52 Everton Brow)
6 VB (59/61 Everton Road)
7 VB (Douglas, Isle of Man)
8 VB (Fraser St)

Norfolk Regt

1 VB (Norwich)
2 VB (Great Yarmouth)
3 VB (East Dereham)
4 VB (Norwich)

Lincolnshire Regt

1 VB (Lincoln)
2 VB (Grantham)
3 VB (Grimsby)

Devonshire Regt

1 VB (Exeter)
2 VB (Plymouth)
3 VB (Exeter)

4 VB (Barnstaple)
5 VB (Newton Abbot)

Suffolk Regt

1 VB (Ipswich)
2 VB (Bury St Edmunds)
3 VB (Cambridge)
4 VB Cambridge University VRC

Somerset LI

1 VB (Bath)
2 VB (Taunton)
3 VB (Weston-super-Mare)

West Yorkshire Regt

1 VB (York)
2 VB (Bradford)
3 VB (Leeds)

East Yorkshire Regt

1 VB (Hull)
2 VB (Beverley)

Bedfordshire Regt

1 VB (Hertford)
2 VB (Hemel Hempstead)
3 VB (Bedford)
4 VB (Huntingdon)

Leicestershire Regt

1 VB (Leicester)

Yorkshire Regt

1 VB (Northallerton)
2 VB (Scarborough)

Lancashire Fusiliers

1 VB (Bury)
2 VB (Rochdale)
3 VB (Salford)

Royal Scots Fusiliers

1 VB (Kilmarnock)
2 VB (Ayr)

Cheshire Regt

1 VB (Birkenhead)

2 VB (Chester)
3 VB (Knutsford)
4 VB (Stockport)
5 VB (Congleton)

Royal Welsh Fusiliers

1 VB (Wrexham)
2 VB (Hawarden)
3 VB (Caernarvon)

South Wales Borderers

1 VB (Brecon)
2 VB (Newport)
3 VB (Pontypool)
4 VB (Newport)
5 VB (Newtown,
    Montgomeryshire)

King's Own Scottish Borderers

1 VB (Roxburgh & Selkirk)
2 VB (Duns)
3 VB (Dumfries)
4 VB (Maxwelltown)

Cameronians

(all Glasgow except 2 VB)
1 VB (261 West Princes St)
2 VB (Hamilton)
3 VB (Victoria Road)
4 VB (149 Cathedral St)

Gloucestershire Regt

1 VB (Bristol)
2 VB (Gloucester)
3 VB (Bristol)

Worcestershire Regt

1 VB (Kidderminster)
2 VB (Worcester)

East Lancashire Regt

1 VB (Blackburn)
2 VB (Burnley)

East Surrey Regt

1 VB (Camberwell)
2 VB (Wimbledon)

3 VB (Kingston-on-Thames)
4 VB (Clapham Junction)

Duke of Cornwall's LI

1 VB (Truro)
2 VB (Bodmin)

Duke of Wellington's Regt

1 VB (Halifax)
2 VB (Huddersfield)
3 VB (Skipton)

Border Regt

1 VB (Carlisle)
2 VB (Kendal)
3 VB (Workington)

Royal Sussex Regt

1 VB (Brighton)
2 VB (Worthing)
1st Cinque Ports VB (Hastings)

Hampshire Regt

1 VB (Winchester)
2 VB (Southampton)
3 VB (Portsmouth)
4 VB (Bournemouth)
5 VB (Newport, Isle of Wight)

South Staffordshire Regt

1 VB (Handsworth)
2 VB (Walsall)
3 VB (Wolverhampton)

Dorsetshire Regt

1 VB (Dorchester)

South Lancashire Regt

1 VB (Warrington)
2 VB (St Helen's)

Welsh Regt

1 VB (Haverfordwest)
2 VB (Cardiff)
3 VB (Pontypridd)
4 VB (Swansea)

Black Watch

1 VB (Dundee)
2 VB (Arbroath)
3 VB (Dundee)
4 VB (Perth)
5 VB (Birnam)
6 VB (St Andrews)

Oxfordshire LI

1 VB (Oxford)
2 VB (Oxford)
1st Bucks (Great Marlow)
2nd Bucks (Eton)

Essex Regt

1 VB (Brentwood)
2 VB (Colchester)
3 VB (West Ham)
4 VB (Leyton)

Sherwood Foresters

1 VB (Derby)
2 VB (Chesterfield)
1st Nottinghamshire (Nottingham)
4 VB (Newark)

Loyal North Lancashire Regt

1 VB (Preston)
2 VB (Bolton)

Northamptonshire Regt

1 VB (Northampton)

Royal Berkshire Regt

1 VB (Reading)

Royal West Kent Regt

1 VB (Tonbridge)
2 VB (Blackheath)
3 VB (Woolwich)
4 VB (Chatham)

KO Yorkshire LI

1 VB (Wakefield)

King's Shropshire LI

1 VB (Shrewsbury)

2 VB (Newport)
1st Hereford (Hereford)

Middlesex Regt

1 VB (Hornsey)
2 VB (Hounslow)
17th Middx (Camden Town)

King's Royal Rifle Corps

(all in London)

1st	Middx	(Davies St, W)
2nd	,,	(Putney Bridge Rd)
26th	,,	(attd) (Horseferry Rd, SW)
4th	,,	(Iverna Gdns, W)
5th	,,	(137 Park Road, NW)
12th	,,	(Somerset House)
13th	,,	(58 Buckingham Gate, SW)
21st	,,	17 Penton St, Pentonville)
22nd	,,	(Grays Inn Rd, WC)

1st London (130 Bunhill Row, EC)
2nd London (57A Farringdon Rd, EC)
3rd London (24 Sun St, EC)

Wiltshire Regt

1 VB (Warminster)
2 VB (Chippenham)

Manchester Regt

1 VB (Manchester)
2 VB (Manchester)
3 VB (Ashton-under-Lyne)
4 VB (Manchester)
5 VB (Ardwick)
6 VB (Oldham)

North Staffordshire Regt

1 VB (Stoke-on-Trent)
2 VB (Burton-on-Trent)

York & Lancaster Regt

1 VB (Sheffield)
2 VB (Doncaster)

Durham LI

1 VB (Stockton-on-Tees)
2 VB (Bishop Auckland)
3 VB (Sunderland)
4 VB (Durham)
5 VB (Gateshead)

Highland LI

1 VB (Glasgow)
2 VB (Glasgow)
3 VB (Glasgow)
9th Lanarkshire (Lanark)
5 VB (Glasgow)

Seaforth Highlanders

1 VB (Dingwall)
1st Sutherland (Golspie)
3 VB (Elgin)

Gordon Highlanders

1VB (Aberdeen)
2 VB (Old Meldrum)
3 VB (Peterhead)
4 VB (Aberdeen)
5 VB (Banchory)
6 VB (Keith)
7 VB (Lerwick)

QO Cameron Highlanders

1 VB (Inverness)

Argyll & Sutherland Highlanders

1 VB (Greenock)
2 VB (Paisley)
3 VB (Pollockshaws)
4 VB (Stirling)
5 VB (Dunoon)
1st Dunbartonshire (Helensburgh)
7 VB (Alloa)

Rifle Brigade

(all in London)

7th	Middx	(59 Buckingham Gate, SW)
14th	,,	(Lincoln's Inn)
15th	,,	(Custom House)
16th	,,	(2 Duke St, Charing Cross)
18th	,,	(207 Harrow Rd, W)
19th	,,	(Chenies St, WC)
20th	,,	(Duke's Road, WC)
24th	,,	(General Post Office)
26th	,,	(45A Horseferry Rd, SW)

2nd Tower Hamlets (66 Tredegar Rd, Bow)

$\mathcal{J}$ *Tartan Backings*

Most Scottish line infantry regiments wore in the khaki Tam-o'-Shanter (or Balmoral) bonnet a three-inch square of the appropriate tartan on which was mounted the regimental badge. The tartan patch was not worn in the blue bonnet which came into use in the 1950s nor in the earlier glengarry: in both of these the badge was mounted on a black silk rosette.

Despite the ruling from the Ministry of Defence that 'a patch' of tartan will be worn behind the badge most regiments specify the pattern which this will take and also where and how the coloured lines of the tartan will feature in the patch. In certain regiments, the pipers wear, or wore, a Royal Stuart tartan kilt but they did not normally wear a Royal Stuart patch – in fact, pipers generally affected the glengarry when rifle-company jocks were wearing the TOS. Notwithstanding, in mounting your Scottish badges it is both interesting and colourful to include some Royal Stuart backings where appropriate: the changes of tartan occurring over the years add variety to the display.

Most military tartans are based on the 42nd, or Government tartan and differences were effected by the addition of red, white or yellow lines: exceptions to this are Hunting Erskine (worn by The Royal Scots Fusiliers after 1948), Buccleuch (worn by the pipers of 4Bn KOSB), Cameron of Erracht (worn by The Queen's Own Cameron Highlanders), hodden-grey (worn by The London Scottish) and, of course, Royal Stuart.

Listed below are the Scottish infantry regiments, regular and Territorial, with details of the tartan patches which you can use to back your badges:

Scots Guards (pipers only)	Royal Stuart (I favour the intersection of the multiple-colour lines on the scarlet background).
Royal Scots (pipers)	Royal Stuart
Royal Scots (others)	Hunting Stuart (cut square with a red line running top left to bottom right crossing a yellow line top right to bottom left)

Royal Scots Fusiliers (until 1948)	42nd Tartan (the lack of features in this dark blue/black/green tartan makes it difficult, if not impossible to identify a specific patch)
Royal Scots Fusiliers (after 1948)	Hunting Erskine (the four dark green squares centrally located on the paler green square patch)
Royal Highland Fusiliers (pipers)	Dress Erskine (this is a green and red tartan with such a large pattern that it does not lend itself to a badge-patch)
Royal Highland Fusiliers (others)	Mackenzie (cut square with vertical white line crossing a red horizontal line)
King's Own Scottish Borderers (pipers)	Royal Stuart
,, ,, (before 1900)	42nd Tartan
,, ,, (after 1900)	Leslie (cut square with a thin white line running top left to bottom right, crossing a red line top right to bottom left)
,, ,, (pipers, 4Bn only)	Buccleuch (square of black and white shepherd's check with a super-imposed pale-blue line)
Cameronians (Scottish Rifles)	Douglas (cut square with an upright intersection of white lines)
Black Watch (pipers)	Royal Stuart
,, ,, (others)	42nd Tartan.
	Black Watch soldiers, of course, did not wear either a badge or a tartan patch in the TOS: they wore, instead, simply a red hackle
Highland Light Infantry	Mackenzie (cut square with vertical white line crossing a red horizontal line)
Glasgow Highlanders	42nd Tartan
Seaforth Highlanders	Mackenzie (cut square with a thick white line from top left to bottom right crossing a red line top right to bottom left)
,, ,, (4/5 Bns)	42nd Tartan
Gordon Highlanders	Gordon (cut square with a diagonal intersection of yellow lines)
Cameron Highlanders	Cameron of Erracht (cut square with

	an upright intersection of the yellow lines)
Queen's Own Highlanders	Cameron of Erracht (cut square with an upright intersection of the yellow lines)
Argyll & Sutherland Highlanders	42nd Tartan
London Scottish	Hodden-grey (a plain square of unpatterned material)
Liverpool Scottish	Forbes (cut square with a diagonal intersection of white lines)
Tyneside Scottish (pipers)	Royal Stuart
,, ,, (others)	42nd Tartan

The enthusiastic soldier who sought to embellish his drab battledress by box-pleating the back of his blouse, facing his reveres and whitening his chevrons would also ensure that his badge-backing had the threads pulled at the edges, thus producing a fringed finish. However, in certain regiments such as the Gordon Highlanders, the lines of the tartan patch worn in the bonnet were intended to cross diagonally. The construction of tartan is such that the lines of the pattern run 'along' the material and, thus, the edges of the Gordons' patch would not fray. The zealous Jock, therefore, took a piece of 42nd tartan cut rather larger than the regimental patch and mounted the latter on it. The rear patch, being 'square' could thus be suitably fringed to meet even the most exacting barrack-room standards .

If you consider mounting all your Scottish badges together on a tartan background I would suggest that you use 42nd tartan. It is sufficiently sober to provide a dark background and, having once been styled Government tartan it is appropriate for all units. One collection which I once saw mounted on Royal Stuart tartan was not a success. Royal Stuart tartan design is a very 'busy' one and its multiple colours tend to distract the viewer from the badges whereas, on 42nd the badges, brass or whitemetal, stand out well.

K *Order of precedence – 1994*

The Life Guards
The Blues & Royals (Royal Horse Guards & 1st Dragoons)
Royal Horse Artillery
1st The Queen's Dragoon Guards
The Royal Scots Dragoon Guards (Carabiniers & Greys)
The Royal Dragoon Guards
The Queen's Royal Hussars (Queen's Own & Royal Irish)
9/12th Royal Lancers (Prince of Wales's)
The King's Royal Hussars
The Light Dragoons
The Queen's Royal Lancers
The Royal Tank Regiment
The Royal Regiment of Artillery
Corps of Royal Engineers
The Royal Corps of Signals
Grenadier Guards
Coldstream Guards
Scots Guards
Irish Guards
Welsh Guards
The Royal Scots (The Royal Regiment)
The Princess of Wales's Royal Regiment (Queen's & Royal Hampshires)
The King's Own Royal Border Regiment
The Royal Regiment of Fusiliers
The King's Regiment
The Royal Anglian Regiment
The Devonshire & Dorset Regiment
The Light Infantry
The Prince of Wales's Own Regiment of Yorkshire
The Green Howards (Alexandra, Princess of Wales's Own Yorkshire Regiment)
The Royal Highland Fusiliers (Princess Margaret's Own Glasgow & Ayrshire Regiment)

The Cheshire Regiment
The Royal Welch Fusiliers
The Royal Regiment of Wales
The King's Own Scottish Borderers
The Royal Irish Regiment
The Royal Gloucestershire, Berkshire & Wiltshire Regiment
The Worcestershire & Sherwood Foresters Regiment (29/45th Foot)
The Queen's Lancashire Regiment
The Duke of Wellington's Regiment (West Riding)
The Staffordshire Regiment (The Prince of Wales's)
The Black Watch (Royal Highland Regiment)
The Royal Marines
The Highlanders (Seaforth, Gordons & Camerons)
The Argyll & Sutherland Highlanders (Princess Louise's)
The Parachute Regiment
The Brigade of Gurkhas
The Royal Green Jackets
Special Air Service Regiment
Army Air Corps
Royal Army Chaplains' Department
Royal Logistic Corps
Royal Army Medical Corps
Corps of Royal Electrical & Mechanical Engineers
Adjutant General's Corps
Royal Army Veterinary Corps
Small Arms School Corps
Royal Army Dental Corps
Intelligence Corps
Army Physical Training Corps
Queen Alexandra's Royal Army Nursing Corps
General List

The Plates

Plate 1   Cavalry 1914

A	1st Life Guards	2nd Life Guards	Royal Horse Guards
B	1st King's Dragoon Guards	Queen's Bays	3rd Dragoon Guards
C	4th Royal Irish Dragoon Guards	5th Dragoon Guards	Carabiniers (6th Dragoon Guards)
D	7th Dragoon Guards	1st (Royal) Dragoons	Royal Scots Greys (2nd Dragoons)
E	3rd Hussars	4th Hussars	5th (Royal Irish) Lancers

Plate 2   Cavalry 1914

A   6th (Inniskilling)   7th Hussars   8th (King's Royal
        Dragoons   Irish) Hussars

B   9th Lancers   10th Hussars   11th Hussars

C   12th Lancers   13th Hussars   14th Hussars

D   15th Hussars   16th Lancers   17th Lancers

E   18th Hussars   19th Hussars   20th Hussars   21st Lancers

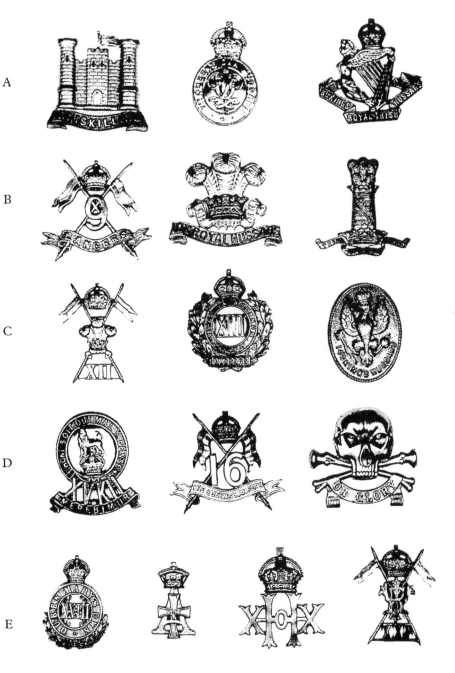

Plate 3   Miscellaneous Cavalry

A   Household   Blues & Royals   Life Guards   Life Guards
      Cavalry   (1st and 2nd)   (ER VIII)

B   1st King's Dragoon Guards   3rd Carabiniers   Royal Scots
      (i) 1915–37   (ii) post 1937   Dragoon Guards

C   7th Dragoon   4/7th Dragoons   1st (Royal)   1st Royal
      Guards   Guards   Dragoons   Dragoons
      (pre-1906)   (1915–19)   (1948–69)

D   Royal Scots   4th Hussars   5th Inniskilling   7th Hussars
      Greys and   (1898–1902)   Dragoon   (1898–1902)
      Royal Scots   Guards
      Dragoon Guards
      (bandsmen)

E   12th Royal   13th Hussars   14th Hussars   14th Hussars
      Lancers   (1915–29)   (1915– 29)
      (pre-1903)

Plate 4   Miscellaneous Cavalry

A 18th Hussars
(1898–1904)

18th Hussars
(1904–1905)

18th Hussars
(1905–1910)

B 13/18th Hussars
(1929–38)

13/18th Hussars
(1938–57)

19th Hussars
(1898–1902)

C 19th Hussars
(1902–1909)

15/19th Hussars

14/20th Hussars
(1929–31)

D 14/20th Hussars
(1931–69)

21st Lancers
(1898–1899)

21st Lancers
(1899–1901)

E 22nd Dragoons

23rd Hussars

24th Lancers

Plate 5   Miscellaneous Cavalry and Royal Armoured Corps

A   25th Dragoons   26th Hussars   27th Lancers

B   25th Dragoons   26th Hussars
    (trial)   (3 trial types, the last Indian-made)

C   Tank Corps   Royal Tank Corps   Royal Tank Corps &
    (1917–24)   (1924)   Royal Tank Regiment
                                        (1924–55)

D   Royal Armoured   Royal Armoured
    Corps (1939–41)   Corps (1941–55)

Plate 6   Helmet Plate and Centres

A   HELMET PLATE QVC

B	Queen's Regiment	Royal Warwickshire Regiment	Somerset Light Infantry
C	West Yorkshire Regiment	Cheshire Regiment	Duke of Cornwall's Light Infantry
D	Dorsetshire Regiment (2 tower)	Royal Berkshire Regiment	Leinster Regiment

A

B

C

D

Plate 7   Helmet Plate and Centres

A   HELMET PLATE K/C

B   Norfolk Regiment   Royal Sussex   Royal Irish Regiment
                            Regiment   K/C

C   Yorkshire Regiment   Oxfordshire &   South Staffordshire
                            Buckinghamshire   Regiment
                            Light Infantry

D   Dorsetshire Regiment   Border Regiment   Manchester Regiment
    (3 tower)

Plate 8 Fusilier Glengarry Grenades

A Northumberland Fusiliers   Royal Fusiliers   Lancashire Fusiliers

B Royal Welsh Fusiliers   Royal Inniskilling Fusiliers   Royal Irish Fusiliers (pre-1903)

C Royal Irish Fusiliers (post 1903)   Royal Munster Fusiliers   Royal Dublin Fusiliers

Plate 9 Fusilier Fur-cap Grenades

A Northumberland Fusiliers

Royal Fusiliers

Lancashire Fusiliers

B Royal Scots Fusiliers

Royal Welsh Fusiliers

Royal Inniskilling Fusiliers

C Royal Irish Fusiliers (post 1903)

Royal Munster Fusiliers

Royal Dublin Fusiliers

Plate 10   Infantry 1914

A	Royal Scots	Queen's Regiment	Buffs
B	King's Own	Northumberland Fusiliers	Royal Warwickshire Regiment
C	Royal Fusiliers	King's Regiment	Norfolk Regiment
D	Lincolnshire Regiment	Devonshire Regiment	Suffolk Regiment
E	Somerset Light Infantry	West Yorkshire Regiment	East Yorkshire Regiment

Plate 11 Infantry 1914

A Bedfordshire Regiment | Leicestershire Regiment | Royal Irish Regiment

B Yorkshire Regiment | Lancashire Fusiliers | Royal Scots Fusiliers

C Cheshire Regiment | Royal Welsh Fusiliers | South Wales Borderers

D King's Own Scottish Borderers | Cameronians | Royal Inniskilling Fusiliers

E Gloucestershire Regiment (and back-badge) | Worcestershire Regiment | East Lancashire Regiment

Plate 12   Infantry 1914

A   East Surrey Regiment   Duke of Cornwall's
                           Light Infantry
                                              Duke of Wellington's
                                              Regiment

B   Border Regiment   Royal Sussex
                           Regiment
                                              Hampshire Regiment

C   South Staffordshire   Dorsetshire Regiment
    Regiment
                                              South Lancashire
                                              Regiment

D   Welsh Regiment   Black Watch   Oxfordshire &
                                              Buckinghamshire
                                              Light Infantry

E   Essex Regiment   Sherwood Foresters Loyal North
                                              Lancashire
                                              Regiment

Plate 13   Royal Marines

A   Royal Marine Light Infantry

Royal Marine Artillery (pre 1922)

Royal Marine Artillery (1922–23)

B   Royal Marines (post 1923)

Colour Serjeants (post 1923)

Royal Naval School of Music

C   Royal Marine Bands Chatham

Royal Marine Bands Plymouth

Royal Marine Bands Portsmouth (Royal Yacht Band)

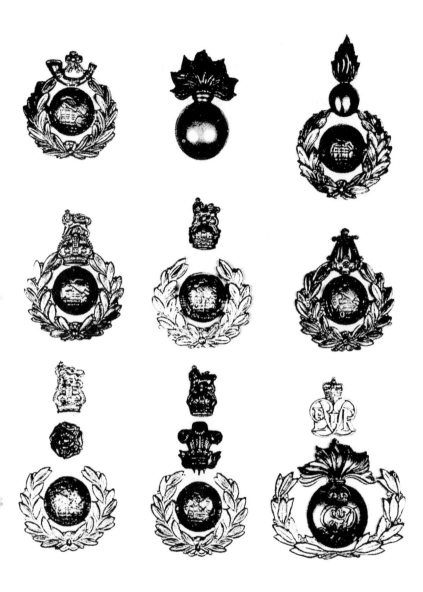

Plate 14   Infantry 1914

A   Northamptonshire Regiment   Royal Berkshire Regiment   Royal West Kent Regiment

B   King's Own Yorkshire Light Infantry   King's Shropshire Light Infantry   Middlesex Regiment

C   King's Royal Rifle Corps   Wiltshire Regiment   Manchester Regiment

D   North Staffordshire Regiment   York & Lancaster Regiment   Durham Light Infantry

E   Highland Light Infantry   Seaforth Highlanders   Gordon Highlanders

189

Plate 15A   Infantry 1914

A   Cameron Highlanders   Royal Irish Rifles   Royal Irish Fusiliers

B   Connaught Rangers   Argyll & Sutherland   Leinster Regiment
                            Highlanders

C   Royal Munster   Royal Dublin   Rifle Brigade
     Fusiliers   Fusiliers

Plate 15B   Airborne Forces

D   Army Air Corps   Glider Pilot   Army Air Corps
     (1940–50)   Regiment   (post 1957)

E   Parachute Regiment   Special Air Service   Special Air Service
                                                       (cloth badge
                                                       for beret)

Plate 16   Infantry 1939 differing from those of 1914

A   Queen's Royal
Regiment

Royal Northumber-
land Fusiliers

King's Regiment

B   Royal Norfolk
Regiment

Bedfordshire & Hert-
fordshire Regiment

Cheshire Regiment

C   Royal Welch
Fusiliers

Royal Inniskilling
Fusiliers

Worcestershire
Regiment

D   Welch Regiment

Black Watch

Loyal Regiment

E   Manchester Regiment   Rifle Brigade

Plate 17 Miscellaneous Infantry

A   Buffs (pagri) Royal Lincolnshire Regiment Royal Fusiliers QVC and Q/C

B   Suffolk Regiment (QVC and K/C—2 tower) Yorkshire Regiment (pre 1908)

C   Yorkshire Regiment (crown pattern of WWII) Green Howards (1950–58) Lancashire Fusiliers (beret-badge)

D   Cameronians (i) pagri (ii) standard (iii) serjeants

Plate 18   Miscellaneous Infantry

A   Royal Inniskilling
    Fusiliers
    (1926–34)

East Surrey Regiment
    (pagri 1891–93)

Duke of Cornwall's
    Light Infantry
    (Pre 1901)

B   Royal Hampshire
    Regiment
    (post 1949)

Dorsetshire Regiment
    (pre 1900)

1st Black Watch
    (serjeants QVC)

C   Essex Regiment

(i) regimental castle
(ii) standard castle

Derbyshire Regiment
    (pre 1901)

D   Northamptonshire Regiment
    (i) regimental castle
    (ii) standard castle

KOYLI (pagri)

Plate 19   Miscellaneous Infantry

A   Wiltshire Regiment   Gordon Highlanders   Royal Irish Fusiliers
     (post 1954)   (Staff)   (early 1900s)

B   Leinster Regiment   Rifle Brigade (i) pre 1903 (ii) pre 1903 f.s.cap
     (WWI variant)

C   Rifle Brigade   (i) 1903–10   (ii) 1910–37   (iii) 1937–56

D   Rifle Brigade 1956–58   Manchester Regiment
                                                                  (Warrant Officers
                                                                  1881–95)

Plate 20   Brigade of Guards

A   Grenadier Guards
     (i) ranks below full serjeant   (ii) musicians and full serjeants
     (iii) warrant-officers (iv) pagri

B   Coldstream Guards
     (i) ranks below warrant-officer   (ii) Warrant-officer   (iii) pagri

C   Scots Guards
     (i) ranks below full serjeants   (ii) musicians and full serjeants
     (iii) warrant-officers   (iv) pagri

D   Irish Guards
     (i) ranks below warrant-officer   (ii) warrant-officers
     Welsh Guards   (i) all other ranks   (ii) pagri

E   Guards Machine Gun Regiment   Guards Machine Gun Battalion
     Officers' Training Battalion

Plate 21 Territorial Infantry

A 4th & 5th Royal Scots

8th King's Regiment
(post 1939)

10th King's Regiment
(1908–37)

B 4th & 5th Lincoln-
shire Regiment

Suffolk Territorial
Force Bns.

4th & 5th Somerset
Light Infantry

C 7th West Yorkshire
Regiment
(1960)

4th, 5th & 6th
Leicestershire
Regiment

Brecknockshire
Battalion

D 4th Border Regiment

5th Border Regiment

5th Royal Sussex
Regiment

E 6th Hampshire
Regiment

6th Royal Hampshire
Regiment

7th Hampshire
Regiment

Plate 21A Territorial Infantry

A 6th King's Regiment 8th King's Regiment
(1908–22)

B 7th West Yorkshire 8th West Yorkshire 7/8th West Yorkshire
Regiment (1908–22) Regiment (1908–22) Regiment (post-
1922)

C 6th East Surrey 8th Hampshire Buckinghamshire
Regiment (1908–20) Regiment Battalion

Plate 22 Territorial Infantry

A Royal Guernsey Light Royal Guernsey Royal Jersey Light
   Infantry   Militia   Infantry

B 4th, 5th, 6th & 7th Tyneside Scottish (i) 1916 pattern
   Black Watch   (ii) late 1915 pattern

C 4th, 5th, 6th & 7th 7th (Robin Hoods) 4th Northamptonshire
   Essex Regiment   Foresters   Regiment

D 7th, 8th and 9th   10th Middlesex   7th Manchester
   Middlesex Regiment   Regiment   Regiment

E 6th Highland Light   5th, 7th & 8th Highland Light Infantry
   Infantry

A

B

C

D

E

Plate 23   Territorial Infantry

A 9th Highland Light   Glasgow Highlanders (two patterns)
    Infantry (1908–39)

B 5th Seaforth High-   4/5th Seaforth High-   5th & 4/5th Seaforth
    landers (pre 1920)   landers (1920–46)   Highlanders
                                             (serjeants)

C Liverpool Scottish   Cambridgeshire   Hertfordshire
    (post 1937)   Regiment   Regiment

D Herefordshire   Herefordshire Light   1st Monmouthshire
    Regiment   Infantry   Regiment (i) 1908–
                                             1922 (ii) 1922–46

Plate 24   Volunteer Battalions

A   5th Royal Scots

1st Royal Warwick-
shire Regiment

1st Royal Fusiliers

B   5th (Irish) King's
Regiment

2nd Norfolk Regiment

3rd Bedfordshire
Regiment

C   5th South Wales
Borderers

2nd Worcestershire
Regiment

2nd East Lancashire
Regiment

D   2nd Hampshire
Regiment

1st South Lancashire
Regiment

2nd Welsh Regiment

Plate 25   Volunteer Battalions

A   4th Black Watch   1st Essex Regiment   2nd Essex Regiment

B   1st Sherwood Foresters   1st Middlesex Regiment   2nd Manchester Regiment

C   3rd Durham Light Infantry   105th Lanarkshire Rifle Volunteers   5th Highland Light Infantry (Glasgow Highlanders)

D   4th Gordon Highlanders   5th Gordon Highlandcrs   1st Dumbartonshire Volunteer Rifle Corps

Plate 26   Pipers

A   Lothians & Border Horse

Scots Guards

B   Irish Guards   Royal Scots

1st Royal Scots
     Fusiliers

C   2nd Royal Scots   1st Cameronians
       Fusiliers   (1921–68)

Royal Highland
     Fusiliers

D   Royal Inniskilling Fusiliers (two patterns)

Plate 27   Pipers

A   North Irish Brigade   Ulster Defence
Regiment   Royal Irish Fusiliers

B   London Irish Rifles (1908–61)   London Irish Rifles
(post 1961)

Liverpool Irish (post 1957)

C   123 (Scottish)   Queen's Own   2nd Scottish General
Transport Column   Highlanders   Hospital
RASC TA

Plate 28   Yeomanry 1914

A	Royal Wiltshire	Warwickshire	Yorkshire Hussars
B	Sherwood Rangers	Staffordshire	Shropshire
C	Ayrshire	Cheshire	Yorkshire Dragoons
D	Leicestershire	North Somerset	Duke of Lancaster's Own
E	Lanarkshire	Northumberland Hussars	South Notts Hussars

Plate 29   Yeomanry 1914

A   Denbighshire Hussars   Westmorland and Cumberland   Pembroke

B   Royal East Kent   Hampshire Carabiniers   Royal Bucks Hussars

C   Derbyshire   Dorset   Royal Gloucestershire Hussars

D   Hertfordshire   Berkshire   Middlesex

E   Royal Devonshire   Loyal Suffolk Hussars   North Devonshire Hussars

Plate 30 Yeomanry 1914

A Queen's Own Worcestershire Hussars West Kent West Somerset

B Queen's Own Oxfordshire Hussars Montgomeryshire Lothians & Border Horse

C Royal Glasgow Lancashire Hussars Surrey

D Fife & Forfar Norfolk Sussex

E Glamorgan Lincolnshire City of London

Plate 31   Yeomanry 1914

A   Westminster   3rd County of   Bedfordshire
        Dragoons   London Yeomanry

B   Essex   North Irish Horse   South Irish Horse

C   Northamptonshire   East Riding   Lovat Scouts (w/m)

D   Lovat Scouts   Scottish Horse   Welsh Horse   Inns of Court
        (brass)   OTC

Plate 32   King's Colonials

A   King's Colonials
                                (front)

B   Australasian Squadron   British-African
                                                Squadron

C   King's Colonials
                                (side)

D   Australian Squadron   British-AsianSquadron

E   New Zealand   King Edward's   British-American
    Squadron   Horse   Squadron

Plate 33 Miscellaneous Yeomanry

A Sherwood Rangers (post 1949)   Staffordshire   Shropshire (post 1950)

B Ayrshire (i) 1915–23 (ii) 1923–66   Leicestershire Imperial

C Leicestershire (i) 1915–22 (ii) 1922–66   North Somerset (Q/C)

D Duke of Lancaster's Own (1954–66)   Lanarkshire Imperial   Caernarvon & Denbigh

E Flint & Denbigh   Royal Bucks Hussars Imperial   Leicestershire & Derbyshire

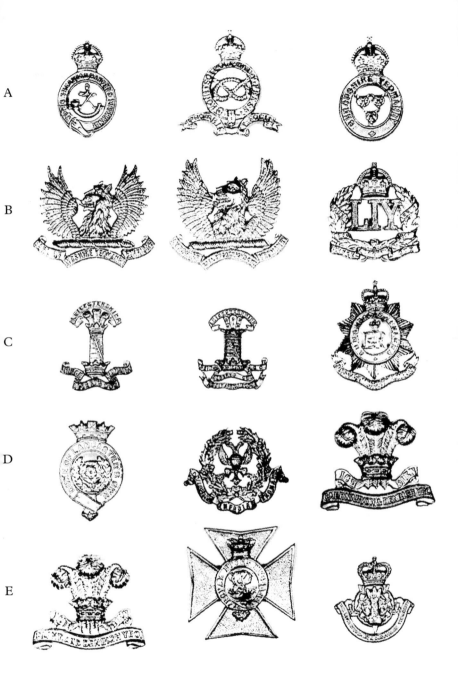

A

B

C

D

E

Plate 34   Miscellaneous Yeomanry

A   Dorset Imperial (1902–05)   Dorset (1920–60)   Royal Gloucestershire Hussars Imperial

B   Hertfordshire (1952–1961)   Berkshire Imperial   Middlesex (Q/C)

C   Royal Devon (mis-spelt)   Lothians & Berwick-shire Imperial   Royal Glasgow (collar worn in cap)

D   City of London
   (i) collar worn as cap   (ii) 1950–60   3rd County of London Imperial

E   23rd London Armoured Car Company   (i) 1938–39   (ii) 1920–38
   (iii) 4th County of London Yeomanry   (iv) 3rd & 3/4th County of London Yeomanry   (v) Kent & County of London Yeomanry

Plate 35   Miscellaneous Yeomanry

A   Essex   (i) Imperial Yeomanry   (ii) 1905–09   (iii) 1916   (iv) 1918–54
      (v) 1954–63

B   2nd King Edward's   Northamptonshire   (i) Imperial Yeomanry
      Horse   (ii) 2nd Regiment

C   East Riding   Queen's Own York-   Lovat Scouts 1900–03
      (1920–56)   shire Yeomanry   and post 1922

D   Scottish Horse   Fife & Forfar   Inns of Court
      (pre 1903)   Scottish Horse   Regiment

Plate 36   Kitchener's Army

A   Tyneside Scottish   Tyneside Irish
    (i) first pattern 1914   (ii) second pattern Jan. 1915

B   Birmingham Pals   25th Royal Fusiliers   Jewish Bns Royal
                                                     Fusiliers

C   Liverpool Pals   Leeds Pals   11th Border Regiment

D   Cardiff Pals   18th Middlesex   14th Royal Irish Rifles
                         Regiment

E   Wandsworth Bn (13th East Surrey Regiment)

Plate 37 London Regiment

A 5th Bn London
   Rifle Brigade
   (i) 1908–20 (ii) 1920–56   7th Bn   8th Bn Post
                                  Office Rifles

B 10th Bn Pad-   10th Bn Hackney Regiment   13th Bn Ken-
   dington Rifles   (1912–37)   sington
   (1908–12)   Regiment

C 14th Bn London
   Scottish
   (i) post 1908   (ii) pagri   (i) pre 1920   17th Bn
                                  (ii) 1920–46

D 18th Bn London Irish   19th Bn St.   20th Bn Black-
   (i) 1937–62   (ii) warrant   Pancras   heath &
                 officer   Woolwich

E 23rd Bn   28th Bn Artists   (i) first   (ii) second
            Rifles   pattern   pattern

Plate 38   London Regiment

A   6th Bn City of London Rifles

9th Bn Queen Victoria's Rifles

11th Bn Finsbury Rifles

B   12th Bn Rangers (i) first pattern   (ii) third pattern

15th Bn Civil Service Rifles

C   16th Bn Queen's Westminster Rifles

Queen's Westminsters (KRRC)

Queen's Royal Rifles, (KRRC)

D

21st Bn First Surrey Rifles

25th Bn Cyclists

239

Plate 39A   Honourable Artillery Company

A   Infantry   (i) pre 1954   (ii) serjeants pre 1954   (iii) beret badge
                                                               (post 1969)

B   Artillery   (i) service dress cap badge   (ii) beret badge post 1953

Plate 39B   Cyclist Battalions

| C | Army Cyclist Corps | Highland Cyclist Battalion | Northern Cyclist Battalion | Huntingdonshire Cyclist Battalion |
| D | Essex & Suffolk Cyclist Battalion | 8th (Cyclist) Battalion Essex Regiment | 9th (Cyclist) Battalion Hampshire Regiment | City of London Cyclist Company |

Plate 40   Arms and Services

A   Royal Artillery   (i) service dress cap   (ii) field service cap
(iii) Territorial Force   (iv) Volunteers

B   Royal Horse Artillery   (i) GR V   (ii) ER VIII   (iii) GR VI
(iv) ER II

C   Royal Engineers   (i) VR   (ii) Volunteers ER VII   (iii) GR VI
(iv) Royal Monmouthshire Royal Engineers (Militia)

D   Royal Signals   (i) pre 1947   (ii) 1947–55
Royal Army Medical Corps   (i) all-brass   (ii) bi-metal

E   Army Service Corps   (i) VR period   (ii) 1901–19
Royal Army Service Corps (ER VIII) Royal Corps of Transport

A

B

C

D

E

243

Plate 41   Services

A   Army Ordnance Corps (pre 1919)
    Royal Army Ordnance Corps   (i) 1919–47   (ii) 1949–55
    Corps of Royal Electrceal & Mechanical Engineers
    (i) 1942–47   (ii) 1947–55

B   Corps of Military Police (ER VII) Royal Military Police (ER II)
    Army Veterinary Corps (1903–18) Royal Army Veterinary Corps
    (1918–55)

C   Army Pay Corps (1898–1900)
    Army Pay Corps (1902–20)
    Royal Army Pay Corps   (i) 1920–29 (ii) 1929–55

D   Corps of Military Accountants
    School of Musketry
    Small Arms School Corps
    Army Educational Corps

E   Royal Army Educational Corps (1948–55)
    Military Provost Staff Corps
    Army Dental Corps (1921–48)
    Royal Army Dental Corps (1948–55)

Plate 42 Services and Women's Corps

A Royal Pioneer Corps   Intelligence Corps
   ArmyPhysical Training Corps
   Army Catering Corps   (i) all brass K/C (ii) 1973 pattern

B Royal Defence Corps (i) and (ii)
   National Defence Company   (i) E.R VIII   (ii) GR VI

C Mobile Defence Corps   Non-Combatant Labour Corps
   Non-Combatant Corps   Royal Flying Corps

D Women's Army Auxiliary Corps
   Queen Mary's Army Auxiliary Corps
   Auxiliary Territorial Service
   Women's Royal Army Corps
   Queen Alexandra's Royal Army Nursing Corps

E Women's Transport Service (FANY)
   Royal Army Chaplains Department (post 1940) (i) Christian
   (ii) Jewish

A

B

C

D

E

Plate 43   Schools and Training Establishments

A   Royal Military   Royal Military   Royal Military   Royal Military
       Academy   College   College (Staff   Academy
                                                   and Band)   Sandhurst

B   Royal Military   Mons Officer   Army Appren-   Welbeck College
       School of   Cadet School   tices School
       Music

C   Duke of York's   Queen   Royal   21st Officer
       Royal Mlilitary   Victoria's   Hibernian   Cadet
       School   School   Military   Battalion
                             Dunblane   School

Plate 44   War-raised Units

A   13th Duke of Cam-   Imperial Yeomanry   Fincastle's Horse
    bridge's Own   (slouch-hat)   29th Bn Irish Horse
    Company IY   IY

B   Machine Gun Corps   Motor Machine Gun   Household Battalion
                         Corps

C   Anson Bn RN   Drake Bn RN   Hawke Bn RN   Hood Bn RN
    Division   Division   Division   Division

D   Howe Bn RN   Nelson Bn RN Machine Gun Bn
    Division   Division   RN Division

Plate 45 War-raised Units

A Remounts (i) and (ii)   1st Armoured Motor Battery

B Reconnaissance Corps
   (i) standard (ii) Yorkshire
      units
         Highland   Lowland
         Regiment   Regiment

C Infantry Training   No 2 Commando   No 2 Commando
   Battalions   (other ranks)   (Officers)

              No's 50–52 Commandos   Popski's Private
                             Army

D 'V' Force   Long Range   Raiding Support   Control Com-
            Desert Group   Regiment   mission
                                         Germany

E United Nations Emergency Force

Plate 46   Home Guard

A   Upper Thames   Rutland   Huntingdonshire   Isle of Man
    Patrol   (post 1951)

B   Radnor (i) 1940–45 (ii) post 1951   Ulster (1940–45)

C   1st American Squadron

Plate 47   Infantry Brigades 1958–69

A	Lowland	Homc Counties	Lancastrian
B	Fusilier	Forester	East Anglian
C	Wessex	Light Infantry	Yorkshire
D	Mercian	Welsh	North Irish
E	Highland	Green Jackets	Parachute Regiment

Plate 48   Miscellaneous Cavalry and Yeomanry

A Queen's Own Hussars

Queen's Royal Irish Hussars

9/12th Royal Lancers

B The Royal Hussars (PWO)

Berkshire & Westminster Dragoons

QO Warwickshire & Worcestershire Yeomanry

C North Somerset & Bristol Yeomanry

QO Lowland Yeomanry

Inns of Court & City Yeomanry

D QO Dorset & W. Somerset Yeomanry

Hertfordshire & Bedfordshire Yeomanry

Suffolk & Norfolk Yeomanry

E Westmoreland & Cumberland Yeomanry

Plate 49   Miscellaneous Infantry 1970

A   Duke of Edinburgh's Royal Regiment   Green Howards
    Staffordshire Regiment   Worcestershire & Sherwood Foresters
    Regiment   Royal Highland Fusiliers

B   Royal Irish Rangers   Royal Regiment of Gloucestershire and
    Hampshire   Royal Green Jackets   Royal Anglian Regiment

C   King's Own Royal Border Regiment   Devonshire and Dorset
    Regiment   Queen's Regiment   Queen's Lancashire Regiment

D   King's Regiment   Royal Regiment of Wales
    PWO Regiment of Yorkshre

E   Queen's Own Highlanders (Seaforth & Cameron)

Plate 50   Miscellaneous Territorial Units

A   Dorset Territorials   Devonshire Territorials   Hampshire & Isle-of-Wight Territorials

B   Oxfordshire   Ulster Defence   Buckinghamshire
    Territorials   Regiment   Regiment

C   Queen's Royal   Suffolk &   Bedfordshire & Leeds Rifles
    Surrey   Cambridge-   Hertfordshire
    Regiment   shire   Regiment
                           Regiment

D   Royal Wiltshire   London Yeomanry   5/6 Bn Staffordshire
    Territorials   & Territorials   Regiment

Plate 51 Additional Volunteers and Territorials

A 8th Bn Argyll & Sutherland   Glasgow Highlanders (ER II)
     Highlanders

B 5th Bn Cameronians

C 1st Hampshire RGA Volunteers   5th London RFA Brigade

D 3rd Middlesex RGA Volunteers

E Warwickshire RHA   West Riding RHA

Plate 52 Additional Yeomanry

A Staffordshire Imperial   Dorset Imperial (1905–08)
    Hertfordshire Imperial

B Scottish Horse Imperial   Lothians & Border Horse Yeomanry
    3rd County of London Imperial   Surrey Imperial

C Fife & Forfar Imperial   Glamorgan Imperial
    Lincolnshire Imperial

D North of Ireland Imperial   South Irish Yeomanry
    Scottish Horse (Scots Crown)

E Royal Devon Yeomanry (D Sqn Wessex Yeo)   QO Yeomanry
    QO Mercian Yeomanry

Plate 53 Her Majesty's Reserve Regiments

A Dragoons   Dragoon Guards   Hussars

B Lancers   Home Counties Northern/Southern/Eastern
    Rifles

C Scottish   Irish   Irish Fusiliers

A

B

C

Plate 54   Gurkha Brigade 1939

A   1st King George's Own   2nd King Edward's Own
       3rd Queen Alexandra's Own

B   4th Prince of Wales's Own   4th (Gurkha hat)
       5th Royal

C   6th Gurkha Rifles   7th Gurkha Rifles   8th Gurkha Rifles

D   9th Gurkha Rifles   10th Gurkha Rifles

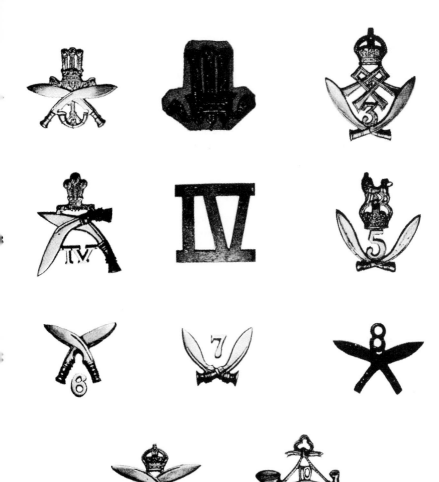

Plate 55   Brigade of Gurkhas 1970

A   2nd King Edward's Own   6th Queen Elizabeth's Own
      7th Duke of Edinburgh's Own

B   10th Princess Mary's Own   10th (Beret badge)
      Queen's Gurkha Engineers

C   Queen's Gurkha Signals   Gurkha Army Service Corps
      GurkhaTransport Regiment

D   Gurkha Military Police   (i) First pattern   (ii) Second pattern
      Gurkha Parachute Company

E   Gurkha Independent Company, Parachute Regiment
      Staff Band   Boys' Company

Plate 56 Options for Change

A Royal Dragoon Guards   Royal Dragoon Guards (senior NCOs)   Queen's Royal Hussars   King's Royal Hussars

B Light Dragoons   Princess of Wales's Royal Regiment   Royal Irish Regiment

C Royal Gloucestershire, Berkshire & Wiltshire Regiment   The Highlanders (Seaforth, Gordon & Cameron)

Plate 57   Miscellaneous additional badges

A   Royal Pioneer
       Corps (1985)

Royal Logistic
    Corps

Adjutant General's
    Corps

B   Army Legal Service

Army Legal Corps

C   Piper – Queen's Royal
       Irish Hussars

Royal Gurkha Rifles

Queen's Own Gurkha
    Transport Regiment

D   Royal Mercian & Lancastrian
       Yeomanry

Scottish Yeomanry

Army Junior School of
    Music

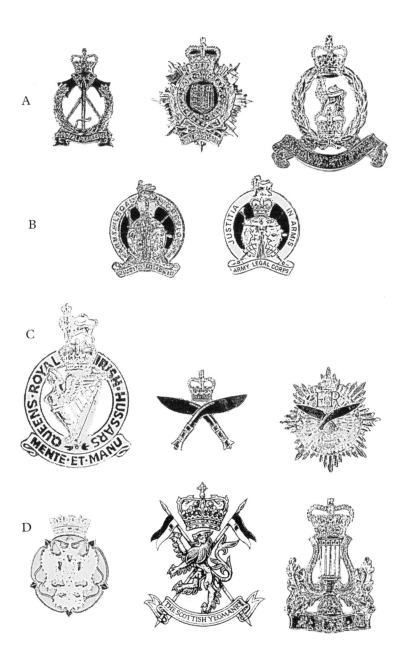

Index

Regimental Index

In the case of regular cavalry regiments, these are grouped under a single heading 'Cavalry' and, again, separated as Dragoons, Dragoon Guards, Hussars and Lancers under 'D', 'H' and 'L'. They are not separately listed under their full Army List title: for example, the 4th Queen's Own Hussars is not listed under 'Q'.

Infantry regiments are recorded under their most frequently-used title. The Middlesex Regiment is not, for instance, also listed as The duke of Cambridge's Own (Middlesex Regiment).

Figures in italics refer to illustrations.

North Staffordshire Regt, 26, 44, 51, 55; *14*
Northumberland Fusiliers, 27, 30; *8, 9, 36, 39b*
Northumberland Fusiliers, Royal, 30, 53; *16*
Northumberland Hussars, 83; *28*
Nottinghamshire & Derbyshire Regt, 25, 40, 53, 58, 61, 67; *12, 18, 22, 25*
Nottinghamshire Hussars, South, 84; *28*
Nottinghamshire Yeo, Sherwood Rangers, 81; *28*

Officer Cadet Bn, 21st, 121; *43*
Officer Cadet School, Mons, 120; *43*
Officer Trg Unit, Guards, 18; *20*
Ordnanace Corps, Army, 101; *41*
Ordnance Corps, Royal Army, 101, 131, 134; *41*
Oxfordshire & Bucks LI, 24, 40, 56, 67; *7, 12, 21a*
Oxfordshire Hussars, QO, 88; *30*
Oxfordshire LI, 24, 40; *12*
Oxfordshire Territorials, 71; *50*

Paddington Rifles, 74; *37*
Parachute Regt, 49, 50; *15b*
Pay Corps, Army, 101; *41*
Pay Corps, Royal Army, 102; *41*
Pembroke Yeo, 84; *29*
Physical Trg Corps, Army, 103; *42*
Physical Trg Staff, Army, 103
Pioneer Corps, 103; *42*
Pioneer Corps, Auxiliary Military, 103; *42*
Pioneer Corps, Royal, 103, 131, 134; *42, 57*
Police, Corps of Military, 101; *41*
Police, Royal Military, 101, 131; *41*
Poplar & Stepney Rifles, 76; *37*
Popski's Private Army, 125; *45*
Post Office Rifles, 73; *38*
Prince of Wales's Own Regt of Yorkshire, 32, 55; *49*
Princess of Wales's R Regt, 133; *56*
Prison Staff Corps, Military, 102
Provost Staff Corps, Military, 102; *41*

Q Alexandra's Imp Mil Nursing Service, 104

Q Alexandra's R Army Nursing Corps, 106; *42*
Queen Mary's Army Aux Corps, 106; *42*
Queen Victoria's Rifles, 74; *38*
Queen Victoria's School, Dunblane, 120; *43*
Queen's Lancashire Regt, 56; *49*
Queen's Own Buffs, 52
Queen's Own Cameron Hdrs, 46, 56, 68; *15a, 23*
Queen's Own Highlanders, 56, 58, 110, 133; *27, 49*
Queen's Own Lowland Yeo, 89, 108; *48*
Queen's Own Mercian Yeo, 97; *52*
Queen's Own Warwicks & Worcs Yeo, 88, 97; *48*
Queen's Own Yeo, 97; *52*
Queen's Own Yorkshire Yeo, 94, 97; *35*
Queen's Regt, 56, 133; *49*
Queen's R Regt (West Surrey), 20, 29, 52, 63; *6, 10, 16*
Queen's Royal Hussars, 132; *56*
Queen's Royal Rifles, 75; *38*
Queen's R Surrrey Regt, 29, 36, 52; *50*
Queen's Westminster, 75; *38*

Radnor HG, 118; *46*
Raiding Support Regt, 125; *45*
Rangers, 74; *38*
Reconnaissance Corps, 124; *45*
Remounts Service, Army, 124; *45*
Reserve Regts, HM, 122
    Dragoons, 122; *53*
    Dragoon Guards, 122; *53*
    Hussars, 122; *53*
    Lancers, 123; *53*
    Guards, 123
    Home Counties, 123; *53*
    Northern, 123; *53*
    Southern, 123; *53*
    Eastern, 123; *53*
    Rifles, 123; *53*
    Scottish, 123; *53*
    Irish, 123; *53*
    Irish Fusiliers, 123; *53*
Rifle Brigade, 48, 56; *15a, 16, 19*
Robin Hood's Bn, Foresters, 67; *22*
Rough Riders (City of London Yeo), 91, 96; *30, 34*
Royal Anglian Regt, 57; *49*

293